French Architecture

BY

PIERRE LAVEDAN

SCOLAR PRESS
LONDON

L'Architecture française

First published 1944 by Editions Larousse, Paris

This translation published 1956 by Penguin Books Limited,
Harmondsworth, Middlesex, England

This edition published 1979 by Scolar Press
39 Great Russell Street, London WC1B 3PH

Copyright © Penguin Books Limited 1956

ISBN 0 85967 366 9 (cloth)
0 85967 365 0 (paper)

PUBLISHER'S NOTE

This edition is a reprint of the text of the Penguin edition
of 1956, but contains a new selection of plates.
The only other alterations are the new Foreword, the
deletion in the text and index of references to the
plates of the 1956 edition, and the insertion of new
plate references in the index.

Printed in England by
Whitstable Litho Ltd
Whitstable, Kent

Contents

CONTENTS

List of Figures

List of Plates

(Between pages 160 *and* 161)

Foreword to 1979 Edition

T his short book first appeared in French in 1944 (Larousse, Paris, in the series 'Arts, Styles et Techniques'). It was published in English translation, as a Pelican, in 1956. It is this translation which is reprinted in this edition, with a new selection of illustrations.

The book is both a history of French architecture and a work of theory. It is based on three main ideas. The first is that architecture is usually taught in the context of the history of art, beside that of painting or sculpture. But the circumstances in which these activities are carried on are utterly different from each other, and they should be taught, and learnt, separately. The painter is master of his canvas and he can express himself freely on it. But the architect is not the master of his building. To begin with, he is dependent upon the person who gives him the order, upon the money that person can afford, and upon that person's tastes. The architect works for someone other than himself, for a client. Furthermore what the architect conceives is not carried out by him, but by a contractor and by workmen with limited, though specialist, skills. This idea is developed in Part One of the book.

The second fundamental notion is that in architecture what counts above all else is purpose, the function of the building. To build a church is not to build a dwelling-house or a municipal building. Buildings therefore can only be studied with reference to their eventual use.

Thirdly, the same problems present themselves in all ages and in all countries, at least in all countries of the same civilization. Much more so than with painting, in architecture one has to be suspicious of nationalism and to be susceptible to foreign influences. The true framework is Europe, heir of Rome and Christianity. In 1944 I discussed points of contact between French and English architecture, and today I would emphasize this further.

Thirty years have passed since the first edition of this book. Many new buildings have appeared. Rather than rewrite the text I have tried to take account of these new developments in the illustrations. A number of new plates have been added to cover the period 1940–1977.

Pierre Lavedan
Paris, May 1977

PART ONE
Technique and Style

*

No judgement can be passed on a building without a knowledge of how it was built

*

CHAPTER ONE

TECHNICAL PROBLEMS

I. Materials

In the first place, what is a building made of? The materials an architect uses may be grouped according to their nature (stone, wood, iron, etc., and a mixed material, reinforced concrete); according to their use (structural and facing materials); or according to the date of their appearance. Certain materials are traditional, almost as old as the Earth, such as stone and wood; others, such as iron and reinforced concrete, are products of the modern age.

The use of building materials is determined by their cost, their structural and their aesthetic qualities.

The latter problem may be left aside for the moment. Structural qualities comprise resistance to crushing, to bending, and – in the case of wood and iron – to stretching. Cost depends on how the materials are extracted or manufactured and conditions of transport. Cost of transport varies with distance, and determines to what extent the building shall depend on local materials. Rural and humble buildings are always an expression of their geographic setting, but this does not hold for urban or large buildings. A country church in the Pyrenees is very different from a country church in Lorraine. On the other hand, the same type of house is found to-day in Lille, Marseilles, Oslo, and Algiers. The essential characteristic of town architecture is its independence of local materials, which is due to the progress of industrial technique and means of transport. Thus marble comes to play an ever increasing rôle in Parisian architecture. But there was transport in the Middle Ages. 'We have an exaggerated idea of the lack of communication in medieval Europe,' says Puig i Cadafalch. Of course there were no railways, and roads were fewer and less well made than they are now; but waterways were relatively more developed. Charlemagne had columns brought from Rome and Ravenna for his church at Aachen; the basic materials had been taken from the fortifications of Verdun, demolished at his order. Abbot Suger dreamed of bringing columns from Diocletian's palace at Spalato to Saint-Denis; he gave up the idea only because he thought that he had found finer examples nearer at hand. Even for more modest churches like Saint-Pierre at Coutances or the Abbey of Hambye (Manche) there was no hesitation in going to Bernières for Caen stone, which had to be transported by sea round the Cotentin and then up a river, a journey of some 200 miles. The favourable formation of the mountains and uplands of France, her wealth of navigable waterways, and the easy connexions between her various river basins have all made important contributions to the history of French architecture.

¶ STONE

The distinction must be made between natural and artificial stone.

Natural stone is that extracted from a quarry. It is called *freestone* when it is square-hewn; *rubble* when its surface is rough-hewn. The term covers a very large range of varieties.

First and foremost are the calcareous stones (composed of lime and carbonic acid). These are the real freestones. They are found in the quarries in beds or layers. France is a fine source of these, and it may be said, without putting undue emphasis on a questionable geographic determinism, that as long as architecture meant construction in stone, the superiority of France in this art was conditioned by her rich resources, particularly those of the Paris basin. Its geological past has made it a vast quarry, brought to light by the Seine and its tributaries. To the north, near the Oise and the Aisne, are the thick strata of so-called coarse limestone, which cover the Valois and Soissonnais regions. The railway between Chantilly and Creil has been cut through this; there are quarries at

Saint-Maximin, Senlis, and Trossy; quarries at Saint-Leu, used as early as the Merovingian period for making sarcophagi in upper Normandy, in the thirteenth century for the portals of the transepts of Chartres, in the fifteenth century for those of Sens, despite the distance involved (over 120 miles), in the sixteenth century at the Château of Gaillon, in the seventeenth century in the Luxembourg and the vault of the chapel of Versailles. At the confluence of the Oise and Seine are the quarries of Poissy and those of Conflans, with the Banc-Royal ('Royal Bed'), the source of the stones of Saint-Denis, Notre-Dame-de-Paris and the corner stones of the pediment of the Panthéon, which measure over 9 × 9 × 6 feet, nearly 486 cubic feet each, and weigh 24 tons. On the site of Paris itself, the left bank of the Seine was lined with quarries now exhausted. Rondelet held that five distinct kinds of stone were extracted from them: *lias*, very fine-grained and homogeneous, without traces of fossils, cut up into blocks from 18 to 21 feet long and 6 feet wide but rather thin, and hewn in the quarries of the Barrière d'Enfer and the Avenue de l'Observatoire which became the Catacombs; *cliquart*, very hard but less fine-grained (Arcueil, Bagneux); *roche* (Bagneux); *banc franc*; and *lambourde*. To the south of Paris, Château-Landon (Seine-et-Marne) produced a hard, heavy, compact stone of a yellowish grey, capable of taking a high polish; it was used in the Panthéon (paving), the Arc-de-Triomphe at the Étoile, and the Sacré-Cœur of Montmartre.

All round the city, in a larger radius, is another circuit of incomparable materials. In Picardy, the magnesian chalk of Amiens cathedral; in Champagne the more resistant chalk of Reims cathedral. To the east, in Burgundy, are the limestones of Tonnerre. Further away can be found the coral limestones of the Côtes-de-Meuse at Nancy and throughout Lorraine. To the south is the Berry stone; to the west the Turonian chalk of the Loire valley, the rather friable *tufa* used for the Loire châteaux; and in Normandy the magnificent Caen stone. Outside the Paris basin, similar resources are found in the Aquitanian Basin and the region around Lyons (Mont-d'Or hills).

Marble is a variety of limestone easily dressed, fine in polish, and varied in colouring. It is much less rare in France than is generally believed, but its quality is very unequal, so that it is used not only for columns but also as facing material and ordinary paving. The marbles from the Pyrenees are the finest. More than 250 kinds are known, principally the Saint-Béat (a white marble exploited since the time of the Roman Empire) and the Sarrancolin (red veined with grey, and flesh-coloured veined with yellow). They have been used in a number of palatial buildings in the Paris region: the Louvre, the Opéra, as well as at Versailles and the Trianon. In the sixteenth century they were brought by water, first down the Garonne and then by sea; there is a contract of 1553, in which two watermen from Moissac undertake to convey Saint-Béat marbles for the Louvre down the Garonne from Toulouse to Bordeaux. In Provence and the Alps there are more than 150 varieties of marble. Others are less famous, but no less used, for example the marbles of the Boulonnais, the Ardennes, and the Comblanchien (Côte-d'Or).

In the absence of calcareous stones, siliceous or volcanic stones are used. The Paris area still supplies a *millstone grit*, a very hard variety – the derivation of the name is obvious. There are several varieties of this stone; that used for building is the fine yellow variety riddled with holes. The Vosges mountains have a *sandstone*, of a fine red colour (Strasbourg Cathedral); the Massif Central has one very similar (Rodez Cathedral). Granite, which is more difficult to cut, but extremely hard, furnishes an inexhaustible mine for the Cotentin (Mont-Saint-Michel), Brittany, and the Limousin (Limoges Cathedral). Auvergne has its volcanic stones, both basalts and trachytes.

The main artificial stones are bricks and mortars. Certain regions possess neither any quarries nor any hard geological strata. This was once the case in Mesopotamia. In France it is so in the Flemish region and in Languedoc. This gap is filled by the manufacture of artificial stones, whose principal variety is brick, or baked clay. Gallo-Roman bricks were square; as a rule they were made in three sizes, $23\frac{1}{2} \times 23\frac{1}{2}$,

$17\frac{1}{2} \times 17\frac{1}{2}$, and $8\frac{1}{2} \times 8\frac{1}{2}$ inches, and were about 2 inches thick; but there was no hard and fast rule, and for columns circular and quadrant bricks are even to be found. Medieval bricks, much larger than the present-day ones, are generally almost square, 13×10 inches and 2 inches thick, according to Viollet-le-Duc. To-day bricks have fixed proportions; each dimension is double the preceding one (as in $2 \times 4 \times 8$ inches), so that a brick may be laid in any direction. Brick architecture has given us such masterpieces as the belfrey of Bergues in the north, and the great monuments of the Garonne area such as the Jacobin (Dominican) church at Toulouse, and the cathedral of Albi. The use of artificial stones has been greatly developed in our time and they are now made with many materials other than clay.

Mortar is also an artificial material, ordinarily used for binding, but sometimes, and nowadays more and more, by itself. The elementary type is the mud mortar composed of a soil mixed with water, which hardens as it dries. To this chopped straw (' cob ') is sometimes added. This was used in the Middle Ages, in the absence of brick, in many of the timber-framed houses, to fill in the spaces between the posts and the laths. Its use continues even to-day in country districts throughout certain provinces (e.g. Limousin). Rondelet noticed it in the eighteenth century in the Ain, Rhône, and Isère regions; elsewhere he declares that in the Ain he restored, in 1764, a country-house built with a mud (*pisé*) as hard as Saint-Leu stone.

Mortars of lime or cement are more frequently used. The former is a mixture of lime and sand in varying proportions. Cement, obtained by Vicat in 1820 by the burning of limestone in the presence of clay, is a special lime, a composite of silica, alumina, and lime, a thin powder which, when mixed with sand and water, becomes extremely hard on exposure to air. Here again France is highly favoured, with the Vassy cement, which hardens rapidly, and those of Mantes and the Boulonnais. Concrete is a mixture of sand, cement, and water with pebbles of variable size, though never larger than an egg.

¶ TIMBER

The main kinds of timber employed for building are oak and pine in Paris, and chestnut, elm, beech, ash, and walnut, according to local resources. From this point of view, too, France is well provided. From antiquity, Gaul was renowned for the abundance and quality of her oaks; the Romans used them extensively. The belt of forests which spreads right round Paris is no less prominent than that of her quarries; and although the abundance of building materials does not account entirely for her development, it has at least assisted it. Since the nineteenth century colonial woods, notably okoumé, have appeared on the home markets; simultaneously, a modification in technique has made it possible to unroll the wood along its circumference, rather than sawing it lengthwise; the machine operates like a pencil sharpener. In this way extremely thin sheets of wood of large surface are obtained, and a new process has been evolved: the use of veneers and plywood. A board may now be made of three or five layers of which the expanding or contracting movements (in heat or damp) neutralize each other.

Timber is the only material with which an entire house may be built – framework (posts and beams), facing of the façades and inside walls, floors and roofing, doors and windows, and even the greater part of the furniture. Yet in France its use is declining. In the Merovingian and Carolingian periods it still played a considerable rôle; then, gradually, it was eliminated in favour of stone masonry (in particular, the substitution of the vault for the wooden ceiling) and confined to the framework. At the end of the Middle Ages, it was only in domestic architecture that it still formed the framework of house-façades in certain regions, but even there it has had to give way to stone.

Modern France has perhaps made a mistake. Wooden houses are much more common abroad. A third of the population of the United States lives in them and the same is true of northern Europe. That is why an effort has been made in recent years to bring the attention of French architects back to timber. At the Exhibition of 1937 one of the most interesting pavilions demonstrated its possibilities, particularly in relation to French and colonial varieties. It has many advantages: it is easily worked; it allows the easy mass-production of component parts which lowers the cost considerably; although of slight density it is highly resistant; finally, because of its cellular structure, it is a remarkable insulator.

It also has its drawbacks; for instance, there is the risk of rotting by fungi. It may be noted that on this point medieval technique was far superior to that of the nineteenth century; nowadays it is not unusual to see timber work rot within thirty years, while there is timber of the fifteenth century still perfectly preserved. The danger of fire is much diminished by the process of fire-proofing, and American statistics show that in a million houses, 75 per cent of which are of timber, the proportion of wooden houses burnt is lower than that of houses of stone.

The Middle Ages used mainly oak, which seems to have been of a kind different from that of to-day: the trees had very straight trunks and the diameter, though not large, remained constant from the base to the upper branches. The timber, once felled and trimmed, was kept in the timber yard for several years. Usually, medieval timber was not of very large squaring, which contradicts the modern idea that the thicker the timber, the better the resistance.

¶ IRON

Iron has been used almost always as a binding element in masonry (antique temples, the colonnade of the Louvre, Saint-Sulpice, the palace of the Place de la Concorde, the Panthéon portico); but it only really became a building material with the advent of modern metallurgical methods, the burning of iron ore in the presence of coal in blast furnaces. This technique was invented in England in the eighteenth century. Here France is at a disadvantage because she has little coal. Actually, under the heading 'Iron' three materials should be distinguished – cast-iron, iron, and steel.

Cast-iron is the direct result of the smelting of ore in the blast furnace. It is a liquid which solidifies on cooling, and can therefore be given the desired form by pouring it into moulds. This process was successfully carried out in sand moulds for the first time about 1710 by the Englishman, Abraham Darby. Its earliest application on a large scale, in 1779, was in the first metal bridge to be thrown over the Severn, a single arch with a 100-foot span. Cast-iron was then used in Paris for the Pont des Arts (1803), the Pont d'Austerlitz (1806), and the Halle aux Blés (Bélanger, 1809) for a large dome with an interior diameter of 108 feet. Cast-iron is brittle and reacts badly to bending stress, but on the other hand offers good resistance to crushing forces. It is therefore used primarily for vertical supports, pillars, or columns (Labrouste, Bibliothèque Sainte-Geneviève).

Iron, ductible and malleable, is obtained by oxidizing white-hot cast-iron (puddling). It may be pulled out into wires or rolled into sheets, which can then be assembled by rivets and bolts. Iron resists simultaneously pressure, bending, and stretching. The first French steam-hammer was set up in the Creusot factories in 1839. In 1840 there was a strike lasting several months in the timber yards. The Creusot establishment then began to produce iron girders, and iron framing gradually replaced wooden framework. Iron was first used for bridges and rail-tracks. In the Bibliothèque Sainte-Geneviève Labrouste combined cast-iron supports with iron roofing. Then came the great monuments of iron architecture, the Crystal Palace in London, the market halls of Paris, the Galerie des Machines, the Eiffel Tower, etc. Iron has various drawbacks. It expands when hot. It has to be painted often to prevent rust. It is not fire-proof. And thousands of screws, bolts, and rivets are necessary to assemble the parts. This, however, has been made considerably easier by the present use of oxy-acetylene welding.

Steel is iron combined with 1 or 2 per cent of carbon. It is harder and more elastic than iron and, what is more, almost impervious to rust. The greatest American sky-scraper, the Empire State Building (102 floors, 1,248 feet high) has a steel frame. In France, when Otua (Technical Office for the Utilization of Steel) organized a competition in 1935 for the covering of a hall of 29½ acres (the area of the Place de la Concorde) by a flat roof without interior supports, it was found that steel was the only solution.

¶ REINFORCED CONCRETE

Reinforced concrete, the most recent architectural material of importance, is a combination of concrete and iron. Bars of iron of variable thickness, from less than one inch in diameter to normal beams and rails, are placed in a wooden mould (shuttering). These are kept in place by transverse tie bars. Into this mould is poured liquid concrete, which hardens in about three weeks. Reinforced concrete was invented in 1849 by a French gardener, Joseph Monier, working in the Orangerie of Versailles; he replaced wooden flower-tubs by wire tubs coated with cement. In 1867 he applied for patents which were sold abroad. The Germans still call this material 'Monier concrete' after him. In 1850, reinforced concrete was used for the first time in the building of a block of flats at Saint-Denis (3, rue des Poissonniers), by François Coignet. Since then, the technique has been greatly perfected and tested, notably by Hennebique, Cottancin, Freyssinet (pre-stressed concrete, etc.).

The advantages of reinforced concrete are many. It can be prepared anywhere, by workmen of a grade relatively easy to find. Iron and concrete have the same coefficient of expansion, so their cohesion is perfect. Iron enclosed in cement does not rust, and cement enclosing iron becomes as flexible as the iron itself; that is to say, the whole acquires qualities which neither of the constituents possessed. Because of the iron, supports may be much narrower than if they were not reinforced. And for the first time in the history of architecture, a building can be considered as a single block; any combination of masses, any overhanging is possible; the architect is restrained only by fear of absurdity.

Nor are the drawbacks negligible. The external appearance

is frankly ugly, so much so that architects hesitate to leave concrete bare and it is generally disguised beneath a facing. For wide spans it becomes difficult to set up the shuttering, which limits the use of the concrete, and makes iron more suitable to this purpose. Above all, concrete cannot be repaired: once cracked it is finished. Moreover, since its use is so recent we cannot judge how lasting it is.

II. Structure

The two basic problems are those of support and covering. Walls, pillars, columns, and posts are supports. The principal kinds of covering are ceilings and vaults, supporting roofs and flat roofs.

¶ WALLS

The wall has a double function: it encloses the building and at the same time supports the covering. It can be made either of a single type of material (stone or brick), or of a combination of different materials.

Let us consider first the simplest case, that of a wall made exclusively of stone. The stones are arranged in superimposed courses or beds. The points of contact between two stones of the same bed are called 'joints'. The manner in which the stones are cut and laid is defined as the 'stonework'. The word may apply in the first place to the size of the stones. 'Large stonework' is made up of square-hewn stones whose dimensions vary from 24 to 40 inches. In the Middle Ages it was used in the great cathedrals of northern France. In 'medium-sized stonework', the stones are 10 to 20 inches long by 8 to 10 inches high; this is more or less the pattern of the stones from the quarries of west and south-west France, which were 1 × 1 × 2 feet. This was frequent in the Romanesque period because small stones are easier to transport and manipulate than big ones. The stones of 'small stonework' are not more than 4 to 6 inches long.

The word stonework may also refer to the way in which the stones are laid. The most usual way is 'ashlar'. In this, the horizontal layers are parallel; the vertical joints, on the other hand, are unconnected but in line with one another. Ashlar is said to be 'isodome' when the layers are of the same depth, 'pseudisodome' when they are unequal. In modern and medieval buildings, the large and medium sized stonework is always regular. Small stonework, on the other hand, offers several variations of considerable historical importance. It is called herringbone masonry (*opus spicatum*) when the stones of each bed are inclined; in one bed the joints lean to the right; in the bed above or below they lean to the left. This arrangement is less firm than the usual ashlar work but has the advantage of giving a certain variety to the appearance of the wall-surface. Reticulated stonework (*opus reticulatum*) is composed of cubic stones, laid diamond fashion; it has the appearance of a net (*rete*).

Finally, the word 'stonework' refers to certain peculiarities in the way the stone is cut. We speak of 'grooving' when there are furrows round the joints and beds of the stones. This grooving may be applied either to both joints and beds or to the beds only (Palace of Versailles, Gabriel wing). A building is 'rock faced' when the outer surface of the stone is left undressed: this is 'rustication'; it is 'vermiculated' when the surface is grooved with S-shaped furrows. Grooving and rustication were much used in classical architecture; the Pitti Palace in Florence set an example which was copied at the Luxembourg in Paris and subsequently used very commonly. In medieval architecture grooving and rustication did not exist, but medieval stones often show the trace of tools and in many cases bear the mason's marks, letters, or signs which are helpful in discovering the building's history.

The problem of building a wall consists in ensuring that the stones of which it is composed hold firmly together. In Greece, the cut of these stones was so perfect that it alone would have sufficed to secure the equilibrium of the wall, but in spite of this they were also bound by metal or wooden cramps. The same method has sometimes been used in the

Middle Ages (Saint-Front at Périgueux). But the most common method of securing this cohesion is the use of mortar. The thickness of the layers of mortar can date a building; if the layer of mortar is too thick, the weight of the stone squeezes it out of the joints; it forms a protruding rim which is normally removed, but which was left at certain periods, such as the Carolingian and the eleventh century.

Stability may also be increased by the arrangement of the stones in the wall. A frequent arrangement is to put two stones breadthwise for one depthwise; the stones projecting

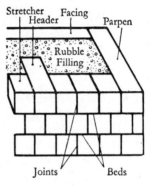

Figure 1. Masonry

into the body of the wall, with only their ends visible, are called 'headers' or 'parpens'; those showing their larger sides are 'stretchers' (fig. 1).

In brick walls, the bricks are always bound with mortar. In medieval buildings the brick-courses are regular, separated by very thick beds of mortar, sometimes of as much as $1\frac{1}{2}$ to 2 inches. Nowadays, as for stone, the brick courses are alternately laid: one course lengthwise, one breadthwise, or, in the same course, two bricks lengthwise, one behind the other, plus one breadthwise. But many combinations are possible. If placed at different depths into the wall, the bricks may trace motifs in relief (Paris, Institut d'art et d'archéologie). Moreover, there are many kinds of bricks, both glazed and coloured.

The wall may be composed of different materials: stone and rubble, stone and brick, wood and masonry, iron and masonry, reinforced concrete and masonry. In these combinations the first material is the supporting element, the second the filling element.

(a) *Stone and rubble*. For reasons of economy, mortar has served for filling as well as for binding. Formerly, when medium-sized stonework was used for thick walls, only the surface or *dressing* was of ashlar; the inside was filled with a mortar mixed with pebbles known as rubble. This was the Roman method, which was still used in the Middle Ages. Cohesion is maintained by headers projecting into the rubble (fig. 1).

(b) *Stone and brick*. The combination of stone and brick, even for large buildings, is characteristic of certain periods of French architecture. We find it, for example, during the reign of Louis XII, in the façade of the Château of Blois; during the reigns of Henri IV and Louis XIII in the houses of the Place Dauphine and the Place des Vosges in Paris, and in the first Château of Versailles, the one which Saint-Simon called the 'petit château tricolore' (stone, brick, and roof of blue slate). In such combinations the stone is naturally used for those parts where the load is greatest, wall-angles and door and window frames. The vertical superimposition of stone-layers is called *chaînes* (piers), and these are often set with alternately long and short stones, in which case they are called *harpes*.

(c) *Wood and masonry*. It is unusual for wood to be used alone. In heavily wooded regions (Switzerland, Sweden, parts of Russia) it has been possible to make walls with piled tree trunks (the Russian *isba*); they are more often made of planks or panels assembled within a framework of thicker timber. In France, this framework has most frequently been filled in with masonry (mortar, plaster, bricks). The components of the framework are the vertical 'uprights', the horizontal 'beams' which support the 'summers' on which in turn rest the joists of the floorboards. A closer network may be obtained by placing smaller vertical 'scantlings' (small upright and diagonal units) between the uprights and the beams. The 'braces' are brackets forming a right angle between the stringer beams and the uprights.

(d) *Iron and masonry; reinforced concrete and masonry.* Nowadays we are accustomed to seeing the skeletons of buildings made entirely of vertical and horizontal components of iron or re-inforced concrete. As in the case of wood, the framework can be filled in with masonry, so much the lighter since the wall here is a screen rather than a support. Sometimes even glass is sufficient.

¶ COLUMNS AND PILLARS

If the wall has only to support and not to enclose, it can be replaced by a series of small supports, columns or pillars, joined together only at the top. The saving in material is con-siderable.

The column, of circular section, is the simplest kind of support. When in stone it may consist of a single block (mono-lith), or of horizontal layers called 'drums'. There are also brick columns. For their construction the Romans used to bake quadrant bricks, four of which put together formed a layer. The column, the basic element of Greco-Roman and classical architecture, is composed of three parts – the base, the shaft, and the capital. The shape and decoration of the latter, despite the efforts of Colbert to create a specifically French order, remained the same in the classical period as they had been defined in antiquity: Doric, Ionic, Corinthian, and Composite. The simple, isolated support of wood or concrete (post) is generally square in section.

The pillar is a complex support. It may consist of a circular, rectangular, or cruciform nucleus, to which are added either half-columns (called 'engaged' columns) or rectangular half pillars (pilasters). The architects of the Middle Ages and classical period evolved a large variety of pillars; in theory each of the elements of which they are formed should have a carrying function, that is, it should correspond to an element in the covering (fig. 2). Pillars are very rarely coursed through-

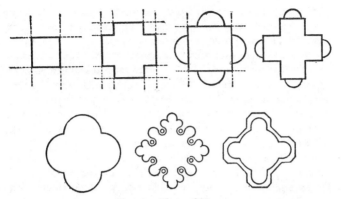

Figure 2. Plans of Piers

out; the freestone is a facing only, the interior being of rubble.

To span the gap between two supports, either a stone or beam (lintel or architrave) or a series of smaller stones or pieces of wood (arch) are thrown. These are the two fundamental types of covering, and the problem is the same when the space to be spanned lies between two walls. The problem of covering must therefore be considered as a whole.

III. Covering

The two types of covering, ceiling and vault, correspond to the two methods of spanning an empty space, either in one piece or by a composite of smaller units.

¶ THE CEILING

The architrave is the horizontal beam joining two isolated supports, such as two columns of the Parthenon, of the church of the Madeleine, or of the Odéon theatre. By analogy, to cover a room, beams of stone, wood, iron, or reinforced concrete are thrown from one wall to another. These transverse beams are then linked together at right angles in a similar way

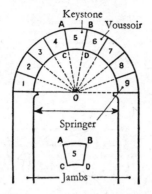

Figure 3. The principle of the vault

of the voussoir, CD, is narrower than its upper one, AB; naturally subject to the force of gravity and pressing downwards, it can only make way for itself by pushing the neighbouring stones aside, that is, to the right and left.

The arch of a vault may be designed in many ways. The circular arch is self-defined; a vault consisting of a succession of semicircular arches is called a 'barrel vault'. An arch is 'horseshoe' when its curve is more than a semicircle; it is 'depressed' or 'segmental' when it is less than a semicircle. The 'pointed arch' is formed by two halves of a circular arch joined together after the keystone, which exerts the greatest pressure, has been removed; the vault consisting of a series of pointed arches is called a 'pointed barrel' vault. One can also, by cutting through the upper and lower parts of an arch of very large radius by two horizontal, parallel lines, give it the appearance of an architrave or lintel; this is the 'flat arch'. On the other hand, one can pile stones together, so that they overlap each other; these stones, subject only to the force of gravity, are cut at their lower edges to give them the appearance of an arch (corbelled or cantilevered arch); these are false arches and architraves (fig. 4).

The 'dome' is a vault of hemispherical shape. Concentric rings are placed one over the other in such a way that the

Arches, or at least true arches, present a very difficult problem for the architect – that of resistance to lateral thrusts. All the efforts of their science, particularly in the Middle Ages, were concentrated on finding a remedy to counteract these thrusts.

The simplest solution consists in setting the vault on to very thick walls, pierced with as few openings as possible, so that the very mass of their masonry exerts resistance against the oblique thrusts of the vault. This is what the first Romanesque architects did. The process is costly, for masonry is paid for by cubic measure, and it results in badly-lit buildings. Therefore other solutions were quickly sought for.

(a) It seemed that a good step forward would be made if the thrust of the vault, borne equally along the whole length of the walls, could be localized at certain points. This gave rise, at first, to the invention of the transverse arch or *doubleau*. This is the name given to arches built below the vault, perpendicular to its axis, to reinforce it. The inventors of this system argued that these arches supported the vault and bore the greater part of the thrust, and it was therefore sufficient to reinforce the walls at the points corresponding to the arches. These supports were the 'buttresses'. It is possible that the Romanesque architects were mistaken, and that the ribbing system gave no support at all, that it even tended to exert forces on its own account and to detach itself from the fabric; but at least the intention of those who used it is perfectly clear (fig. 6).

(b) A better solution was found in the 'groined vault'. This is the name given to the intersection of two barrel vaults whose summits are in the same plane and which project downward salient ridges called groins. The advantage of this is obvious – the thrust is localized at the four points where the groins end and it becomes possible to hollow out the masonry in the intervening space. Unfortunately the groined vault is difficult to build. The groin voussoirs are of an awkward cut, as each voussoir is formed of two facets with different curvatures, and the meeting of the four groins in the centre of the vault presents a new problem – the complex shape of their common keystone. This is why the groined vault, perfectly well known to the Romans (e.g. the Basilica of Constantine, the great halls of the Thermae of Diocletian), made only a relatively short appearance in Romanesque art.

(c) Then the 'rib-vault' was tried. 'The rib is to the groined vault as the transverse arch is to the barrel vault.' (Lasteyrie.) In the same way that transverse ribs are arches thrown perpendicular to the vault, these cross-ribs are arches intersecting crosswise, and meeting diagonally below the groins of the vault. Combined with two transverse ribs before and behind, with two other arches known as wall arches (*formerets*) to right and left, they form a closed, inviolable system (fig. 6). In

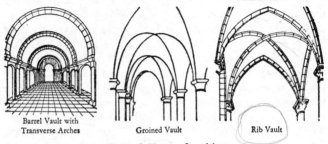

Barrel Vault with
Transverse Arches

Groined Vault

Rib Vault

Figure 6. Types of vaulting

practice this process may be applied in many ways. It may be the crossing of only four ribs (quadripartite vault); or of six (sexpartite vault, with a supplementary rib in the middle); or of eight (octopartite vault); or even more (ridge ribs (*liernes*), intermediary ribs (*tiercerons*), star vaults). The principle is always the same – the intersection of arches keyed under the vault which is to be supported (fig. 7).

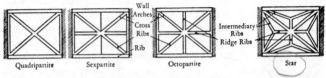

Quadripartite   Sexpartite   Octopartite   Star

Wall Arches
Cross Ribs
Rib
Intermediary Ribs
Ridge Ribs

Figure 7. Types of rib-vaulting

The idea of those who used it was that the cross-rib, like the transverse rib but more precisely, should distinguish the supporting from the supported agent. With the thrust completely localized, it was sufficient to build the wall only at the abutment of arches. All the rest could be left open, that is to say filled in by huge glass screens. Furthermore, the vault itself, apart from the ribs, could be made of light materials stretched over the ribs like a drum skin on a wooden frame. In other words, the cross-rib was a self-sufficient framework, independent of its covering, comparable to the metal or reinforced concrete skeletons of modern buildings. This at least is the interpretation given by Viollet-le-Duc. If it is exaggerated, if it has proved wrong on certain points, it is none the less true that, in practice, Gothic architects succeeded in erecting buildings made of as little material as possible, virtually glass cages, and that, in its anatomy, the Sainte-Chapelle is a building of the same quality as the church at Le Raincy.

Another problem is that of the origin of the rib-vault. In contradiction to what has long been held, this perfect method was not the discovery of French architects in the first quarter of the twelfth century. For many years and in many countries architects had thought, if not of localizing the thrusts, at least of easing the burden of a vault by arches intersecting below it. From the seventh century, ribs were found under several Georgian (Caucasus) domes, but their function is purely decorative; they are supported by the vault, but do not give it support. In the ninth and tenth centuries the ribbed Hispano-Moresque domes made their appearance, notably in the mosque of Kairouan, in that of Tunis, and in Europe, at Cordova. Generally they are of very small dimensions (10 to 13 feet in diameter) and, here again, it is not certain that the ribbing is more than an ornament attached to the lower part of the cupola. But they may have suggested a better idea; at any rate they were imitated in France, near the Spanish frontier, in the church of Sainte-Croix at Oloron and the Hôpital-Saint-Blaise. Another province of Mohammedanism, Persia, displays similar ribbing in the Jouma mosque at Ispahan (date disputed).

On the other hand, proper supporting arches existed in Armenia at the same time. At Ani, the Shepherd's Chapel (second half of the tenth century) is a small circular building the upper storey of which is vaulted with a dome resting on six arches radiating from a central key-stone. Again, at Ani, in the porch of the church of the Holy Apostles (mid eleventh century), two bays are each covered with a vault resting on two diagonally intersecting arches. Other Armenian buildings are of similar structure (Horomos Vank; Aradesh), either of the same period or later, but based on an older prototype. All these arches are of square or rectangular cross-section, very strong and often of considerable span, and therefore absolutely different from the Arabic ribbing. In Christian Europe itself the oldest example of rib-vaulting appeared in the eleventh century in Lombardy, perhaps as early as the middle of the century if the springers of Sannazzaro Sesia belong to the original construction (1040–60); certainly at the end of it, at San Nazzaro, Milan (1075) or at San Giacomo at Corneto (1095). At nearly the same time, between 1060 and 1075, over the ground-floor room of the north bell-tower of Bayeux cathedral a vault with a strong convex curve is reinforced by arches intersecting crosswise, presenting the same rectangular section as the Armenian rib-vaults and springing not from the corners, but from the middle of the sides as at Horomos Vank. This connexion seems beyond doubt. Section and arrangement are similar at Loches, in the bell-tower of the church of Saint-Ours (late eleventh century), at Cormery (Loir-et-Cher, same date). In the church of Sainte-Croix at Quimperlé, begun in 1083 – a building of markedly oriental plan in which the four arms of the cross radiate from a circular rotunda – two very flat arches intersect under the dome. Nothing came of all these attempts. To succeed, the ribbing had to be applied neither to a dome, nor to the room of a bell-tower, but to the bay of a church. This was attempted in England at Durham Cathedral, begun in 1093. Thus, if it is held that the Gothic style is characterized solely by the use of ribbed vaults, this cathedral would have to be called the first Gothic structure.

¶ ROOFING

Neither the vault nor the ceiling would be sufficient to protect a building from the weather. They themselves need to be protected, and this is the function of the roof, which may be either of tiles or slates attached to a wooden framework (pitched roof) or of horizontal masonry in the form of a terrace (flat roof). These two roofing methods make buildings look quite different. Moreover, until the twentieth century, they depended on geographical factors and the demands of the climate, rather than on aesthetic choice. The pitched roof is appropriate to northern countries; its slope prevents snow from accumulating. The Mediterranean region is characterized by the terraced roof.

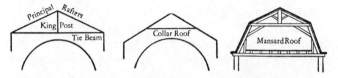

Figure 8. The principle of roofing

A roof framework is a series of 'trusses' in metal or wood. A truss is a rigid construction in the shape of an isosceles triangle. The base of the triangle BC is the 'tie-beam'; the sides AB, AC are the principal rafters; the height AD is the 'king-post'. The rafters, which might tend to flatten out and be forced apart, are kept in place by the tie-beam and king-post. In order to make the triangle fit the vault more snugly, the tie-beam can be set as much as half-way up the lateral sides; in this case, the structure is like the letter A. This system is known as the 'collar-roof' (fig. 8). The trusses are joined together by a horizontal ridge piece, on which are laid the lighter pieces (rafters and planks) on to which the slates or tiles are fixed. The sloping roof may be straight or broken (curb-roof or 'Mansard'). The appearance of the roof depends to a great extent on the quality of the tiles; those produced nowadays are a glaring red and do not weather like those of earlier periods. In place of tiles or slates, sheets of metal (lead on certain cathedrals) or slabs of stone, have also been used. It must also be remembered that many great buildings have neither vault nor ceiling, and all the framework of their roofs is exposed on the inside.

The terraced roof was practically unknown to French architecture until the sixteenth century, when, as we shall see, it was introduced together with other imitations of Italian buildings. Apart from the difficulty of making it water-tight, its use is highly unsuitable in combination with the chimney-stacks indispensable in a cold country. The unhappy result is demonstrated in the Place de la Concorde. Nowadays, with the advent of reinforced concrete and its influence on masonry, flat roofs are used much more; regional differences in architecture tend to be eliminated and the same kind of roof may be seen in Oslo and Algiers.

CHAPTER TWO

AESTHETIC PROBLEMS

WHATEVER the technical methods used for carrying out a building programme, it is rare for architects worthy of the name to be content with satisfying material needs. One of the great masters of the fifteenth century, Alberti, author of one of the first modern treatises on architecture, says that an architectural work must have a double aim – *commoditas* and *voluptas*: *commoditas*, the precise adaptation to an end, what we should call functionalism; *voluptas*, the pleasure of the eye and mind, which would be art for art's sake if building were not intrinsically a useful craft. It is the *voluptas* added to the *commoditas* which distinguishes an architect from an engineer. Compare, writes Perret,* Chartres cathedral with the hangars of Orly, which are the work of a very great engineer but not of an architect. 'On seeing these hangars in the distance, one wonders what those two half buried pipes can be. On seeing the cathedral of Chartres from the same distance, one wonders what this great building is. And yet one could easily put Reims, Paris, and Chartres in a single hangar at Orly and within its area that of five cathedrals.'

In what, then, does architectural *voluptas* consist? For Alberti all beauty comes from harmonious proportions which are, in the last analysis, mathematical. Architecture, especially, is nothing but a series of mathematical proportions. The same holds for music. The architect must 'search for proportions which remain harmonious in music, and avoid on the other hand those which would grate on the ear as dissonant'. The difference between the hangars of Orly and the cathedral of Chartres, continues Perret, 'is that the Orly hangars as an architectural work lack Scale, Proportion, Harmony, Humanity.' And finally, let us quote a contemporary who is often considered the most utilitarian and strictly functionalist of

* *Revue d'art et d'esthétique*, No. 1, 1935.

men, Le Corbusier. 'Beauty? Proportion, that *nothing* which is *everything* and gives life to all. ... We must enlighten people's minds on the radiant forces of divine proportion. I consider that no one has the right to become an architect unless he feels that grace is bestowed on him.'*

So everyone is in agreement as to the aim – to create an architectural beauty which is not simply utilitarian – as they are about the means; and here the same words always come up again – ratios, proportions.

But there are ratios – as there are chords in music – which are harmonious and others which are not. There are proportions which are good and others which are bad. How is one to choose? Here architects become much more reserved and willingly make way for critics and commentators. These do not fail to discover intentions in their works, which are possible or even probable, but are often unconscious or have never been confirmed by the architect in words. Let us then limit ourselves to indicating, in a purely historical spirit, the principal attempts made to discover this beauty. They are of several kinds.

Mathematical Beauty

First to be examined are those attempts based on the idea that beauty is something absolute with an independent existence, coming from the application of certain geometrical formulae or the observance of certain mathematical ratios. It is a method submitting to authority, and leading to the formulation of rules, the observance of which is the guarantee of success. Critics often confuse the different concepts of ratio and proportion, which are carefully distinguished by mathematicians.

(a) *Scale* is important, said Perret. Scale is a ratio, the relation between two magnitudes. The standard of comparison is often the normal height of a man; but it can also be another part of the building or the building as a whole, or the background against which it is set. For example, when we say that

Quand les cathédrales étaient blanches, Paris, 1937, p. 302.

the portal of a Gothic cathedral is on a human scale, we mean
that it takes man for its measure, that it is calculated to allow
the passage of a man through it. In 1771 the canons of Notre-
Dame in Paris had the lintel of the centre portal destroyed
because it hindered the passage of the canopy under which the
archbishop went when processions came out of the church.
The gates of the Louvre, in contrast, are 32 feet high; their
dimensions are no longer calculated in relation to those who
pass through, but in relation to the building as a whole; tall
portals and large buildings go together. The same principle
was applied to Greek temples. The houses of the Place
Vendôme in Paris were made to frame a statue of Louis XIV.
They are 64 feet high and the statue was 56 feet high with its
pedestal. This ratio was upset when the 147-foot Vendôme
column was substituted for the statue. The content became
higher than the container. We say that the column is no longer
in scale with the square; and in this case, in contrast to the two
previous examples, it cannot be compared to anything, it is
out of scale and cannot be justified. It is out of harmony.

(b) *The module.* The module is a unit chosen as the measure
of all or part of an architectural composition. Generally it is
an element in the composition itself, for example the diameter
of the column in a colonnade. The necessity of deciding on a
module has been stressed by Vitruvius and all architectural treatises since the Renaissance. Actually, they have examined hardly anything but the proportions of the column.
The requirement of a module would in itself be commonplace
enough – some may calculate in diameters of columns as
others calculate in heads for a statue, or in feet or metres for a
building. But this doctrine goes further. It fixes the number of
modules to be given to the various elements of the order to
obtain a satisfactory effect. Here the figures given by Vignola
have most often laid down the law. The height of the column
must be seven times its diameter in the Tuscan order, eight
times in the Doric order, nine times in the Ionic order, and
ten times in the Corinthian order. The relation between the
parts of the order must also be fixed. For an order with pedestal, the total height is divided into nineteen parts, four of

which are given to the pedestal, twelve to the column, and three to the entablature; for an order without pedestal, four parts are given to the column and one to the entablature. Indications of this kind, which at the time constituted imperative rules, abound in the treatises of the seventeenth and eighteenth centuries. The entablature must be one quarter the height of the column; the diameter of the Doric column must be one eighth of its height, and so on.

(c) *Geometrical figures.* The perfection of certain geometrical figures has led architects to follow them in their designs. Viollet-le-Duc* holds that Romanesque and Gothic architects based their churches on geometrical patterns. Good proportion, he says, is that which expresses the idea of stability; the triangle, being the most stable figure, is therefore the most satisfactory, and the great cathedrals are systems of related triangles. The Middle Ages appear to have preferred three kinds of triangle: the right-angled isosceles triangle in which the angles at the base are 45°; the Egyptian isosceles triangle in which the proportion of the base to the height is four to two-and-a-half, the angles at the base being 52°; and the equilateral triangle, the highest pitched of the three, which has angles of 60° at the base.

Analysing Saint-Sernin at Toulouse, Viollet-le-Duc showed that all its dimensions are based on a system of equilateral and right-angled isosceles triangles. The apex of the great nave is that of an equilateral triangle having the width of the church for its base. The apex of a right-angled isosceles triangle constructed on the same base corresponds to the level of the capitals of the galleries. The cathedrals of Amiens and Paris, he considered, were planned with the aid of Egyptian and equilateral triangles (*IXᵉ Entretien sur l'architecture*). The right-angled isosceles triangle, the flattest of the three, was eliminated in the Gothic period, which strove upwards, with the exception of Bourges cathedral which is still half-Romanesque in spirit.

Are these remarks the result of Viollet-le-Duc's imagination, or are they based on historical fact? The regulations out-

Dictionnaire d'Architecture française, article on 'Proportion'.

lined in the notebooks of Villard de Honnecourt – the only document we possess, besides the works themselves, dealing with the practice of the architect's profession in the Middle Ages – do indeed seem to indicate that the theories of Viollet-le-Duc contain at least a semblance of truth. Philibert Delorme, Mansart, François Blondel, also used geometrical patterns. The dome of the Invalides was planned on a system of tri-angles. François Blondel, in his *Traité d'architecture* (1675), himself points out the combination of circles which he used for the Porte Saint-Denis in Paris; they are, as a matter of fact, simple enough – the building, square in outline, is inscribed in a circle, the centre of which is also the centre of the circle of the great archway of the gate; the height of the archway is equal to twice the diameter of this small circle, etc.

(d) *Proportion* and the '*golden section*'. If one wishes to deter-mine the height of a building in relation to its breadth and length, one has to combine their proportions. Many combina-tions are possible, and mathematicians as early as classical antiquity, notably Pythagoras and his followers, discussed this subject widely. Since the treatise of the Bolognese monk Fra Luca Pacioli di Borgo, *De divina proportione* (Venice, 1509), theorists have been occupied chiefly with the proportion described as 'divine', which concerns only two lengths, *a* and *b*, the elements of the second ratio being one length of the first ratio and the sum of its two lengths: $\frac{a}{b}=\frac{b}{a+b}$. Numerically it may be expressed thus: $\frac{0\cdot618}{1}=\frac{1}{1\cdot618}$. Graphically, it is expressed by a line so divided that the smaller part is to the larger as the larger is to the whole, or it corresponds to a rectangle of which one side is to the other as 0·618 is to 1 (or as 1 is to 1·618). This is known as the 'golden section'. It is possible that certain architects may have used it to establish their schemes of proportion; the formula seems really rather to have been employed by painters: it presupposes an almost abstract inde-pendence as far as the dimensions of the site are concerned, which architects in practice do not enjoy.

The French classical treatises, particularly that of François Blondel, generally consider the height to be given to a build-ing in relation to the area it covers. They follow the three

systems of proportions already indicated by Alberti – the
arithmetic mean (the intermediary term is half the sum of the
other two, e.g. 2, 3, 4); the geometric mean (the intermediary
term is the square root of the product of the two others – 4,
6, 9); and the harmonic mean (the intermediary term is obtained by dividing twice the product of the two others by
their sum – 3, 4, 6). Generally the length is the largest dimension, the breadth the smallest, and the height the medium
one. But of these three systems, which should one choose?
François Blondel did not commit himself.

We can at least believe that beauty is dependent on certain
mathematical proportions. 'Beauty,' says Blondel, 'is born
from dimension and proportion; far from being dependent on
material or delicacy of treatment and execution, it bursts forth
and makes itself felt even in impurity, so to speak, and amid
the confusion of the material itself and the work of the
building.'*

(e) *The optical scale and the best angle of vision.* We can express
in figures the distance – relative to the height – from which a
monument should be seen; this will be the number of degrees
in the angle from which it is perceived. It may be that the
aesthetic superiority of certain proportions can ultimately be
explained by physiological factors. The problem is too complicated and too specialized to be dealt with here. As for the
angle of vision, it is certain that the human eye is made in such
a way that it can only see a building well at a distance of three
times the height of the building, that is to say, at an angle of
18°. If the distance is greater, the building gradually loses its
individuality, its outline becomes confused with the neighbouring ones. And if the distance is less, say twice the height
(an angle of 27°), one can still see the whole, but nothing of its
character, and the monument no longer appears in its setting.
At a distance equal to its height (angle of 45°) one sees only
details. Alberti held that the ideal breadth of a square should
be three to six times the height of the surrounding buildings,
so that from its centre there would be at the most a proportion
of one to three, that is, an angle of vision of 18°. In the seven-

Cours d'architecture, p. 774.

teenth century Jules Hardouin-Mansart, in the plan a.
tion of his great royal squares, guessed and insti.
applied this rule, later established by physiologists.

Symmetry and Harmony

Another element of beauty – probably also coming from an
unconscious obedience to mathematical or physiological laws
– consists in the observance of certain rules of symmetry and
order. This can be checked by examining the building from
several points of view, and we shall see that in this respect the
medieval and classical ages did not always react in the same
way.

¶ I. THE PLAN

The analysis of a plan not only gives a rough estimate of its
date, but sometimes indicates an author's nationality – a
Frenchman does not create in the same way as either a German
or an Italian.

It is rare for a medieval building to follow rigorously the
law of symmetry. Yet it may be argued that the right and left
halves of a church are alike. Not always. In the first place, the
axis is frequently not even rectilinear. Deviations are so frequent that some writers have tried to maintain that they are
systematic and symbolic, and see in them a reference to the
dying Christ whose head leans to one side on the cross. To-day
this idea seems to have been abandoned and we are forced to
admit that in the course of the various stages of construction
the master builders simply neglected to continue to follow the
original axis.

What is more, even in a church with a true axis, it is not
unusual to see chapels and sacristies added on right and left
and the growth of subsidiary buildings in no way corresponding to the elements on the other side of the axis. In the
cathedral of Chartres, the thirteenth-century sacristy is asym-

metrical; the chapel of Saint-Piat, added at the back in the
fourteenth century, is not even a direct extension of the rest.
At Paris, the two lateral façades of the cathedral are not alike
and do not have the same number of porches. It is the same at
Reims. The church, again, most often formed part of a whole:
it was surrounded or flanked either by the cemetery, by
abbatial or canonical buildings, or by an episcopal palace,
schools, or other buildings, each of them planned with regard
to its own special relation to the church, without any respect
for symmetry.

The same holds for dwellings. The cloister plan is the most
geometric of medieval plans, but the buildings surrounding
it present no kind of symmetry in relation to each other, not
even in the ground-plan, and even less in their mass. They
project in all directions, sometimes parallel and sometimes
perpendicular to the galleries. This is even more true of the
inner court of a castle or a house, which does not always provide a regular setting, where the buildings are simply juxta-
posed and not grouped according to an abstract order. A
medieval building is like an old family house, to which each
generation has added a room, perhaps a whole wing, according to its owners' needs. The only definite rule is necessity,
that is to say the demands of everyday life. It is all as if
medieval architects held variety and irregularity to be the very
expression of life.

It is quite a problem to establish at exactly what date a strict
symmetry was imposed on plans in France. We do not find it
at either Amboise, Blois, or Gaillon, but we do at Chambord
(1526). Possibly it appeared at the end of the fifteenth century
at the Château du Verger in Anjou; there the rectangular
great court is surrounded on three sides by the wings.

Once symmetry had been achieved for a simple building
like a house or a palace, from the mid sixteenth century onwards architects devised great undertakings in which the
elements were exactly ordered and balanced around multiple
axes reminiscent of the vast Roman complexes, the Thermae of
Diocletian or of Caracalla. Such is the Tuileries planned by
Philibert Delorme; such is the château of Charleval, on an

even greater scale, conceived by Du Cerceau for Charles IX. At that time Italy could boast of only one experiment of the same order, Bramante's Vatican, which is a rearrangement. But in Spain we must not forget Herrera's Escorial, which really constitutes the first grand architectural composition realized in Europe.

In the seventeenth and eighteenth centuries, intention and design materialized – Versailles, Marly, the Invalides, the École Militaire were built. Here we must take into account two influences: the arts of garden planning and town planning. At Versailles gardens and town, both designed by Le Nôtre, preceded and inspired the great château of Le Vau and Jules Hardouin-Mansart.

For those who cannot build towns or palaces or lay out gardens, there is always paper. The competitions for the *Prix de Rome* have enabled generations of architects to express their need for symmetry and their dreams of grandeur. 'It would be possible,' L. Hautecœur once said, 'to write a history of architectural composition in the nineteenth century based on the *Prix de Rome*. We may question certain results of these exercises; one of them we cannot deny: no school knows how to draw up a plan like the French school.'

¶ II. THE FAÇADE

A façade may, like a plan, be considered merely as a play of lines, rising vertically instead of being read horizontally. But up to what point has one the right to separate its appearance from the building itself, and to submit it to a universal rule of symmetry? Should not the façade limit itself to the expression of a given internal arrangement, as a quotient expresses the result of a division? It is the old controversy of the relation of form and content. Those who believe that they are inseparable say that only in this way is architecture sincere and logical, leaving one to suppose that it is false and illogical otherwise. In this context Viollet-le-Duc praised the truth and logic of the Middle Ages and opposed to them the insincerity of later centuries.

It is true that in the façade of a Gothic house the distribution of the openings, for example, is made not according to symmetry but according to actual needs; here a small window, there a large one, at one point a single opening, at another several grouped together. On the contrary, in a seventeenth-century façade, such as that of the Château of Maisons by François Mansart, the harmoniously distributed windows have no connexion with the interior. We even find Hardouin-Mansart, in the Place des Victoires, putting up a façade in space, a wall with nothing behind it. The architect Daviler, in his *Traité d'architecture*, one of the most famous of the late seventeenth century, laid down the principle that 'the beauty of a building comes before domestic economy, and therefore the organization of space must follow the rules of fine decoration rather than the practical needs of the family'.

But did the Middle Ages never do the same? To pass judgement here we must examine what is certainly architects' and not masons' work, that is the churches, above all the large ones. We find in them many inconsistencies in the arrangement of the openings. The cathedral of Paris has a nave and four aisles, and three porches; but in the cathedral of Reims, which is divided into a nave and two aisles, the two buttresses at the end of the façade are capped with gables and decorated like the three porches, giving the impression that there are really five.

In fact, the arrangement of openings is not the only element brought into play. There are Romanesque and Gothic churches in which false gables rise into space from the centre of the façade, walls behind which there is nothing at all – as in S. Michele at Lucca, at Tarragona, and even in France, at Saint-Père-sous-Vézelay. And the convex gable of the great church of Vézelay itself can hardly pass as part of the main block of the wall.

Viollet-le-Duc maintained that all Gothic architecture was no more than a series of theorems rigorously deduced one from the other, starting from the rib-vault. More recent historians have shown that this was not the case at all and that the Gothic style, like the classical style, was only the expres-

the royal squares), roof with dormer windows. The variety with which these three themes are treated shows the prodigious invention of an art often wrongly considered as bound to a few generalized formulas.

The stressing of the centre and extremities of the façade can be solved in as many different ways. In Lescot's Louvre, centre and extremities are clearly stressed by their curved pediments, but all three are of the same height and what is more are all placed below the main roof-line. In the Hôtel Lamoignon (Paris, about 1580), the central pediment is much lower than the pediments of the wings; but it is triangular, while the others are curvilinear. At Maisons, François Mansart clearly emphasized the supremacy of the centre, but the pediment still stands out against the roof, which is, moreover, raised at this point. At Vaux-le-Vicomte (Le Vau, 1661), only the centre is given a pediment, but the accent is strengthened still more by a large dome. On the colonnade of the Louvre there is a single pediment in the centre rising openly above the great horizontal line of the terrace. At Versailles (garden façade) there is no pediment, the supremacy of the centre is stressed by a group of six columns forming a projection, while the secondary motifs, placed a little in front of the ends, have only four columns. In the École Militaire (Gabriel, 1752), a colonnaded projection, a pediment, and a four-sided dome simultaneously mark the centre of the composition. We mention here only monuments of the first rank, but in the provinces of France there are countless modest eighteenth-century châteaux to which a small pediment, even without antique orders, straight away lends an air of elegance and nobility.

Moreover, we find the same desire for clarity and balance in the French ecclesiastical buildings of medieval or modern times, which often distinguishes them from the churches of other countries. In the façade of the cathedral of Paris (Notre-Dame) the vertical and horizontal divisions are as solidly stressed as in any composition of the classical period. We are reminded of a tragedy by Racine. No one would dream of making the same comparison before the Milan cathedral or St Peter's at Rome. Certainly one may prefer them to the

Parisian cathedral, but for quite other reasons, for they are neither so easily read at a glance nor so well proportioned and at the same time so well ordered. On the other hand, one immediately recognizes the work of a French architect abroad, even in a simple barracks like that built by Jardin at Copenhagen, not far from the Rosenborg palace.

¶ III. VOLUME

Finally, a building is composed not merely of lines but of volumes. A full-scale model must be made from the plan. A building is not just a façade, but three-dimensional. And it must do more than remain erect, it has to fulfil intellectual demands.

(a) We must consider first of all the number and nature of the volumes of which it is the aggregate, two problems rather than one. Volumes are sometimes simple and sometimes complex, sometimes few in number and sometimes many; the two gradations do not necessarily go together. Romanesque architects liked simple volumes. They kept to a few uncomplicated geometrical forms, but they varied and sometimes accumulated them. At the beginning of the Gothic period, in the first Cistercian churches, volumes were simple and few in number. Everybody is familiar with the cardboard houses which children play with. To set up a model of a Cistercian building one would have only to make a few straight cuts in the sheet with the scissors – one rectangle with a pitched roof for the nave and apse; two smaller rectangles, their upper parts slightly sloping, for the side aisles; two others of an intermediate height for the arms of the transepts. All this forms five elementary blocks – in the gamut of construction games the Cistercian church would be reserved for beginners. After it might be suggested seventeenth or late eighteenth-century buildings, easily reduced to a few simple volumes – the Petit Trianon is a cube. Then would come the Gothic cathedrals of the thirteenth century. Flamboyant Gothic and Rococo would be reserved for those who, virtuosi in cutting out and setting up, are skilled enough to produce a flowering of bell-turrets and pinnacles, progressively more complex volumes, a wild growth foreign at once to logic and geometry.

Reinforced concrete permits the most extraordinary overhangings, and the architect often yields to the temptation of stressing the resources of this material by multiplying irregularities. Some works remain close to the cube, while others are cascades of cubes – simple geometrical elements of complicated assembly.

(b) We must look next at this grouping of volumes. It is not sufficient for the building to be solid in fact, it must seem so and convey that impression. Though we can amuse ourselves for a few moments looking at a juggler balancing a pyramid on its vertex, continually correcting the instability of its position by a reflex movement, the sight of a building built in that way would worry us and we would not enjoy living in it. Eye and mind agree in demanding an appearance of stability. The latter may however vary within certain limits and the different periods of French art have played on this very cleverly, to reconcile respect for appearance with the conquest of space, which is the true aim of the architect. All the same, there is no ground for such clear-cut distinctions between the two as are often made.

It is the custom to speak of the *verticality* of Gothic and to attribute to classical art a preference for a balanced horizontality. This distinction requires some amendment.

We may lay down as a principle that in every period architects have been anxious to achieve the conquest of space as completely as possible; that is to climb progressively higher, but each in the measure of his technical means. Let us compare the thirteenth and seventeenth centuries, taking only comparable examples, the churches. In the thirteenth century architects rivalled one another to surpass the vaulting of the neighbouring cathedral. This competition would be expressed in present-day sporting language as 'trying to break a record'. That of Chartres is broken by Reims, which is broken by Amiens, broken in its turn by Beauvais. But the same rivalry existed in the seventeenth century. This time the stake was the height of the dome; each architect strove to raise his own to the highest possible point. He perched it on a drum, made a second drum rise up from the first, tapered the lines of the cupola, capped it with a lantern. In short, they all piled Pelion on Ossa, all rushing to the assault of the heavens. The spirit which drove Mansart in the Invalides, or Soufflot in Sainte-Geneviève, was just the same as that which possessed their ancestors in the thirteenth century.

The difference does not lie in the aim; it lies in the means, or rather the methods. It can be grasped well by comparing the geometrical figures on which the various types are based. The Romanesque architect took the pyramid for his model. His lines ascended and his will to soar upwards was doubtless as great as that of his Gothic colleague, but the ascent was gradual. In the choir the volumes make up a pyramid in which each step is supported on the previous one; it is at the very centre of the building, at the transept crossing, that a lantern-tower crowns the mass of the building. The progression enchants by its harmony and regular ascent. It is of the same kind and quality in Mansart and his rivals. The dome is set well in the centre of the composition, and the dome of the Invalides rises up from a solid cubic pedestal; by joining up the base and the summit one would obtain an equilateral triangle.

The difference between Romanesque and Gothic architecture is the same as that between nineteenth-century iron construction and the reinforced concrete of to-day. The Eiffel Tower is, indeed, one of the highest buildings made by man; but it rises in stages and its contour is still that of a pyramid pitched on four feet set wide apart. A chimney of reinforced concrete – that, for example, of the Usine des Tramways Départementaux of Haute-Vienne, or an American sky-scraper with vertical steel walls – does not often climb so high, but its ascent is less gradual. Greater verticality is not synonymous with greater elevation.

'Verticality' should not be used too readily as a criterion to make distinctions of period. There is nothing more vertical than a Romanesque Catalan tower, such as that of Cuixa, or than the bell towers of Saint-Étienne at Caen, whereas the

Gothic tower of Saint-Sernin at Toulouse is inscribed in a pyramid. Even in church cross-sections, that of the single-naved Gothic churches of the Midi (Toulouse cathedral and the cathedral of Perpignan) is much nearer to a square than that of many Romanesque churches. In the most classical domestic architecture certain distinctions can be established: the superimposing of different orders stresses horizontality; the colossal single order, with the shafts of its pilasters linking up two storeys, is a search for verticality.

Decoration

There remains one last problem, so complex that we shall content ourselves with an indication of how it arises – that of decoration. To give architecture this *voluptas*, is it necessary to employ means other than the architectural – one might say architectonic – combinations that we have just analysed? Does the architect need the sculptor and the painter? The reply varies according to the period, but not perhaps according to the greater periods.

It would be incorrect, on this score, to contrast as a whole the Middle Ages with the classical centuries, though everyone knows the magnificent sculpture of the Gothic cathedrals, and that the classical theorists always affirmed that good proportions were enough for beauty. The sculptured scenes unfolded on the tympana of the churches of the thirteenth century are not a decoration, that is to say superfluous, but a part of the building. They are like a poster on a poster board. At a time when the majority of the faithful were illiterate, the Bible or Gospel stories were inscribed in stone to give them instruction. The architect knew that he had to reserve a place for them; it remained for him to choose it, to outline its frame and, since he was in charge of the work, he had the right to keep an eye on how this frame was filled.

Many historians – and some of the best – hold that the relation between architecture and decoration is defined by a kind of law distinguishing three stages: a first stage in which the supremacy of architecture is fully stressed; a second in which equal stress is put on architect and decorator; and a third marked by the triumph of the decorative over the architectural spirit. But the evolution of neither medieval nor classical architecture shows us anything of the kind. It would be wrong to say that the architectural spirit at the end of the Middle Ages, during the Flamboyant period, was in regression. Never has technique been more perfect or daring. If decoration seems more abundant it is because the architects converted into decoration indispensable elements of their technique; they loaded their buttresses with pinnacles or gables, because the slenderer they were the more they had to be ballasted. This anticipates the application of Fénélon's formula: to turn constructive essentials into decorative themes. But the former remain the dominant factor. The eighteenth century shows that the flowery character of the Rococo, often compared to the Flamboyant, was followed by the doubly austere trend of neo-classical art, the ruthless enemy of all decoration.

Rather than such a succession of three stages, it seems that there is an alternating pattern in the forces influencing building. An ornate period is followed by an austere one. It is like the swing of a pendulum. The law of the three stages arose from an assimilation of art to biology, from a comparison of the destiny of form with the destiny of man, whose decline is marked less by weakening than by the proliferation and independence of the cells, each of which seeks to live on its own account. Once again this is making a principle out of a metaphor. Forms have no life of their own. They are given life by man, and, when we are speaking of art, by human taste. But the law of human taste is one of periodic change and return, the law of contrast which governs the generations. Miserly father, prodigal son; after Louis XIV, the Regency; after Romanticism, Realism; after 1900, Cubism.

Therefore, rather than a necessary evolution of art in a given direction, a series of ebbs and flows can be discerned. But this law, like all the laws of history, can be put forward only with prudence; it is no more valid than any other generalization, or than the law of probability. Architecture is a conflict between the constructive and the decorative impulses, and sometimes it is one and sometimes the other which carries the day; but there are certain countries in which the masterpieces, or at least the most characteristic works, coincide with the triumph of one or the other of the two elements. In France, however, these two impulses have always balanced each other, but rightfully giving the architect, that is the builder, the foremost position in the construction.

CHAPTER THREE

HISTORICAL PROBLEMS

How can the various periods of French architecture be distinguished if its general characteristics remain the same throughout its history? By differences of technique, by variation in the use of ornament, and even by the plan. All these differences result from changes in political, economic, or spiritual conditions, or from external influences.

The last, because of their importance, must be mentioned immediately after technique, the evolution of which has been sketched above. The various provinces of the artistic world have never been entirely cut off from one another. France, for her part, has both given and taken much, given much to the living and taken much from the dead. Four external influences have acted on her architecture – the East, Classical Antiquity, Italy, and England. This applies only to architecture; they would not, of course, be the same for painting.

The Influences

¶ THE EAST

The first influence to be felt in France after the fall of the Roman Empire was that of the East. It was felt throughout the early Middle Ages and up to the thirteenth century. What is implied by the comprehensive term 'East'? Generally speaking, at this time, it was the near East that counted. In the beginning (notably during the Merovingian period) it was mainly Syria, the land of Christ and the first Christian communities. At this time the Mediterranean was a closely united world, crossed in every direction by a multitude of currents.

People travelled from one shore to the other, exchanging products and ideas. There were colonies of Syrian merchants in France throughout the south, at Marseilles and Narbonne, and we have accounts of others at Orleans and Tours. In Paris, in 591, a Syrian merchant, Eusebius, managed to get himself elected bishop and distributed all the ecclesiastical positions in his diocese to his compatriots. From Syria, also, came the monastic system. So it is in no way surprising that the first Christian basilicas in Gaul reproduced certain peculiarities of the Syrian churches. Moreover, it must be noted that in this matter North Africa seems often to have played an intermediary rôle. A little later more complicated plans (centralized plans – Saint-Front at Périgueux is a replica of the church of the Holy Apostles at Constantinople) came from Byzantium, Asia Minor, and Transcaucasia, together with certain vaulting techniques, notably the rib-vault. From the ninth century onwards, particular importance must be attributed to Armenia. Armenians occupied the papal throne. The cult of Armenian saints spread through Europe. In the tenth century, St Gregory, Armenian bishop of Nicopolis, after resigning his office, came to live as a hermit near Pithiviers, whose parish church possesses one of the oldest examples of rib-vaulting.

Another oriental influence to keep in mind is the Arabic. The Arabs were often only intermediaries, but it was through them that the more distant influences of Mesopotamia and Persia were transmitted to Europe. France was the first to profit by them, since the outpost of the Arab empire to the West was her neighbour Spain. The importance of what is known as Mozarabic art – in theory the art of the Christians subject to Arab domination, in fact the contribution of Arabic art to Christian art – becomes more evident every day. Certain rib-vaults of the south of France are transpositions of the ribbed cupolas of the mosque of Cordova. A little later the Crusades were to put the Franks directly in contact with Islam, and French military architecture profited greatly from the technical superiority of the enemy.

¶ CLASSICAL ANTIQUITY

The influence of classical antiquity (Greek and Roman) was much more continuous. At the very start French architecture succeeded Gallo-Roman architecture and from this heritage it gained a broad classical basis. All the same, the memory of it was lost all the more quickly in that the principal buildings, the churches, escaped in it; receiving their spiritual significance from the East they received thence also their models for building and decorating. The reconciliation of Christianity and paganism in church building itself was to come in the sixteenth century. It was one of the results of what is called the Renaissance. The word is ambiguous, but we will give it simply the sense of a resurrection of antiquity. Historians of thought and of art in general admit that the Renaissance of the sixteenth century was preceded by several others – there was a Carolingian Renaissance and a Gothic Renaissance, but neither influenced architecture. We can speak rather of a Romanesque Renaissance, considering the importance of classical Roman influences in the decoration of certain twelfth-century Romanesque churches, notably in Burgundy and Provence.

But from the sixteenth century onwards architects proclaimed their intention of taking the monuments of antiquity as their models. The only Roman treatise on architecture which has come down to us, that of Vitruvius, already known in the Middle Ages, was at this time frequently translated and edited. The first French edition was that of Jean Martin, 1546 – *Architecture de Vitruve ou Art de bien bâtir, mis du latin en français*; Jean Goujon took a large part in it and composed a preliminary epistle to the reader. Architects began to go to Rome to study and measure the antique monuments on the spot – Philibert Delorme was one of the first. Later on they were to be admitted to the French Academy in Rome. The essential part of the architectural treatises consisted of comments on the five orders of Vitruvius – Tuscan, Doric, Ionic, Corinthian, and Composite. The Italians naturally had the upper hand here, though Vitruvius arrived in France not across the Alps but over the Pyrenees, since the edition of Jean Martin was preceded in 1539 by the *Raison d'architecture extraite de Vitruve et autres architectes nouvellement traduite d'espagnol en français*. Note, in this context, that the Renaissance declared itself much earlier in Spain than in France and relations with Spain were much more highly developed at the beginning of the sixteenth century, so that it would perhaps be fitting to grant Spain a larger part in the diffusion of classicism in France than is generally done. Nevertheless the most famous examples were in Italy. Only in Rome did Bramante dare to build at San Pietro in Montorio on the Janiculum a church in the form of a circular temple, like that of the Forum Boarium or the Greek *tholoi*. The great commentaries on Vitruvius are the four great Italian treatises on architecture by Alberti, Serlio, Palladio, and Vignola; and it is on this account that they enjoyed immense prestige in France for more than two centuries.

Yet Italy herself, by the second half of the sixteenth century, began to detach herself from antiquity. France in her turn was to finish by paying it only lip service, striving to live her own architectural life. Towards the beginning of the eighteenth century there was a new eclipse of antiquity, followed in the third quarter of the century by a new Renaissance. The vogue for neo-classical art lasted roughly from 1775 to 1840; it was killed by the Romantic Movement.

¶ ITALY

Now we must turn to Italy itself which so far has only been mentioned as a mediator. To Italy, or rather to northern Italy or Lombardy, was long attributed an important part in the formation of the French Romanesque architecture of the eleventh century. Puig i Cadafalch has shown that Lombard art was only a geographical aspect of a much more general movement, the first Romanesque style, which was itself only one of the manifestations of the East in Europe; it appeared at Ravenna, but it originated in Mesopotamia and Sassanian Persia. Moreover in this first Romanesque **art**

Catalonia held a greater place than Lombardy; she offers the first examples of wholly vaulted churches – a fact which is all the more important for France because at this time Catalonia, included in the Carolingian empire, was under French suzerainty. The exceptional use of rib-vaults in Lombardy has also been pointed out; but this seems to have had little influence in France. The sources of French Gothic art, at least of French rib-vaults, are elsewhere.

It is only from the end of the fifteenth century, especially after Charles VIII's expedition to Naples, that we can speak of an Italian influence on French architecture. Italy introduced herself to the French under a dual mien and with a twofold prestige: as the home of antiquity and – perhaps of even greater account at the time – from the very charm of life in Italy and from her houses. Although the Italian architects brought back by Charles VIII, Fra Giocondo and Domenico da Cortona called Boccador, did not build much in France, all the decoration of the early Renaissance (*c.* 1500–25) is borrowed from one of the most famous monuments of Italian architecture at the end of the fifteenth century, the *Certosa*, or Carthusian monastery of Pavia, near Milan. Evidently Louis XII's expedition to Lombardy was of even more importance than the Neapolitan journey of Charles VIII. With François I it was della Robbia, Serlio, Primaticcio, and Vignola who came to France. They did not transform the technique of French building but they modified its spirit and taught the new decorative style of stucco and painting, of which Raphael and Giulio Romano had given accomplished examples in the Vatican and the Palazzo del Té at Mantua. But under Henri II, French architecture was already becoming independent. In 1559 Du Cerceau wrote in the dedication to the king of his *Livre d'architecture*, 'Since your Majesty takes pleasure and delight in employing such excellent craftsmen from your own nation, it will no longer be necessary to have recourse to foreigners.' France wished to act for herself, while following both antiquity and her own traditions.

Whereas the Wars of Religion put a stop to almost all artistic development in France towards the end of the sixteenth century, Italy, starting from the religious inspiration of the Counter-Reformation, elaborated a new style which no longer had anything antique about it apart from a few decorative formulas: this became known as 'Baroque'. The whole of Europe was to be overwhelmed by it, although in France its influence was not absolute, nor did it last for any length of time. The decisive episode was the invitation given by Louis XIV to Bernini, the greatest master of the Baroque, to put forward plans for the completion of the Louvre, the Italian artist's arrival in Paris, and the eventual failure of his projects. For the second time France liberated herself from Italian influence. 'Before the reign of Louis XIV,' writes Patte, 'Italy alone was regarded as the home of the arts and letters.... People rushed there from every side as if to imbibe the true principles of the fine arts at their source.'

¶ ENGLAND

There remains England. Her rôle is extremely important in the formation of French Gothic in the twelfth century, for England was then Norman and a province of France. After having done so much for Gothic art, England later came entirely under the influence of the Renaissance. Perhaps she was – at least in architecture – the European country which remained most faithful to this tradition and submitted least to Baroque. English historians of the Renaissance legitimately prolong the period to two centuries. Even if the discoveries of Herculaneum and Pompeii were largely responsible for the appearance of neo-classical art in France at the end of the eighteenth century, the example of England must not be underestimated. At that time a wave of Anglomania swept over France. In a different way it was England again, in 1750, which set the example for a return to the Middle Ages and Gothic taste; the first monument of this trend is the house which Horace Walpole built at Strawberry Hill, between 1750 and 1776, a hundred years before Viollet-le-Duc. Nor must we forget the vogue for English landscape-gardening at the end of the eighteenth century. Thus the two styles of French art in the nineteenth century, neo-Classicism and Romanticism, are at least in architecture largely of English origin.

The Evolution of French Architecture

To conclude this first part we can now outline the evolution of French architecture and indicate its stages. We say stages, not styles. A stage is distinguished by its technique, plans, and feeling; a style by ornament, i.e. secondary characters. Stages or periods can be sub-divided into styles.

The history of French architecture is divided into three main periods, the Middle Ages, the period which we call classical, and the modern period. To the last corresponds the use of new materials (iron, steel, reinforced concrete), the appearance of new schemes arising out of the industrial revolution, and often, too, the supremacy of the engineer over the architect. Its starting-point cannot be placed in any particular year, or even decade; it is roughly the second half of the nineteenth century, but certain aspects were already visible under Napoleon I (for example, the subordination of the architect to the engineer or the government administrator) whereas the use of reinforced concrete was not really to spread until the twentieth century. In the same way, between the Middle Ages and the classical period lies the sixteenth century, whose beginning in some ways still belongs to the Middle Ages and whose end was already classical. We must never lose sight of the fact that the whole history of human effort cannot be arbitrarily divided and that in art there has never been a moment when pioneers and reactionaries have not lived side by side.

¶ THE MIDDLE AGES

Since it is not yet known what will be the destiny of modern art, the medieval and classical periods, whose complete evolution we can alone survey, constitute the two principal objects of this study. The medieval period is characterized by the predominance of religious art. We know it chiefly through its churches, and this is not due to chance alone, for art was entirely turned towards God and there was no similarity in conception between the house of God and that of man, be that man even a king. Neither did it place its ideal of beauty in large perfectly symmetrical compositions; it was less sensitive than classical art to abstract and learned theories; it did not separate art from craft. It kept nearer to life, but while still preferring diversity to unity, it preserved in the highest degree the feeling for an architectural whole – all crafts could collaborate in producing a building, but only under the authority of the architect, who was the real master of the work.

Obviously some of these remarks must be modified according to the different phases, for the medieval period was a long one. It lasted for more than ten centuries and its aspects were many. Often they are not defined except in relation to technique: pre-Romanesque art (open timber roofs), Romanesque art (barrel vaults, groined vaults, domes), Gothic art (rib-vaults). This succession is broadly correct, but there is much more to it. Between Romanesque and Gothic there was not only a difference of technique, but of spirit. There is a whole stage of Gothic which is no more than Romanesque with the addition of rib-vaults; it has none of that verticality we have spoken of and maintains the wise caution of the Romanesque. The technical was subordinate to the spiritual evolution. The Romanesque differed from the preceding style because it imposed on its intellectual disorder a strong, dominating idea – an abstract logic, which later gave way to the spontaneous naturalism of Gothic. The great cathedrals of northern France in the thirteenth century are not simply an assembly of rib-vaults – they are the architectural equivalent of the revolution brought about by St Francis of Assisi. Nature was revealed to the world together with pity. A sea of light flooded the building, as a great breath of humanity swept through the mind of man. In church porches, ornament based on familiar plants replaced the syllogisms of Romanesque decoration; the smile of the Virgin Mary replaced the hieratic immobility of the Throne of Wisdom. Towards the fifteenth century, nature

and sentiment increasingly dominated the purely intellectual;
life sprang up everywhere and the decorative exuberance of
the last Gothic period (Flamboyant Gothic) was but a manifestation of this.

This luxuriance was to be prolonged almost until the middle
of the sixteenth century, with the same constructional patterns
but with new decorative forms, borrowed both from Italy and
from antiquity. This was the first Renaissance; if we consider
only decoration we could call it a break with the Middle Ages;
speaking of the building as a whole, we are still dealing with
medieval architecture.

We can therefore split up this long medieval period in the
following way: pre-Romanesque architecture (about the fifth
to the tenth century), Romanesque architecture (eleventh and
twelfth century), Gothic architecture, with its various subdivisions (thirteenth century), Flamboyant, and early Renaissance.

¶ THE CLASSICAL PERIOD

During the first third of the sixteenth century signs of change
began to appear. We can see them all the better since we know
the developments to come and are able to distinguish the innovations which were to last from those which were to remain
unfruitful. The classical period began with the reign of Henri
II and the second half of the sixteenth century.

An attempt must be made to establish its general characteristics, at least in comparison with the Middle Ages. The
same materials continued to be used with the same structural
methods. The rib-vault was not abandoned. The most typical
monuments appeared simply to go back to Romanesque construction, with barrel vaults, groined vaults, and domes, but
used with a much more confident knowledge.

Here, in fact, we come to a major issue. Although it is true
that, from the mid sixteenth century, art ceased to be confused with craft, it was very far from rejecting or scorning it.
It is modern and not classical architecture that brought about
the divorce between art and craft. In France at least the classi-

cal architect was not a simple designer of plans and façades completely ignorant of technique. There were, of course, men like Pierre Lescot and Perrault, but they are exceptions. On the contrary we can see:

(a) The importance of dynasties of architects passing on structural secrets from father to son. Philibert Delorme was the son of a master mason of Lyons; the Du Cerceaus, the Mansarts, and the Gabriels, were all architect families.

(b) The place given to technical considerations in treatises on architecture, such as those of Philibert Delorme, Daviler, and Rondelet. Rondelet wrote what amounts to a practical encyclopedia. Philibert Delorme began by publishing, in 1561, his *Nouvelles Inventions pour bien bâtir et à petits frais*.

(c) The rôle of engineers in the history of architecture. In the seventeenth century François Blondel was a naval, Vauban a military engineer; in the eighteenth century Boffrand was an engineer of 'Ponts et Chaussées'. The science of the engineer and the art of the architect were no more distinct from each other than art is from actual practice. The Académie d'Architecture gave equal place to both. Hence the constant progress of architectural technique, notably of stereotomy, and the welcome given, when the moment arrived, to the industrial innovation. It was an architect, a decorator if ever there was one – Bélanger – who, under Napoleon, was responsible for the use of iron in the dome of the Halle aux Blés, against the will of the members of the Académie des Sciences. This led to technical and progressive architecture.

Over and above mere craft and technique, highly perfected though they may be, there were certain qualities which classical architects called art and to which they gave the foremost position. They proclaimed them to the world; but is it so certain that medieval architects did not privately think the same? We can only say that the spirit of this art is not that of the last years of the Middle Ages. The Middle Ages passed from geometry to life; classical art passed back from life to geometry, from the concrete to the abstract. It had a taste for regular and logical arrangement, for symmetry, for formal beauty. Its decoration was no longer borrowed from nature. It rediscovered geometrical combinations, but it took its models from Greco-Roman antiquity. Art ceased to be considered as the spontaneous expression of an individual temperament. It was subject to rules. In 1671 Colbert was to found the Académie d'Architecture to register and codify these rules; this younger sister of the Académie de Peinture et de Sculpture was also destined to establish a system of aesthetics.

The phases of the conflict between reason and sentiment, between present and past, divided the evolution of classical architecture into numerous periods. Taste changed more often in these three centuries (1550–1850) than in the ten centuries of the Middle Ages. Its history can be reduced into three acts, each divided into scenes.

(a) *Classical Renaissance and Counter-Reformation* (1550–1650). Philibert Delorme, in imitation of the great Italian classicists of the Renaissance, such as Bramante, had produced an art made up of simplicity and intellectualism. The Wars of Religion interrupted this effort, which could have given France a hundred years earlier an architecture owing nothing to anyone but herself. However, the Counter-Reformation, born from the decisions of the Council of Trent, maintained a taste for austerity, if not for poverty. It impressed this mark on the numerous ecclesiastical and conventual buildings of the reign of Louis XIII, a period of major importance to French architecture and one too often neglected. So from Philibert Delorme to François Mansart the distance was not great, though it spanned a century.

(b) *The Baroque Conflict* (1650–1750). But from this moment Italian art – at least, Roman art, which set the tone – had renounced its policy of self-effacement. To the Counter-Reformation had succeeded Baroque, the definitions of which are many, but which seems to us principally a return to life and nature: luxuriance, exuberance, predominance of the senses and of sentiment over reason, that is at the same time a resurrection of the late Middle Ages and a foretaste of Romanticism. Its great masters were Bernini and Borromini. Their influence was such that most art historians have called this period the Baroque period.

We cannot accept this label for France, for her rôle was that of resistance to Baroque, England and Holland also escaped it. It should not be called the Baroque period, but at most that of the Baroque conflict. After Bernini's fruitless journey to Paris, France was freed from it, and her architecture can claim the opposite epithet, that of classical, which means balance and harmony achieved by putting intelligence foremost; it is summed up in the definition of old Boileau – *Aimez donc la raison.*

The word conflict does not imply rapid victory. There was strife and hesitation. France even produced great Baroque artists – Le Vau and Le Brun. The eighteenth century was to see the return of Baroque on the offensive under the name of Rococo. All the same, victory remained with classical reason, still warm from the strife in Hardouin-Mansart, serene and sure of itself in Robert de Cotte and Gabriel. It is because it had been capable of freeing itself from Italian Baroque that French architecture led Europe in the eighteenth century. Clarity, logic, balance, a happy medium, such were to be the characteristics of the art of this period. It respected antiquity but not too much, taking practical necessities more and more into account, and combining good sense with reason.

(c) *Neo-Classicism and Romanticism* (1750–1850). About 1750 this well-balanced classicism was threatened in two ways: on the one hand a return to pure antiquity was demanded, on the other a return to the Middle Ages. Both sides tended to destroy the balance, the one in favour of logical reasoning, cut off from life, the other of sentiment against reason. This, at least, is the most general aspect of the conflict, which went far beyond the architectural sphere.

But from our particular point of view, it can also be seen in a different light. The adherents of the neo-Classical and the neo-Gothic were in agreement on one point – an offensive by the historical spirit against living architecture, as though the problems of architects were not concrete and immediate, as though the art of building were outside time, as though it were only a question of choosing among the models of the past. Some proposed Rome and Greece; others Flamboyant Gothic;

and some, less vehemently – the so-called eclectics – the Venetian Renaissance.

This sudden change of position is partly explained by an event of major importance, the disappearance of the old Académie d'Architecture, suppressed by the Convention in 1793, and its replacement by the Académie des Beaux-Arts, the Fourth Class of the Institute, in which the architects, reduced to ten, were closely dependent on their colleagues, painters, sculptors, musicians, who, though artists too, were not technicians; they had but one common field, decoration. It was then that the divorce between art and craft was brought about; architecture was uprooted, cut off from the life-giving trunk of technique. And amid the last convulsions of classical architecture modern architecture was to be born.

PART TWO

Religious Architecture

*

Introductory : Its Purpose

CHRISTIAN church building differs widely, by its very purpose, from the antique temple or the Mohammedan mosque. In Greco-Roman paganism the temple was the house of the god; the faithful did not enter it. The sacrifice – the basic element of the cult – was celebrated outside on an altar which generally stood before the entrance. The Mohammedan religion does not involve sacrifice; the mosque indeed admits the faithful, but it is only a hall of prayer. The Christian church must both welcome the faithful and serve for the celebration of a sacrifice, the sacrifice of the mass, the rules of which are established by the liturgy. In the beginning, every province had its own liturgy; the Gallican was not the same as the Roman. Little by little, as the bishop of Rome, successor of St Peter, became the head of the Christian communities in the West, the rite of his church was imposed on all the others. Ultimately, it was to satisfy certain liturgical needs that the plan of the church was evolved; and it is the permanence of these needs which renders it practically constant or allows it but little variation. To liturgy is added *symbolism*, which is the desire to record in the actual building of the church certain general aspects of the dogma; hence the form of a cross sometimes given to the building. But symbolism takes only second place.

In early Christian times there were two other ecclesiastical buildings besides the church – the *baptistery*, for the introduction of the neophytes into the Christian community, and the *campanile* or bell-tower. In the Middle Ages the baptistery was the obligatory complement of cathedral churches. It was generally circular or octagonal in plan. From the fourth century, in front of Notre-Dame in Paris, stood Saint-Jean-le-Rond, the episcopal baptistery, destroyed in 1748. Bell-towers were sometimes also separated from the church and a few of them joined to it at a later date; for example the bell-tower of the church of La Trinité at Vendôme or that of the cathedral at Limoges. But at Florence and Pisa there can still be seen, side by side, the three distinct elements: cathedral, baptistery, and bell-tower.

There are two kinds of church plan – the *basilican plan* and the *central plan*. In France the former is much the more frequent. Buildings of basilican plan are those inscribed in a rectangle, for example those of Latin cross shape (fig. 9); they

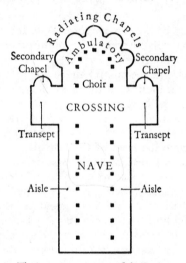

Figure 9. The component parts of the Latin cross plan

have uniaxial symmetry. Centrally planned buildings are those inscribed in a circle or a square or other regular figure (round or octagonal or in the shape of a Greek cross); they are of biaxial symmetry.

¶ CHURCHES OF BASILICAN PLAN

The name derives from the first Christian churches, the *basilicas*, such as are still to be seen in Rome (San Paolo fuori le Mura, San Lorenzo fuori le Mura, Sta Sabina) or in Ravenna (San Giovanni Evangelista, the two churches of Sant'Apollinare). The basic element is a large rectangular hall, the *nave*.

designed to receive the faithful; this is divided internally by rows of columns; and at the end there is a rounded part for the celebration of the sacrifice, the *apse*. Between the nave and the apse there is sometimes a transverse part, the *transept*. These three elements – nave, transept, and apse – make up the plan of the majority of French churches of medieval and modern times as, indeed, of most Western churches. But they are much elaborated.

(a) *Nave*. Up to the twelfth century the nave remained the most important part of the church. It may be either single or flanked by *aisles*.

Aisleless churches are generally small, mere chapels. However, certain large churches of the Romanesque and Gothic periods in the south, for example the Romanesque cathedrals of Carpentras and Avignon, and the Gothic cathedrals of Toulouse, Albi, and Perpignan, have only a nave, with no aisles. In this very important group, the buttresses projecting into the interior of the building form with the wall a series of side chapels which sometimes intercommunicate by means of a narrow passage. Such is also the pattern of certain seventeenth-century churches which have taken as their prototype the mother church of the Society of Jesus, the Gesù in Rome. They include, in Paris, the church of Saint-Paul-Saint-Louis, the church of the Oratoire, and the Carmelite church.

In general, important churches have aisles, most often one to the right and one to the left of the nave (*single aisles*). A few very rich medieval abbeys such as Cluny or Saint-Sernin at Toulouse, and some of the first Gothic cathedrals, like that of Paris, have *double aisles*; that is, two on either side of the nave. The example of the cathedral was, moreover, transmitted to several other Parisian churches, St Séverin, St Eustache, etc. Like aisleless churches, those with aisles may also have additional chapels along the lateral walls, arranged between buttresses which penetrate into the interior.

(b) *Transept*. The transept is a kind of nave thrown transversally between the nave and the apse. It gives the building the shape of a cross. The projecting wings are called *arms*. Sometimes the transept is not evident in the ground plan, but appears only in the elevation; this is so in the cathedral of Paris, where the lateral walls are in a straight line.

Not every church has a transept, and this is true not only of small churches, but of larger ones too (for example, medieval cathedrals in the south, and aisleless seventeenth-century churches). On the other hand some churches have had two transepts. Such were the great twelfth-century abbey church of Cluny and the church of Saint-Benoît-sur-Loire. Generally the arms of the transept end in flat walls; however, there are a few examples of rounded ends, notably in the cathedrals of Noyon and Soissons.

(c) *Apse*. The apse is the essential part of the church. It is there that the altar is placed. At first it constituted the whole sanctuary. Towards the eleventh century the sanctuary took on greater importance and other elements were added to the apse. This fact is related first of all to the development of monastic life. In a monastery many monks have to say mass; they need several altars and therefore several apses. There must also be a place for the Chapter. To this may be added the growing importance of the cult of saints and their relics; in front of these, which were placed in the sanctuary, passed thousands of people, and it was therefore necessary to control their movement. These two factors brought about the multiplication of apses and the appearance of two new elements in the plan: the *choir* and the *ambulatory*.

Already the number of apses had been more or less dependent on the arrangement of the nave and aisles. A church with only a nave normally has one apse, but a church with two aisles and a nave may easily end in three apses. Other apses can be opened out of the transept (*apsidal chapels*). A special arrangement, sometimes called the Benedictine ending, consists in the placing of staggered apsidal chapels on either side of the main apse.

The ambulatory is a semicircular passage running round the apse. It represents the natural prolongation of the aisles. If the church is double-aisled it may have a double ambulatory (Notre-Dame de Paris). On to this passage may open a variable number of apsidal chapels, the axes of which converge towards the centre of the apse – hence their name of *radiating chapels*. In the great Gothic cathedrals (Reims, Amiens, Beauvais, Le Mans) the radiating chapels, seven, nine or eleven in number, form in this way a crown of apsidal chapels at the east end (*chevet*) of the building.

Finally, between the transept and the apse with its ambulatory, in all Gothic churches the part reserved to the clergy came to be enlarged. This is the *choir*, filling two or three bays which in some cases may be flanked, like the nave, by one or two aisles on either side as well as lateral chapels between the buttresses.

¶ CHURCHES OF CENTRAL PLAN

Some are round or octagonal, others square or in the shape of a Greek cross (figs. 10 and 11).

In the Middle Ages, round churches most often derived from the Holy Sepulchre in Jerusalem. The majority date from the time of the Crusades; after the twelfth century they became much rarer. Such was the round church of Saint-Bénigne at Dijon, erected in 1001 at the east end of the basilica of Saint-Bénigne; the central part was surrounded by an aisle topped by two storeys of galleries; only the ground floor remains. On the other hand, the round church of Neuvy-Saint-Sépulcre (Indre), and that of Charroux, are intact. In the twelfth century the religious Order of the Templars, founded in 1118 to defend the Temple of Jerusalem, built round churches in the West in remembrance of the Holy Sepulchre (Laon, chapel of the Templars). Other medieval churches took up the Greek cross, often transforming it into a square by the addition of chapels in the corners, as in Byzantine churches. Examples are the Carolingian church of Germigny-des-Prés and Saint-Front at Périgueux.

From the sixteenth century onwards the central plan came once more into favour, chiefly under the influence of the projects of Bramante and Michelangelo for the reconstruction of St Peter's in Rome. This plan indeed offers two advantages

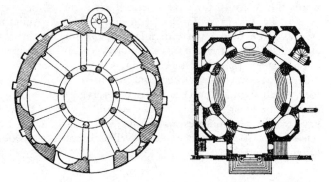

Figure 10. Central plans. *Left:* Church of Neuvy-Saint-Sépulcre.
Right: Church of the Visitation, Paris

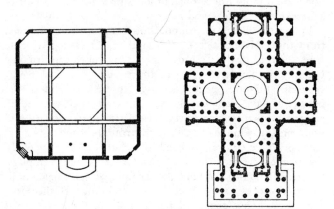

Figure 11. Central plans. *Left:* Saint-Louis de Vincennes.
Right: Panthéon (Sainte-Geneviève)

much appreciated at the time: it naturally imposes the construction of a dome at the intersection of the arms of the cross;
it assures a good view of this dome from without, by shortening the nave. It is thus that one finds in Paris, in the seventeenth and eighteenth centuries, centrally-planned buildings

(Temple Sainte-Marie, rue Saint-Antoine; Chapel of the Collège Mazarin, now Institut de France; Church of the Assumption); and even more frequently Greek cross plans such as the domed church of the Invalides (a cross inscribed in a square) or the Church of Sainte-Geneviève, now the Panthéon (plain cross). The central plan has also been much used in recent years, all the more since the vast free space in its interior gives scope to the possibilities of reinforced concrete (compare the Church of Saint-Louis at Vincennes and that of Saint-Pierre de Chaillot in Paris).

CHAPTER ONE

THE MIDDLE AGES TO THE MIDDLE OF THE SIXTEENTH CENTURY

WE can now begin to look at the buildings themselves. The study of medieval churches falls naturally into three sections, the pre-Romanesque, the Romanesque, and the Gothic periods.

1. Pre-Romanesque Churches

When the barbarian tribes established themselves in Gaul in the fifth century, they found it converted to Christianity and already provided with ecclesiastical buildings. At Reims, a cathedral had been built between 340 and 346. This Gallo-Roman architecture is little known. It seems to have consisted of basilicas similar to those found in other parts of the Roman Empire: rectangular buildings, with or without aisles, with a single apse and covered by an open timber roof. The influence of Christianized Africa appears to have been particularly important. Only one Gallo-Roman church has come down to us, at least in its foundations: the basilica discovered in 1913 at Saint-Bertrand-de-Comminges (*Lugdunum Convenarum*) near Luchon in Haute-Garonne. Some coins hidden under the paving allow us to date it to the fourth century. It was composed of a nave, preceded by a vast narthex, and a pentagonal apse. The very thick walls were made of pebbles and very irregular quarry stones with cement poured over them. They must have alternated with layers of flat bricks and seem to have been faced with painted plaster, fragments of which have been found: scrolls of flowers and foliage standing out in white on a red ground. The baptistery of Saint-Jean at Poitiers may also go back to the fourth century, but was later altered.

The Merovingian period seems to have possessed a rich architecture, although here too only very little evidence remains. We learn of it from documents full of precious details about construction and decoration. Most of our great cathedrals appeared then, but they have been rebuilt at least three or four times since. The cathedral of Clermont existed about 450. That of Lyons goes back to the same period. The episcopal church of Paris was already in its second state in the sixth century. The church of Saint-Martin at Tours was rebuilt about 472. From the sixth century date the church of Saint-Germain at Auxerre, the church of the Holy Apostles at Paris, in which St Geneviève was buried, and Saint-Germain-des-Prés, also in Paris. The seventh century, that of Dagobert, was the century of the great abbeys – Saint-Denis, Jumièges, Saint-Wandrille. Here it is not a question of small buildings or modest chapels. Gregory of Tours tells us that the basilica put up in his native city by Bishop Perpetuus, over the tomb of St Martin, was 160 feet long, 60 feet wide, and 45 feet high. It had fifty-two windows, eight doors and 120 marble columns. The cathedral of Clermont, built by Namatius, was 150 feet long, 60 wide, and 50 high.

These churches were almost all of basilican plan: a rectangle, sometimes divided into nave and aisles. The frequent expression *in modum crucis*, in the form of a cross, indicates the existence of a transept. At first, in front of the nave, there was an open court or *atrium*, but this disappeared early. At the east end there was either a single apse or an apse flanked by two sacristies (*prothesis* and *diaconicon*) in the manner of Syrian churches. The cathedral of Clermont, described by Gregory of Tours, was on this pattern. The same cathedral also had a second apse in front – *in ante absidam rotundam habens*; it was therefore a church with two apses facing each other, like some that could be seen in Africa. Other churches, on the contrary, had a more compact plan – the Daurade at Toulouse was circular.

The walls were generally of stone and the roofing always of timber. But the masons of Gaul were renowned for their skill, and the great arch of Saint-Martin at Autun was still the admiration of professionals in the eighteenth century, so perfect was its technique.

The most original feature of Gallic churches of the Merovingian period was their bell-tower. Bells have always been popular in Gaul. As early as the fifth century they were placed in a special tower, either at the crossing (cf. the *lantern-towers* of Saint-Martin at Tours, the cathedrals of Nantes and Clermont-Ferrand), or in front of the building and detached from it (Saint-Martin at Tours).

The decoration was highly finished, but included little sculpture, as at Rome and Byzantium, and consisted mainly of mosaics, paintings, hangings, and goldsmiths' work. Several texts also allude to this. The name of the Daurade in Toulouse derives from the gold mosaics which filled the church. Gregory of Tours shows us the Bishop of Clermont planning a series of frescoes for his basilica of Saint-Étienne or the Bishop of Tours having the walls of the church of Saint-Martin decorated with scenes from the Gospel or miracles of the saint.

Unfortunately, very little of all this has come down to us, except perhaps the lower part of the walls of Saint-Pierre at Vienne and the east end of the cathedral of Vaison, as well as two columns from the Daurade. We know directly only the baptisteries, but of these there are some very beautiful examples, especially the series in Provence: Marseilles, Fréjus, Aix, Riez, Vénasque, Mélas, and Valence. They form a homogeneous group of about the sixth century and their lower parts at least date from this time. Generally they are octagons inscribed in a square, like the Baptistery of the Orthodox at Ravenna. They must have been covered by domes. Crypts such as that of Saint-Laurent at Grenoble or that of Jouarre (Seine-et-Marne), oratories such as Saint-Victor at Marseilles (mid fifth century) and Glanfeuil (Maine-et-Loire; probably late sixth century) acquaint us with examples of barrel-vaults from this period.

Carolingian architecture – though this period has often been called a 'Renaissance' – is no richer. But it is more important, because in it appeared certain of those innovations which were to constitute Romanesque art. Here again the buildings are known to us principally from texts. Charlemagne, so his biographer Eginhard tells us, ordered the bishops and prelates throughout the length and breadth of his empire to reconstruct the buildings which were falling into ruins. Hence the rebuilding of the cathedral of Reims (816–62) and of those of Le Mans (833–5), Orleans (after 989), Verdun, of the abbeys of Saint-Remi at Reims, Saint-Riquier, Saint-Denis, etc. From this time, also, date Germigny-des-Prés, Saint-Philibert at Grandlieu, etc.

Most of the churches are of basilican plan, often with a transept. The Carolingian cathedral of Reims, the paving of which has been found two feet below the level of the present cathedral, was almost equal to it in importance. The Carolingian basilica of Saint-Denis, the foundations of which were recognized by Viollet-le-Duc, had a nave and aisles almost as large as those of to-day, a vast transept and a horseshoe apse. The church of the Basse-Œuvre, at Beauvais, has remained entirely Carolingian; built in small stonework with inserted bricks, it is a basilica with nave and two aisles, of which only the apse was pulled down in the sixteenth century, to make room for the new cathedral. Elsewhere, for example in Saint-Remi at Reims or the cathedral of Verdun, we find the arrangement of two apses set facing each other, already noticed in the Merovingian period. A variant of this arrangement, proper to the Carolingian period, was the church with a westwork – in the west apse the sanctuary was transferred to the upper storey, so as to leave on the ground floor a free passage into the nave.

The two innovations with a future which now made their appearance in the basilican plan were: (a) the insertion of a choir-bay between the transept and the apse; (b) the ambulatory, which, it appears, was used for the first time above ground in the cathedral of Clermont-Ferrand, rebuilt in 946, and a little later in Saint-Martin at Tours and the church of La

Couture at Le Mans; but it had been previously realized in crypts such as that at Saint-Philibert at Grandlieu (840) and perhaps at Saint-Denis.

The same mixture of tradition and novelty existed in construction. All these basilicas had open timber roofs, but already the simple column was giving place to the composite pier (Saint-Philibert at Grandlieu), the condition of a new architectural system based on dividing the thrusts. Another innovation was in the arrangement of the masses – the façades framed by two towers, which appeared in Gaul in the eighth century (Saint-Martin at Autun, Saint-Germain at Auxerre, Jumièges).

The central plan is represented by the church of Germigny-des-Prés on the banks of the Loire, unfortunately much restored in the nineteenth century. It was a Greek cross inscribed in a square, each arm of the cross ending in an apse. As a whole it is very close to the Catalan church of San Miguel at Terrasa. The founder, Theodulf, was himself a Catalan. Here too appeared an important structural innovation, the dome on squinches, which is also found at Terrasa.

The decoration of these buildings, as in the Merovingian period, was still painting. The great mosaic of Germigny is of a monumental style largely inspired by Byzantine art. The frescoes of the life of St Stephen in the crypt of Saint-Germain at Auxerre (tenth century) are perhaps the earliest example of French painting to come down to us.

II. Romanesque Churches

It is from the eleventh century onwards, with the Romanesque style, that we really reach French architecture. French Romanesque architecture is a province of European Romanesque architecture, perhaps the most important province, because it is here that we find the most finished works. It was to be replaced gradually by Gothic architecture.

¶ GENERAL CHARACTERISTICS OF ROMANESQUE CHURCHES

Romanesque churches are recognizable by certain characteristics of construction, plan, volume, and decoration.

The basic constructional factor is that they were vaulted entirely in stone. The forms of Romanesque vaults are numerous. We find, as in the East, the dome with its two techniques – on squinches or on pendentives. But the characteristic Romanesque vault is the old barrel-vault of the Romans, transformed and perfected to become the barrel vault on transverse ribs, and the groined vault. These have already been examined in the section on structural problems. We have seen how they led logically to the invention of the cross-ribbed vault which, although the basic element of future Gothic architecture, is in principle no more than a masonry technique known from the Romanesque period. The cross-ribbed vault was first found in buildings of pure Romanesque spirit, that is those which offer all the other characteristics of Romanesque art.

It is rare for Romanesque churches of any importance to be without aisles. Usually they have a nave and two aisles, so that three vaults are placed side by side and can give each other mutual support. In this respect several arrangements are possible: (*a*) the main vault may be very much higher than the lateral ones; the advantage of this is in direct lighting, but equilibrium is less well assured (Vézelay); (*b*) the three vaults may be of equal height; the main vault can then no longer have direct lighting, and there is thus a *blind nave* (Poitiers, Notre-Dame-la-Grande); (*c*) the aisle-vaulting may be different from that of the nave (half-barrel vaults: Arles, Saint-Trophime); the aisles may be divided into two storeys, the ground floor having a barrel or groined vault and the first floor, acting as a gallery, a half-barrel vault (Issoire); finally they may be covered with barrel vaults placed at right angles to the axis of the building (transverse barrel vaults: Tournus, Saint-Philibert) (fig. 12).

Romanesque supports are not simple columns, but piers of

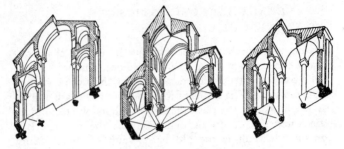

Figure 12. Possible combinations of Romanesque vaulting: Issoire,
Vézelay, Poitiers

more or less complex cross-section – square or cruciform piers
sometimes flanked by pilasters or half-columns. These piers
are linked by arches separating nave from aisles (nave arcades).
In certain buildings, for example in Normandy, the supports
are alternated; this means that strong and weaker supports
succeed each other.

Finally, Romanesque churches, at least the main ones, are
always very carefully built of large masonry. In the few
regions which like Languedoc have no quarry stone, they are
built of brick.

The plan of Romanesque churches is almost always that of
the basilica, but the transept and choir developed in a way
until then unknown. The most common systems were that of
apses built parallel to one another, on the same axis as the nave
and generally decreasing in depth in proportion to their distance from the central apse, or that of the ambulatory with
radiating chapels. These are usually of an odd number, three
or five; in a few churches in Auvergne they are of an even
number. Romanesque radiating chapels are separated from
one another by a window. A few large buildings also have
apses along the arms of the transept; in Saint-Sernin at
Toulouse there are nine apses, two on each transept arm and
five radiating chapels.

Externally, the Romanesque church has a three-dimensional
value, that is to say it is conceived as large-scale sculpture, as a

series of volumes taking possession of space. These volumes are nearly always reduced to simple geometrical forms – the cube, the cylinder or half-cylinder, the truncated cone or pyramid, etc. Their grouping exactly translates the disposition of the interior; one can deduce the plan of the building by simply looking at the exterior. The combination of masses in Romanesque buildings always gives an impression of balance rather than uplift; horizontality dominates verticality. As we see them rise against the sky, like a pyramid, they give simultaneously an impression of harmony by the perfection of their component parts and of stability by the regularity of their progression.

Finally, the Romanesque building is furnished with important decoration in painting and sculpture, of which it is sufficient here to recall the two major characteristics. First of all, its harmony with the architecture; all its lines are subordinated to those of the construction which it is their function to underline. Secondly, its abstract, stylized character – Romanesque sculptors and painters, far from applying themselves to copying nature, transposed it into intellectual, if not geometrical, forms.

⁊ HISTORICAL FACTORS

It has often been said that Romanesque architecture is a monastic architecture. But if the religious orders played a considerable part in its formation and development, we also find among the founders of great Romanesque buildings all the kings of France from Hugh Capet to Philip Augustus and, particularly, Robert the Pious; many great feudal lords, especially the dukes of Normandy and above all William the Conqueror; and bishops, who almost all, in the eleventh and twelfth centuries, undertook the rebuilding of their cathedrals. However, the rôle of the monks remained predominant, or rather there was a coincidence between the zenith of Romanesque art and that of the monastic orders, especially Cluny. The abbey of Cluny was founded in 910 and its rule was to be gradually imposed on the whole Benedictine Order.

Cluny held that all the resources of art must be employed for the glory of God. A little later the Cistercian Order, founded by St Bernard, was to demonstrate an altogether different spirit – voluntary humility and simplicity and a distrust of art, which was considered a sin of pride.

The Romanesque period was also that of the great pilgrimages. Security having been virtually re-established in Europe, it became possible to visit the famous sanctuaries. If Jerusalem was too far away, the pilgrims went to Rome or to Santiago de Compostela in Spain. These pilgrimages, above all that of Santiago, exerted an influence of capital importance on the development of Romanesque art; they facilitated exchange between the different countries and propagated types of churches and decorative formulas. This explains in particular that throughout the Romanesque period there was a simultaneous influence of France on Spain and of Spain on France. We have noticed above the part played by oriental influences in the formation of western medieval art.

Romanesque architecture consists of two periods – the eleventh century, a century of experiment, and the twelfth, a century of achievement. The experiments had already begun in the tenth century and the transition between Carolingian and Romanesque art was imperceptible. The famous phrase of the chronicler Ralph Glaber on the year 1000 and the 'white crown of churches' which Christianity had assumed has only a symbolical value. More importance as regards the division between the two phases of the Romanesque period should be attached to 1095, the date of Pope Urban II's journey to France and of the consecration, premature it is true, of numerous churches in the course of construction.

The Eleventh Century

Not everything was tentative in the eleventh century. It is natural that we should pay the greatest attention to the pioneer works, which mark out the stages of the way to the great masterpieces of Romanesque art. Therefore, only a brief mention need be made of certain regions of the north and east of

France which, on the example of Germany and Switzerland, remained attached to the results previously achieved by the Carolingian architects – Montiérender (998), Vignory (about 1050), Château-Landon (date uncertain), and Saint-Germain-des-Prés in Paris. The really interesting areas are Burgundy, Normandy, and the Loire valley.

We could add Roussillon, that is French Catalonia, though at this time it was very far from being incorporated in the nation. It was here that, in 1009, at Saint-Martin du Canigou, the complete vaulting of the nave seems to have been achieved for the first time in France. The example had been set half a century earlier on the other side of the Pyrenees (Sta Maria at Amer, 949). Eleventh-century buildings in Catalonia and Burgundy belong to what M. Puig i Cadafalch has called the first Romanesque art, which is characterized by building with small stones, and by an external decoration of small arches resting every so often on flat pilasters (the *Lombard band* or *levenae*). These characteristics are found in a much vaster area, including in France lower Languedoc (church of Saint-Martin de Londres, Hérault), the Rhône valley, and Savoy (the church of Aime), as well as the Rhine valley and Lombardy. But among these, innovations can be found as often as the older styles.

Eleventh-century Burgundy saw the construction of three buildings of the first quality – Cluny, Saint-Bénigne at Dijon, and Saint-Philibert at Tournus. Unfortunately the first two have not survived. The great church of Saint-Bénigne at Dijon (consecrated about 1018) was a juxtaposition of a basilica and a circular church, on the pattern of Constantine's Holy Sepulchre in Jerusalem. The basilica, only the aisles of which were vaulted, had already disappeared by the thirteenth century; the circular church survived until the Revolution. It was a large building covered by a dome and surrounded by two ambulatories with barrel and groin vaults, and two storeys of galleries. Cluny, the greatest abbey of medieval France, had three successive churches – Cluny I, dedicated to St Peter and St Paul in 915, 916, or 917; Cluny II (Saint-Pierre-le-Vieux), built by Abbot Mayeul in the last quarter of the tenth century; Cluny III, undertaken by St Hugh from 1088. Cluny II, already very important, had an east end with seven parallel apses, giving on to both the transept and the choir, a non-vaulted nave, a two-storeyed narthex almost as long as the nave, with a lower storey certainly vaulted with groined vaults. Doubtless this was an imitation of Saint-Philibert at Tournus, which is still to-day the finest example of the science of the Burgundian builders in this period. It is a complex structure of uncertain chronology. The narthex, which belongs to the early eleventh century, also has two aisled storeys, of three bays each; on the ground floor, the groined-vaulted nave is flanked by transverse barrel-vaulted aisles; over the upper storey, the aisles have half-barrel vaults. The nave, at the time of its consecration in 1019, was covered by an open timber roof, but in the second half of the century it was given a roof made up of a succession of transverse barrel vaults, balancing each other like the arches of a bridge. The small Burgundian churches, less often altered, have been better preserved than the large ones. There is, in particular, between Tournus and Cluny, a whole group of small vaulted buildings of the eleventh century – Chapaize, Uchizy, Farges. Further north, at Châtillon-sur-Seine, is the charming church of Saint-Vorles, of about the year 1000, an interesting example of a church with a westwork (western portico).

One of the most active regions in the Middle Ages was Normandy, especially from the tenth century onwards and the establishment of the Normans in France. The importance of Norman Romanesque architecture is even greater than the surviving monuments would lead us to believe, for many of those which now have a Gothic appearance passed through a Romanesque period. The great age of Norman Romanesque architecture is the eleventh century. This is the period of the great abbeys and cathedrals – the abbey churches of Jumièges (1037–67), Bernay (begun before 1049, consecrated before 1077), Fécamp (1082–99), Saint-Ouen at Rouen (begun in 1060), Saint-Étienne at Caen (Abbaye-aux-Hommes, begun about 1064, consecrated in 1077), La Trinité at Caen (Abbaye-aux-Dames, 1062–6), Mont-Saint-Michel (1032–4), and the cathedrals of Coutances (nave consecrated in 1056 and the whole in 1091), Bayeux (1077), and Évreux (1076). With the eleventh century, Norman Romanesque art had almost reached the end of its course, for most buildings after this adopted the cross-ribbed vault and the Gothic style.

Paradoxical though it may seem, Norman Romanesque art has only recently become well known. It was long assumed that it knew nothing of ambulatory or radiating chapels; to-day we know that these existed in the cathedrals of Avranches and Rouen, in the abbey churches of Fécamp, Jumièges, and Mont-Saint-Michel. The disposition of Norman churches, which is highly varied, often consists of three storeys; nave, arcade, gallery (or triforium) and clerestory. There were galleries at Saint-Étienne at Caen, Cerisy-la-Fôret, and Fécamp; a triforium (a small arcade gallery or even a blind storey) at Bernay, Mont-Saint-Michel, Lessay, and La Trinité at Caen. Finally, it was supposed that in the case of covering, Norman architects remained faithful to the open timber roof until the mid twelfth century and that when they began stone vaulting they used the cross-ribbed vault straight away. That most of their churches had only open timber roofs is correct. But in La Trinité at Caen, the choir had groined vaults from the first. At Saint-Étienne in Caen it was probably a groined vaulting rather than a wooden ceiling which was replaced by rib-vaulting in the twelfth century; the same applies to La Trinité at Fécamp. It may be added that, in the very special arrangement of masses (towers on the west front and lantern-tower at the crossing) as in the very sober character of the decoration, based essentially on geometrical elements (tangent or intersecting circles, chevron and embattled ornament), Normandy is the province which from this period presented the most original aspect.

The middle Loire, particularly Touraine, possessed one of the most venerated of French sanctuaries, Saint-Martin at Tours, where, at the end of the tenth century, appeared an element of major importance for the Romanesque plan: the ambulatory with radiating chapels. The countryside, which had suffered heavily from the Norman invasions, began to

rebuild the moment peace was re-established. Technical innovations were not lacking, encouraged by the soil's abundance in materials. We have already mentioned the limestone of
Touraine, the soft light tufa. Experiments began from the end
of the tenth century, at Reignac and Langeais (Saint-Jean-
Baptiste), as yet very humble churches: at first, particular
parts of the building were vaulted, the choir, the crossing, and
the narthex (Saint-Mexme at Chinon, first quarter of the eleventh century). The porch of Saint-Benoît-sur-Loire, further
upstream, with its two storeys and nine groin-vaulted bays,
probably goes back to 1026. In any case, the church of Saint-
Gildéric at Lavardin (Loir-et-Cher) was certainly vaulted in
stone from 1042, and was the first example of this in central
France. The dome was also made the subject for experiments.
Four-sided domes with cruciform ribbing – prelude to the
cross-ribbed vault – were launched a little later, about 1060,
almost simultaneously at Loches (collegiate church of Saint-
Ours) and at Cormery. Touraine had accomplished so great a
feat in the eleventh century that she had almost nothing more
to do in the twelfth.

In the second half of the eleventh century completed buildings appeared which were to serve as prototypes for the main
Romanesque period – Saint-Savin-sur-Gartempe, Montier-
neuf at Poitiers, the choir of Saint-Benoît-sur-Loire with its
double transept, which is an anticipation of Cluny III. Above
all, from the third quarter of the eleventh century, we see the
creation of the most perfect type of Romanesque church, the
pilgrimage church, with barrel-vault on transverse ribs for the
nave, galleries over the side aisles, and an ambulatory with
radiating chapels. We find it at Sainte-Foy at Conques
(Aveyron), built under Abbot Odolric (1039–65) by Master
Hugh, which has all the value of a prototype. It also existed
in Saint-Martial at Limoges (1063–96), which was destroyed
during the Revolution. We find it again at Saint-Étienne at
Nevers, completed in 1097, which also has direct lighting in
the nave, an advantage and boldness lacking in the other
buildings of the series.

The Twelfth Century

The flowering of the Romanesque style in the twelfth century is magnificently varied. Some have tried to make its different aspects coincide with the geographical divisions of France and attempted to set up a map of the *regional schools* of Romanesque architecture. The multiplicity of these attempts, the extraordinary jig-saw puzzles that have been produced, the enclaves, the overlapping and the inlets, are so many proofs that this approach to the problem was wrong. A geography of Romanesque architecture can be no more than a simplified method of presentation. There are general types which are found all over France and even outside her boundaries. We can only be certain that some great monuments have exerted a strong influence in the country around them, but generally within a restricted perimeter.

It is these general types which we must concentrate on recognizing. If we leave aside the churches which kept to the open timber roof and which are found mostly in the east (Dugny, Meuse), or those which already seem to belong to the Gothic style, the Romanesque churches of the twelfth century can be divided into three main groups: (a) churches with barrel vaults or groined vaults without galleries in the aisles; (b) churches with barrel vaults or groined vaults with galleries in the aisles; and (c) churches vaulted with a series of domes.

This classification does not correspond to any geographical division. But within the first of these groups, the more frequent reappearance of certain arrangements of detail, particularly the decorative vocabulary and the sculpture, allow us to establish subdivisions which may correspond to provinces.

¶ I. CHURCHES WITHOUT GALLERIES, WITH BARREL OR GROINED VAULTS

This is the largest group; it is here that one can most easily recognize family resemblances, notably in the churches of Burgundy, Poitou, and Provence.

BURGUNDY. The variety of structure in Burgundian churches, now brought clearly to light by Charles Oursel, has definitely dismissed the theory of regional schools of Romanesque architecture. There are in the twelfth century two or even three types of Burgundian Romanesque churches, each of which has a great building as prototype.

(a) *The Cluny Group*. Nave and aisles are of unequal height and the nave has direct lighting. The nave has a pointed barrel vault and the aisles have groined vaults. The elevation is one of three storeys – nave arcade, triforium, clerestory. Its prototype was the great church of Cluny III, begun by St Hugh in 1088, consecrated in 1095 before its completion and then again in 1131. With St Peter's in Rome it was the largest building in Christendom. It was demolished in 1810. Certain details of its grandiose plan were peculiar to it alone (narthex, double aisles flanking the nave, double transept, ambulatory with five radiating chapels). But its structure and system, as well as its decoration full of echoes from classical Roman art (fluted pilasters, superimposed orders) served as models for a whole series of Burgundian churches – Paray-le-Monial (contemporary with Cluny and built in imitation of it), Saint-Andoche at Saulieu (1119), the cathedral of Autun (1132), the church of Notre-Dame at Beaune; the cathedral of Langres (1150–1220; the nave already has ribbed vaults). Certain Cluniac reminiscences (fluted pilasters) may also be seen in the Bourbonnais at Saint-Menoux and Souvigny.

(b) *The Vézelay Group*. The church of the Madeleine at Vézelay, although it also has nave and aisles of different heights and direct lighting in the nave, is noticeably different from the first group. The pointed barrel vault gives way to the groined vault; the triforium disappears and the elevation is simplified to two storeys. We no longer find either fluted pilasters or superimposed orders. The building of Vézelay was undertaken from 1096 onwards; two consecrations took place, in 1104 and 1132. The choir was rebuilt in the Gothic manner in the second half of the twelfth century. Perhaps Vézelay itself may have had as its model the church (destroyed in 1793) of Saint-Martin at Autun; indeed this group is sometimes known as 'the Martinian churches'. It includes also the church of Anzy-le-Duc, the two churches of Saint-Martin and Saint-Lazare at Avallon, as well as Saint-Philibert at Dijon (about 1150). The system of groin-vaulted naves, relatively rare, was to be taken up again a little later in the Rhine valley, notably at the church of Maria-Laach.

(c) *The Group without Clerestory*. Finally, in a last group of Burgundian churches, nave and aisles are almost of the same height, so that direct lighting of the central nave becomes impossible. This is the case in the Cistercian church of Fontenay near Montbard (1139–47), Notre-Dame at Châtillon-sur-Seine, etc. The plan of Fontenay also offers certain peculiarities which characterize the Cistercian Order, notably the square east end and the rectangular shape of the small chapels opening off the arms of the transept.

It may be added that over and above these structural differences there are certain characteristics common to the majority of Burgundian churches: the cross-sections of moulding, numerous borrowings from Roman antiquity in the decoration, and the richness of their sculpture, especially in the magnificent tympana, except in the Cistercian churches which remain deliberately poor and bare.

POITOU. In the area watered by the left bank tributaries of the middle Loire (Cher, Indre, Vienne), Poitou and Berry, from which Saintonge cannot be separated, continue during the twelfth century the lovely series of buildings inaugurated at Saint-Savin-sur-Gartempe. Most of these churches have their balance assured by the equal height of nave and aisles, covered by a single roof; but this cannot be regarded as a local characteristic, in the first place because it is an extremely general formula, as easily found in Spain and Germany as in France, and, above all, because a number of Poitou churches are different. Some of them have no aisles. Others are vaulted with a series of domes (Saint-Hilaire-le-Grand at Poitiers). And finally, even in the churches with nave and two aisles, the disposition may vary: groin-vaulted aisles (Poitiers, Notre-Dame-la-Grande; Chauvigny); aisles with half-barrel vaults (Preuilly; Saint-Eutrope at Saintes); aisles with transverse barrel vaults (Saint-Gautier, Indre).

It is better to look for the family resemblance (a) in the composition of volumes: plans with ambulatories and radiating chapels are translated into magnificent pyramids, in most cases crowned by a high tower at the crossing; (b) in the use of arcading not only outside (east end of Chauvigny; façade of Notre-Dame-la-Grande), but inside, where they form a kind of triforium (example set by Saint-Benoît-sur-Loire); (c) in the disposition of the sculpture, found here on capitals as everywhere else, but tympana are seldom found in the doorways, the effort being concentrated on the voussoirs of the arch, with no fear of imposing the most extraordinary distortions on the human figure to enclose it within the frame of a keystone. These churches also have in the interior extremely large free surfaces, ideal for painting, and indeed Poitou preserves some of the loveliest of Romanesque frescoes.

PROVENCE. The Romanesque churches of Provence have in common first of all the simplicity of their plans. Several, even among the largest, have no aisles (Avignon, Notre-Dame-des-Doms, 1069, rebuilt in the twelfth century; cathedral of Digne). Those which have aisles have no trace of an ambulatory, finding three parallel apses sufficient (Vaison; Saint-Paul-Trois-Châteaux). Another common point is the simplicity of their lines, for they prefer above all straight lines and right angles. The bell-towers are square and sturdy. An east end from Provence could never be mistaken for one from Burgundy or Poitou. Often the apses are polygonal (Cavaillon; Saint-Paul-Trois-Châteaux) dominated in any case, and without transitional interruption, by the mass of the nave whose flat roofs underline the almost cubist effect. Finally, they are alike in their decoration, the nearest to Roman antiquity, if not to classical Greece, in all France – geometrical motifs (ovoli, the Greek key-pattern, beads, meanders) which seem to have come straight from the Erechtheum; and rather heavy, thick-stemmed floral motifs. More than one feature from antique temples reappears even in the panels reserved for narrative sculpture, the triangular pediments of Saint-Restitut, Saint-Gabriel, or Notre-Dame-des-Doms at Avignon; and the friezes on columns at Arles or at Saint-Gilles in Languedoc.

¶ II. CHURCHES WITH GALLERIES

We have already met, as early as the eleventh century, churches with a gallery over the aisles, in Normandy (Saint-Étienne at Caen), in Central France (Sainte-Foy at Conques and Saint-Étienne at Nevers). These buildings constituted an important series in the centre and south during the twelfth century. Some ten of them can be found in the Puy-de-Dôme country (Notre-Dame-du-Port at Clermont-Ferrand, Orcival, Saint-Nectaire, Issoire); then this type spread south via Beaulieu (Corrèze), Figeac, Saint-Sernin at Toulouse, and as far as Santiago de Compostela, so that they are often called *pilgrimage churches*. All have an ambulatory and radiating chapels and generally, over the crossing, a bell-tower resting on a dome. But they also show appreciable differences in the arrangement of masses and decoration, even in the disposition of the gallery and its opening over the nave. The masterpiece is Saint-Sernin in Toulouse (choir consecrated in 1096; work continued until the mid twelfth century). The plan, with its double aisles, great transept with two small apses on each arm, and large ambulatory with five radiating chapels, is exceptionally spacious. Quite apart from its magnificent sculpture, Saint-Sernin attracts us by its architectural perfection, the balance of the lines of the interior, the superb pyramidal composition of the east end, dominated by a fine octagonal bell-tower, the prototype for all future bell-towers in Toulouse.

¶ III. DOMED CHURCHES

A last group of Romanesque churches includes those in which several domes unite to cover the nave. They would form quite a homogeneous series in the three provinces of Quercy,

Périgord, and Angoumois, had not some important buildings escaped a considerable distance from this geographic background: Saint-Hilaire at Poitiers, Solignac in the Limousin, and the cathedral of Le Puy.

The oldest building in the Quercy-Périgord-Angoumois group seems definitely to be the cathedral of Cahors, consecrated in 1119. It is the simplest in its plan – a nave of two bays, two domes (Gothic choir). Similarly, the church of Saint-Étienne at Périgueux, of the mid twelfth century, was no more than a succession of four squares covered by four domes. The plan is slightly complicated at Souillac, Solignac, and the cathedral of Angoulême where a transept appears with domes again over the arms (three at Souillac, four at Solignac, five at Angoulême). All these are set on pendentives and the buildings have no aisles. This means of covering has evidently been chosen to obtain the greatest uninterrupted space possible. There is no direct echo here of Byzantine buildings. Saint-Front at Périgueux – Greek cross with aisles, covered with five domes – is almost the only imitation on French soil of St Mark's, Venice, and the Holy Apostles at Constantinople (its date is disputed; probably 1120–70).

Saint-Hilaire at Poitiers and the cathedral of Le Puy have domes on squinches and Latin-cross plans with aisles. Saint-Hilaire (eleventh-century building, roofed about 1130) even has triple aisles. The cathedral of Le Puy is the most important of the series. Its nave is covered by a series of six domes on squinches. The oriental influences are easily discerned here, in the structural technique as in the decoration, but they were transmitted by the Arabs.

If this picture of twelfth-century French architecture is not complete, if it misses out such important provinces as Normandy or the Île-de-France, it is because at this time they had outgrown and, in its essentials, abandoned Romanesque for Gothic or at least for rib-vaulting. Their main buildings are a mixture of Romanesque traits and rib-vaulting, but, even thus defined, they must be studied together with the Gothic to which they gave birth.

III. Gothic Churches

The Gothic style was that which in western Europe succeeded the Romanesque, from which it was derived.

Characteristics and divisions. How can a Gothic church be recognized? The pointed arch was first put forward as a criterion. This is a mistake, because there are purely Romanesque churches – notably in twelfth-century Burgundy, as we have seen – which already have pointed arches; on the other hand certain Gothic churches of the sixteenth century, such as Saint-Eustache in Paris, have round-headed arches. Then came the rib-vault, in which two or more intersecting arches are thrown below a vault. It must be recognized that this form was used in Armenia and Lombardy, and even in England and Normandy, in buildings that were by no means Gothic. If a technical definition is needed, it must include at least the association of the rib-vault and the pointed arch, allowing for exceptions in late examples like Saint-Eustache. Some would add the flying buttress, but this is nonsense, since many Gothic churches have none. The formula seems insufficient, because Gothic is less a technique than a style, that is to say a spirit rather than a certain number of processes and forms. It differs from the Romanesque not only by the ribbing of its vaults and the outline of its arches, but by an upward thrust which is often called verticality; by the spirituality expressed in the predominance of void over solid; by a very plentiful decoration which tends more and more to escape from the architecture and live its own life; and finally by the naturalism of this decoration, where real and familiar objects replace the stylization and geometrical patterns of the Romanesque. Such are at least the characteristics of the Gothic buildings which eventually served as prototypes for others, those of the north of France. They are found elsewhere, less characteristic, but sufficiently to prevent a Gothic church being taken for one that is Romanesque.

The perfection of this style was not achieved all at once. We have to distinguish at least the following four periods:

Twelfth-century style, in which Gothic hesitated to detach itself from Romanesque.

Thirteenth-century style, where the structural characteristics, as we have described them, were gradually clarified, while the sculptural decoration still remained subordinated to architectural domination.

Late medieval style, where the virtuosity of Gothic architects reached its greatest development, but in which the decoration had a life of its own, independent of the architecture.

Renaissance Gothic, where the medieval structure remained with new decorative elements borrowed from antiquity.

Historical factors. Viollet-le-Duc saw in the great Gothic cathedrals the expression of an episcopal and communal art, the result of an alliance between the higher clergy and the communes; and in the Romanesque a monastic art. He saw a contrast of secular and monastic art, and a popular if not actually lay character in Gothic buildings. The first Gothic cathedrals do in fact coincide with the first communal charters. Suger, to whom we owe Saint-Denis, freed the townspeople; but he was an abbot, not a bishop; on the other hand, the Bishop of Laon was on the worst possible terms with the commune of his cathedral city. Above all, the first great Gothic structures, Saint-Denis, Saint-Martin-des-Champs, Saint-Germain-des-Prés, were monastic churches, and the chief propagators of the new art and the rib-vault were to be monks, the Cistercians. Hence we must reject the historic assimilations of Viollet-le-Duc.

More worthy of attention is it that this is the period of the Crusades. Like them, Gothic cathedrals are a manifestation of enthusiasm, of a faith which sought to find an outlet in action. St Bernard, co-founder of the Cistercian Order, also preached in the cause of the Second Crusade. Numerous documents attest to this extraordinary fervour. For example, at Saint-Denis when the columns extracted by the workmen had to be drawn away from the quarry 'all the inhabitants of the place, noblemen and commoners, harnessed themselves piously to the ropes, like beasts of burden. ... All along the way, leaving

their work aside, craftsmen ran to help transport these masses
of stone, in order to merit the favours of God and the Holy
Martyrs. ...' It was the same at Chartres and elsewhere.

Nevertheless the cathedrals are planned and organized
works, due to the genius of one man and not to the creative
instinct of the masses, as German Romanticism would have it.
Their architects are beginning to be known by name. They in
no way sought anonymity, but signed their works with a
pattern of labyrinths, unfortunately almost all lost to-day.

The Twelfth Century

France did not invent the rib-vault, but she developed a style
from it; she did not succeed at the first attempt, and it is in fact
rather difficult to fix the moment at which the Romanesque
building with rib-vaults gave place to the Gothic building.

The earliest experiments took place from the end of the
eleventh and the beginning of the twelfth century, in Normandy and England. Indeed, Normandy, after having
conquered England (1066), had become a province of her
conquest and remained so until the beginning of the thirteenth
century. We have noted her inventive spirit and her fine
Romanesque buildings, characterized by their galleries, alternating supports, their façades framed between two towers, a
lantern over the crossing, and covered sometimes with an open
timber roof and sometimes with groined vaults. In the second
half of the eleventh century, in the cathedral of Bayeux, two
arches keyed under the dome of the lower room of the north
bell-tower already offer the principle or at least the appearance
of the rib-vault. The Anglo-Norman architects were the first
to apply the system to a building as a whole, without, however,
grasping its advantages or understanding its consequences:
the opening up of the walls and the lightening of the masonry.
The example was doubtless set in England itself, by the cathedral of Durham, begun in 1093; choir, transept, and nave were
vaulted in turn and the building must have been complete
with its pointed arches in 1133. Elsewhere, about the same
time, the work of rebuilding after collapse or fire afforded the

opportunity of applying this process to various parts of the cathedrals of Winchester, Peterborough, and Gloucester.

But French Normandy is more important than English Normandy in the development of French architecture. She was by no means backward. At Jumièges the chapter-house of the abbey, a rectangle 30×40 feet, was rib-vaulted between 1101 and 1109 at the latest, and in this period can most likely be placed the rib-vaults, very similar in profile and design, of the choir of the old church of Saint-Paul at Rouen and the central tower of Duclair. Throughout Normandy churches are partly roofed in this way. But what great building can we name as being the first to be entirely covered with rib-vaults? Perhaps the abbey of Lessay (Manche), which still exists, the choir of which received the body of its founder's son in 1098. Choir and transept at Lessay have thick cross-vaults with roll mouldings, tapered gradually at the ends, linking up rather clumsily with the outside wall. The nave, which came later, has a different type of moulding, more complicated and with more happily calculated springings. The building remains none the less Romanesque in its masses, its round-headed arches, the absence of wall ribs and flying buttresses, and in all its decoration. The elevation is of three storeys, with a false triforium and a gallery with a passage running at the foot of the windows. The cathedral of Évreux, largely rebuilt in 1119, also seems to have had rib-vaults, if we judge by the form of its supports. The Abbaye-aux-Hommes and the Abbaye-aux-Dames at Caen, from the first half of the twelfth century, also offered the perfect type of the rib-vaulted church, this time on another pattern – sexpartite vaults with six ribs instead of four.

In the royal domain, the rib-vault, as formerly the barrel vault, was applied at first only to certain parts of buildings. The ambulatory of Morienval is held to be the first example in the Île-de-France, about 1122; its very coarse ribs, of semi-circular cross-section, spring from capitals of purely Roman-esque tradition; the windows are round-headed and the bal-ance is maintained by columnar buttresses. Between 1130 and 1150 similar applications of detail can be seen in a series of large and small churches north of Paris. Their chronology is very difficult to establish – Rhuis, Acy-en-Multien, Cauffry, Bellefontaine, Saint-Étienne at Beauvais, in the Oise; in Picardy, Airaines, the bishop's chapel at Laon, etc. In Paris, the choir of the important abbey of Saint-Martin-des-Champs was probably the first example of rib-vaulting in the city, about 1135–40 – the semi-circular form continues in the windows, combined with the pointed arches of the main arcade, and the general effect remains entirely Romanesque: on the other hand, stability is assured by wall-buttresses, the oldest in France. In the collegiate church of Poissy, unhappily restored in the nineteenth century by Viollet-le-Duc, the nave seems to have had rib-vaulting about 1140.

¶ THE 1140 GROUP

A few more important buildings undertaken simultaneously about 1140 reap the benefit of these experiments. They differ from one another. They hesitate over the form of arches, over the arrangement of the storeys (three or four) whether with gallery or triforium, and over the method of buttressing. Each has the value of an experiment. But the Norman influence was felt everywhere.

In the royal domain, the cathedral of Sens was perhaps the first great church entirely covered with rib-vaults. It keeps the alternation of supports and the sexpartite vault of Normandy. The elevation is in three storeys and the gallery is replaced by a triforium. This was already the case in certain Norman Romanesque churches (Mont-Saint-Michel) and no doubt in the Gothic church of Poissy. It is the formula of the future, that of the great cathedrals of the thirteenth century. In the meantime, it was not found elsewhere save in the cathedral of Canterbury, a work by the same architect. In France the gallery remained throughout the second half of the twelfth century, at least in the cathedrals; only some abbeys, like Saint-Germain-des-Prés or Vézelay, gave preference to the triforium.

Saint-Germer-de-Fly (Oise) offers a more complicated

arrangement, but one which was to become popular later: gallery and triforium superimposed raise the elevation to four storeys. An important innovation is the quadripartite vault and identical supports, yet another the flying buttresses masked in the roofing of the gallery. Moreover, the rib is used only for the nave and aisles, while the galleries still have groined vaults. The round-headed arch persists side by side with the pointed arch. The chevron motif in the decoration is once again indicative of Norman influence. Saint-Germer was to have a more modest replica a few years later in the delightful church of Chars.

The rebuilding of Saint-Denis by Abbot Suger was the most famous of these experiments, but it is difficult to assess its influence. The work of Suger has been almost entirely destroyed, partly in the thirteenth century, when Pierre de Montereau rebuilt the nave, partly in the nineteenth century with the restoration of Viollet-le-Duc. We know – thanks to the eloquent commentaries of Suger himself – the chronology of the building. Work began about 1137; it was concentrated at first on the façade and the choir, the solemn dedication of which took place in 1144 before an assembly of prelates. Then Suger turned to the nave. He did not set himself up as an innovator, declaring, on the contrary, that he searched all around him to select the best elements. Only the façade (very much restored), the narthex, the crypt, and the plan of the ambulatory may be considered as belonging to the twelfth century. The two bays of the narthex and their aisles all have rib-vaults, each one different from the rest; the aisles are covered by a gallery, a direct echo of Normandy, as is the chevron decoration. As at Saint-Germer, the round-headed openings are combined with the pointed form of the nave arcades. Of the arrangement and structure of the nave we know nothing. Were there three or four storeys? Alternating or identical supports? Sexpartite or quadripartite vaults? Around the ambulatory are five contiguous radiating chapels, inter-communicating as at Avranches or at Fécamp. Each is lit by two windows – hence the additional rib in the vault, making a total of five. This peculiarity reappears in a certain number of churches, whence some writers have tried to establish a 'Dionysian family'. It is found, notably, in the cathedral of Noyon, begun about 1145. But, on the other hand, the elevation of Noyon is of four storeys (gallery and triforium superimposed); the original structure had sexpartite vaults and alternating supports. It is not known whether these features, much more important than an additional rib in the vaulting of a radiating chapel, were borrowed from Saint-Denis.

¶ THE SECOND HALF OF THE TWELFTH CENTURY

(a) *The Royal Domain.* In the second half of the twelfth century the rib-vault spread throughout France; it was treated differently in the various regions, and we can speak in this period of several provincial families – the royal domain, the Plantagenet domain, and the Cistercian group.

The north remained the most important centre, with the great cathedrals of Noyon (begun about 1145), Senlis (begun about 1155), Laon (begun about 1155–60), Paris (begun 1163), and Soissons (begun about 1180). They have in common the sexpartite vault and the gallery over the side-aisles, but each possesses its own peculiarities and its distinct physiognomy.

The two most important buildings are Laon and Paris. The cathedral of Laon, begun a little before that of Paris, recalls the cathedral of Tournai in the disposition of its masses – two towers on the façade, two towers on each arm of the transept, and a high lantern-tower over the crossing – seven in all. The original plan included a large transept with a chapel in each arm and a choir with ambulatory, but without radiating chapels. The interior disposition, like that of Noyon and Tournai, is of four storeys, including both gallery and triforium. But the respective parts have found their equilibrium; the proportions and design of the bays are harmoniously defined; above all, the walls begin to open up and the light of day to penetrate into the church. Still more original is the façade: at the base there are three deep porches; higher up, a rose-window (the first of its kind), the two towers (183 feet high), square at the base and ending in an octagonal belfry; on the sides, colossal figures of oxen reminiscent of the teams which served to hoist the building materials up to the hill. This façade founded a school; it was imitated at Reims and in several German cathedrals, notably at Bamberg.

The cathedral of Paris, a little later in date, begun in 1163 by Bishop Maurice de Sully, keeps all its originality. But the present building, considerably transformed in the thirteenth century, differs very much from that of the twelfth century. Yet in its essentials the original plan remains: it is characterized by double aisles, the absence of a projecting transept, and the double ambulatory; but it had no radiating chapels, those which we see to-day being later additions. The interior arrangement, eliminating the triforium, is reduced to the gallery alone; yet the four-storey principle is present in the subdivision of the window stage – a small rose-window surmounted by a second window; later on they were merged into a single larger window, but Viollet-le-Duc re-established them in the bays nearest the transept. Nave and choir keep the sexpartite vault in the main body, but give up the alternation of supports, which are all thick monocylindrical columns with powerful crocket capitals. The aisles, on the contrary, combine, rather illogically, the quadripartite vault and alternating supports. A particularly original solution is the vaulting of the double ambulatory by a series of triangles. The master builder, in this case, was sufficiently sure of his technique to raise his main vault much higher than those that had preceded it: 104 feet to the 80 feet of Laon; this is the beginning of an upward growth which was to continue for a whole century, the century into which the Gothic art of northern France was to put its best effort. The façade alone, built in the first years of the thirteenth century, has not changed. It has preserved the sturdiness of Norman Romanesque façades, with their double system of vertical and horizontal divisions; solidly framed between two towers, its H-shaped form has a classical and well-balanced look, in contrast with the romanticism of the cathedral of Laon.

The cathedral of Paris naturally served as prototype for

a certain number of churches in the royal domain, which are
more or less reductions of it (Mantes, Arcueil, Santeuil), and
also for two great cathedrals, Bourges and Le Mans. The
cathedral of Bourges, begun about 1190 by the archbishop
Henri de Sully, brother of Maurice, is a sister to that of Paris,
with its double aisles, double ambulatory, the absence of a
projecting transept and (originally) of radiating chapels. The
differences of structure are more marked, depending chiefly
on the fact that the projected galleries were not executed;
they are replaced by a simple series of openings. The five units
rising in stages form a harmonious composition; the great
vault is lighted from both sides by three rows of superimposed
windows. The choir of the cathedral of Le Mans, begun about
1220, prolonged the series into the thirteenth century. It recalls principally the double ambulatory of Paris with its alternating square and triangular bays. The same arrangement may
be found once more in Spain in the cathedral of Toledo.

The cathedral of Laon also has its family. To it can be related two fine buildings of Champagne: Saint-Remi at Reims
and Notre-Dame at Châlons-sur-Marne. In 1162, the abbot of
Saint-Remi altered the Romanesque nave of his church,
covering it with rib-vaults. The arrangement of the new nave
was the same as at Laon, with superimposed gallery and triforium. As for the choir, he entrusted its entire reconstruction
to an architect whose name we do not know, but who may
well have been the same as at Notre-Dame at Châlons;
there is the same plan in both and, at the entrance to each
radiating chapel, two isolated columns allowing a square to
be cut in the centre of each bay of the ambulatory. The façade
of the building, with its two square towers capped with spires,
is very similar to that of Chartres.

(b) *The Plantagenet Domain.* The strong vertical soaring
which characterizes the cathedrals of the north is no longer
found in the western provinces, Anjou and Poitou, which
depended at the time on England, since they belonged to the
territory of the Plantagenets. Their appearance remains thick-
set and Romanesque. The rib-vault took on a special form, of
very curved profile reminiscent of that of a dome, which has

been called a *domical vault*. This was used in the cathedrals of Angers and Poitiers. The elevation shows neither tribune nor triforium; the height of the building is practically equal to its breadth. This characteristic of marked horizontality is even more accentuated in the cathedral of Poitiers by the fact that the nave and aisles are of the same height: it must be remembered that this was already a frequent feature of the Romanesque churches in this region. Here, therefore, nothing is changed but the means of covering; the arrangement and the feeling for space are the same.

(c) *The Cistercians and Burgundy.* Burgundian Gothic architecture of the twelfth century represents a third type. It is dominated by the beliefs and personality of St Bernard, reformer of the Cistercian Order in 1112. He believed above all in austerity and modesty. In contrast to the Benedictines and notably to Suger, St Bernard wanted no luxury, not even for the glory of God. The unrestrained soaring, the precipitous course of the great cathedrals towards the heavens, seemed to him a mark of pride. He was also guided by preoccupation with economy: economy of ornament – and all sculpture was banned; economy of materials – and very often in Cistercian churches we see the pilasters cut half way down and resting on simple consoles; economy of line and masses – nothing but straight lines and right angles; this is what we have already found at Fontenay, but on this point his successors soon showed themselves less adamant; the thirteenth century often saw a return to complicated lines, curving ambulatories, and radiating chapels. The Cistercians adopted the rib-vault very early. It was to be found in the church (destroyed) of Cîteaux, dedicated in 1148; it is found at Pontigny (about 1150), at Preuilly, at Noirlac. The disciples of St Bernard, bearing it with them beyond the borders of France, were to make it known especially in Italy (Fossanova, Casamari) and in Germany (Heisterbach, 1202, now in ruins but of the same plan as Pontigny; Ebrach, etc.). The elimination of the triforium, and the reduction of the elevation to two storeys, were other Cistercian simplifications.

One fact however must prevent us from speaking of a Burgundian Gothic, and that is the variety of Gothic buildings in the province. The Cistercian formulas did not conquer it entirely. In the old Benedictine abbey of Vézelay the Romanesque choir had to be rebuilt about 1160. The plan, as at Saint-Denis, adds radiating chapels with five ribs to the ambulatory. But the elevation, as at Sens and Saint-Germain-des-Prés, is of three storeys with triforium. The stability of this work is assured only by a continuous, semi-circular wall. The work was clumsy, but the renown of Vézelay was such that it was imitated literally, with all its faults, in Spain by the architect of the cathedral of Avila.

The Thirteenth Century

The thirteenth century marked the zenith of Gothic art. It was then that there sprang up round Paris buildings characterized by their forceful upward movement, by the predominance of voids over solids, by a more and more abundant and naturalistic decoration. These great structures tended to become prototypes for the rest of the kingdom; they merit special attention. But in the different provinces local peculiarities may be seen, and Languedoc in particular escaped their influence altogether, creating the most original variety of the Gothic style.

¶ ÎLE-DE-FRANCE, PICARDY, CHAMPAGNE

First to be set down are three great names – Chartres (work begun 1194); Reims (work begun 1210); Amiens (work begun 1220). Later, with Beauvais and the Sainte-Chapelle in Paris, came the Gothic called the 'rayonnant' (radiating) style. There is no 'rayonnant' in England, except in the period (c. 1245–1300) which used in the nineteenth century to be called 'geometrical'; no 'perpendicular' in France; but a close analogy exists between the English 'decorated' of the early fourteenth century and the French 'flamboyant'. Sometimes the thirteenth century is divided into two periods: but this is a superfluous distinction – the 'rayonnant' style is no more than the logical development and outcome of the style of the first part of the thirteenth century, while the latter had added to the Gothic style of the twelfth century elements which were not necessarily included in it.

The general characteristics of the great cathedrals of the Île-de-France in the thirteenth century are as follows:

(a) Few changes in the plan, except that the importance of the choir was marked more and more strongly and the number of radiating chapels increased regularly – five at Chartres, five at Reims, seven at Amiens. Seven was the number to become most usual (Clermont-Ferrand, Narbonne, Beauvais, Cologne), though it was sometimes exceeded (eleven in the old cathedral of Orleans, thirteen at Le Mans). Twelfth-century cathedrals, like Paris, without radiating chapels, added them in the thirteenth century. The nave also was enriched by the addition of lateral chapels between the buttresses, the example for which was probably set by Paris in 1240.

(b) The elevation was simplified, the three-storey system being finally adopted, the gallery being given up in favour of the triforium, a simple passage set in the thickness of the wall. The nave arcades now rested on complex pillars, the nucleus of which was still the column, but to which were added other smaller columns, running from the floor to the springing of the vault. The capital was reduced to a carved band. Windows became even higher and wider; for the first time, at Chartres they took up the whole bay. From then on they had to be divided by mullions, in two or sometimes three parts. In the second half of the thirteenth century, at Amiens, a prolongation of the window can be seen behind the triforium. This *pierced triforium* seems to be the lower part of the window. In the end these two parts were united and this simplifying tendency resulted at the end of the Middle Ages in the disappearance of the triforium and the reduction of the elevation of the church to two storeys – nave arcades and clerestory. The first example of this extension of window space was given in the thirteenth century by Saint-Urbain, at Troyes.

(c) As for the vault, it was now only quadripartite; the bay

was no longer square, but irregular and rectangular·
nave-bay corresponded to an aisle-bay.

The Cathedral of Chartres. In 1194 a fire destroyed the Romanesque cathedral of Chartres, with the exception of the façade
and the belfry. The rebuilding began immediately. The vaults
were completed in 1220, the portals about 1240, the porches
about 1250. The solemn consecration took place on 17 October 1260. The builders are unknown, though the work is of
considerable historical importance. Gothic architecture, which
we have seen hesitating between several systems, here took on
its definite form with the characteristics which we have just
indicated. The great nave soars straight to a height of 120
feet; whereas at Sens, Noyon, and Paris the restraint of the
Romanesque was still felt, art here takes a decisive step towards its liberation from weight. A few technical details alone
reveal inexperience or hesitation: the windows are broken up
into two lancets, the flying buttresses heavily outlined.
Nevertheless admiration was general, and almost immediately
the cathedral of Chartres was imitated in the choir of the cathedral of Soissons, completed in 1212, to which was soon added
a nave in the same style, finished in 1225. The principal difference is that at Soissons the pillar is flanked by only one small
column. This creates an impression of extreme lightness, and
although the cathedral at Soissons is no more than 100 feet high
it seems the equal of the highest cathedrals.

The Cathedral of Reims. The cathedral of Reims, about
fifteen years later than Chartres, replaced a Carolingian cathedral begun in 816, which lasted through the Middle Ages
until it was burnt in 1210. Its rebuilding was begun almost
immediately. The choir was erected between 1221 and 1241.
Then the work slackened off in the second half of the thirteenth century, so that the main façade was reached only at
the beginning of the fourteenth. The whole remained more
or less intact until 1914; four years of bombardment then
turned it into the 'martyr-cathedral'. The names of the architects were inscribed on the paving, in a labyrinth the drawing
for which has been preserved; they were Jean d'Orbais

(1211–31); Jean Le Loup (1231–47); Gaucher of Reims (1247–55); and Bernard of Soissons (1255–90). To them must be added, for the fourteenth century, Robert de Coucy, who died in 1311. The cathedral of Reims is without doubt that to which the general description outlined above applies most exactly. Certainly it has neither the poetry of Chartres nor the virtuosity of Amiens, but its architectural unity, its regular perfection make it the classic type of Gothic.

The Cathedral of Amiens. The history of the cathedral of Amiens is more complicated. Work began about 1220, ten years after Reims, directed in succession from 1228 to 1248 by three architects, Robert de Luzarches, Thomas de Cormont, and Renard de Cormont; their names were registered in a labyrinth. They began with the nave, an unusual procedure, and it was ready for use in 1236. The choir was completed about 1250. The plan (475 feet long, 49 feet wide in the nave, 229 feet wide at the transept, and 80,730 square feet in total area) represents the perfected type of the great Gothic cathedral, notably in the eastern apse (double aisles in the choir, ambulatory of seven bays and seven radiating chapels) which was imitated at Beauvais, Cologne, Tours, Troyes, Antwerp, and by the group of five southern cathedrals, Clermont-Ferrand, Limoges, Narbonne, Rodez, Toulouse, as well as at Gerona and at Barcelona. The structure of the nave maintains the general characteristics of Chartres and Reims, with yet more boldness. The nave arcades rise uninterrupted to over 65 feet and the vaults to 140 feet. The windows, divided into four elements by very slender columns, fill the whole bay. But the choir shows an important innovation, which marks a turning point in the history of Gothic building. Burnt down in 1258, the upper part had to be rebuilt. Then the triforium wall was pierced by windows, the various sections of which corresponded to and prolonged those of the main windows. The nave and choir of Amiens are thus like two wings of a diptych, on which can be read the synopsis of the whole history of French Gothic in the thirteenth century.

The novelties of Amiens were imitated at Châlons-sur-Marne (cathedral begun about 1230 to replace a Gothic

cathedral of the twelfth century), in the choir of the cathedral
of Troyes (1208–1304; nave fourteenth century), at Saint-
Sulpice at Favières, begun about 1250, a very fine building,
though it does not have the rank of cathedral. But its real
offspring, which, moreover, carried the experiment to its
extreme, was the cathedral of Beauvais, whose architects were
harshly reminded of the existence of matter. The choir of
Beauvais, begun in 1247 with an open triforium, was to rise
to a height of 157 feet, say 16 feet higher than Amiens, with
piers yet more slender and set wider apart. Completed in 1272,
in 1284 it collapsed. It was rebuilt with better materials, re-
inforcing the structure with flying buttresses and adding
intermediary pillars. Later, the steeple over the crossing, which
soared to a height of 501 feet, collapsed also. The cathedral of
Beauvais remained unfinished.

Two old buildings also were brought up to date after a
century of existence – Saint-Denis and the cathedral of Paris.
At Saint-Denis Pierre de Montereau rebuilt, with open triforium, great windows, and enormous rose-windows in the
transept, the half-Romanesque nave of Suger. At the Parisian
cathedral, Jean de Chelles, in 1258, contented himself with
adding a bay to the north transept, but he closed it by a great
rose-window which completely filled it. Pierre de Montereau
did the same with the south.

Two more modest churches consecrated this victory over
matter. First of all in Paris, the Sainte-Chapelle du Palais,
built between 1245 and 1248: the upper storey, without aisles
or flying buttresses, is no more than a glass screen. It again is
the work of Pierre de Montereau (died 1267), who in his work
at Saint-Denis, the cathedral of Paris, the Lady Chapel (no
longer extant) at Saint-Germain-des-Prés, and perhaps that at
Saint-Germain-en-Laye, shows himself one of the greatest
architects of the thirteenth century. Above all must be remembered the church of Saint-Urbain at Troyes, in which not only
do the voids triumph over the solids with dazzling facility,
but a modification in the very elevation of the building can be
seen, this time eliminating even the pierced triforium. Between 1262 and 1266 the architect Jean Langlais reduced the

walls to a simple skeleton of stone and made the windows come down to ten feet from the ground. The flying buttresses were now no more than thin stays. Every part of the building was of extreme delicacy, fitted together like a carpenter's joints. In technique, Gothic architecture was to go no further.

¶ THE PROVINCES

The experiments carried out in the Île-de-France, Picardy, and Champagne were exploited by the other provinces. We cannot follow them in detail here, or enumerate all the buildings. We shall restrict ourselves to presenting two groups – Burgundy and Normandy.

Burgundy borders on Champagne and could easily profit from her example. This explains why the church of Notre-Dame at Dijon, begun in 1230 and almost completed in 1251, though it was not consecrated until 1334, resembles the churches of the first half of the thirteenth century which we have mentioned, and notably the great church of Braine, which itself resembled the cathedral of Laon. To the more developed art of the late thirteenth century belong the nave and transept of the cathedral of Auxerre, the choir of the cathedral of Nevers (fourteenth century), which with its thirteenth-century nave presents the same contrast as the choir and nave of Amiens. The choir of Saint-Thibault-en-Auxois (late thirteenth century), with its two storeys of windows separated by an unlit triforium, but where in fact light comes down almost to the ground, filtered through the mullions which continue through the entire height, is midway between Saint-Sulpice at Favières and Saint-Urbain of Troyes. The present nave of the cathedral of Saint-Jean at Lyons is, in great part, a reconstruction of the thirteenth century.

Normandy, which in the twelfth century had set an example for the master builders of the royal domain, was reconquered in 1204 by Philip Augustus and from then on tended to merge into the pattern of Gothic architecture. It was influenced simultaneously by the monuments of the Île-de-France and of Burgundy. However, its churches maintained certain characteristics peculiar to themselves, such as the square lantern-tower over the crossing, the sharply-pointed arches, the decorative system, and the deep and numerous mouldings. The cathedral of Rouen was rebuilt in the thirteenth century; in the nave, above the main arcade, there are wide openings simulating a gallery, in reality open at the back on to empty space over the aisles. The church of La Trinité at Fécamp also replaced a Romanesque church. The nave, finished in 1219, still has galleries. South of the Seine, the finest of thirteenth-century Norman Gothic buildings are the cathedrals of Lisieux (rebuilt from the nave in 1170 and after; choir about 1226–35), Bayeux (Romanesque nave transformed at the beginning of the thirteenth century; choir after 1230), and Coutances (formerly a Romanesque cathedral; nave 1218–38; choir and transepts completed in 1251 and 1274). The nave of the cathedral of Coutances had galleries now, walled up; the elevation of the choir is reduced to two storeys. The same applies to the nave of Bayeux. The case of Coutances is a good example of the complexity of the relations between the great Gothic buildings. Like Paris, Bourges, and Le Mans, it has two ambulatories and the composition of its choir shows singular analogies with the east end of the cathedral of Le Mans, consecrated in 1254, without our being able to say which influenced the other. The system of the open triforium is represented in the province by two magnificent buildings – the cathedral of Sées (third quarter of the thirteenth century) and the church of Saint-Ouen at Rouen (work begun in 1303).

¶ THE SOUTH OF FRANCE

The rib-vault was known in the south almost as soon as in the north, but it was not then exploited in any way. It appeared in the porch of Moissac (1130–40); but its first important application was in the nave of the cathedral of Toulouse, rebuilt about 1211. Gothic thus suffered a time-lag of nearly a century here; this fact is linked up with the very success and very perfection of the Romanesque, which dispensed architects from the need to search for other forms. Yet, when the moment came, they were capable of developing from the new formula highly original works which hold a considerable place in the geography of Gothic architecture.

It is true that certain cathedrals were content to imitate those of the north. Bayonne, begun about 1260, is reminiscent of Soissons and Reims. The dominant influence was that of Amiens. We recognize it in the group of five cathedrals attributed more or less justifiably to Jean Deschamps – Clermont-Ferrand (begun in 1248), Limoges (begun in 1273), the choir of Narbonne (begun in 1272), the choir of Toulouse (begun in 1275), Rodez (begun in 1277). The choir of the church of Saint-Nazaire (after 1270), at Carcassonne, is inspired by St Louis' Sainte-Chapelle in Paris.

But there are other buildings which in their structure and feeling for space are in open contrast with northern Gothic. They have no aisles and consequently no interior supports, the church is no more than a great hall in which the priest at the altar is seen and heard from all points – a factor which greatly favoured the preaching of the mendicant orders, the Dominicans and Franciscans – and in which the buttresses simply mark along the walls sites for side-chapels. The nave of the cathedral of Toulouse, substituted for a Romanesque nave at the beginning of the thirteenth century, is already a great rectangle of 164×63 feet covered by three square-section rib-vaults. The span of these vaults (63 feet) considerably exceeds that of the northern cathedrals, but their height is very much less, since it is only equal to their breadth. The stability, the horizontal accent of the Romanesque is still maintained. Moreover Toulouse is not really the prototype of the series, since it has no side chapels or inwardly projecting buttresses. The first examples seem to have been set outside France, in Catalonia, by the two churches of the Dominicans and Franciscans at Barcelona; so we must speak of Catalan rather than of southern Gothic. It is true that they draw largely also on Romanesque and Cistercian

Burgundy. In Languedoc the formula was to produce the three cathedrals of Saint-Bertrand-de-Comminges (1304), Perpignan (1324), and Albi (begun 1282, completed late fourteenth century). Less important but perhaps more characteristic are the parish churches of Toulouse (Notre-Dame-du-Taur; Notre-Dame-de-la-Dalbade) and above all the churches of the numerous new towns springing up at this time (see below) in the district: the church of Notre-Dame at Villefranche-de-Rouergue (1260, one of the first buildings of the series); those of Saint-Vincent and Saint-Michel at Carcassonne, the old cathedral of Mirepoix, the church of Beaumont-de-Lomagne. Examples can be found as far north as Montferrand (Puy-de-Dôme). For a long time some of these buildings probably had only an open timber roof, such as we see to-day in the church of Lamourguié at Narbonne. The church of the Dominicans in Toulouse is also only a rectangular hall with an apse and side-chapels; but it is divided internally by a row of slender columns. In short, there were many churches in new towns and many churches belonging to the mendicant Orders. A common trait was that neither the one nor the other had much money to spend. And this, in fact, is a particularly economical formula for a church, which is another reason why the decoration of these buildings is generally extremely plain and almost completely devoid of sculpture.

IV. The End of the Middle Ages

The art of the late Middle Ages is generally called *Flamboyant*. The word comes from 'flame'. In the first place a Flamboyant building may be recognized by a tracery of certain windows, in which the opposition of curve to counter-curve reminds one of the undulating form of a flame. Its basic form is the ogee; others, more complicated, are known as dagger and falchion tracery. The Flamboyant system is not merely decorative. There are in it more important constructional characteristics:

The form of the arches: the depressed is substituted for the pointed arch.

Tracery of the vault: supplementary ribs (ridge ribs, and intermediary ribs) bring greater complexity to the basic quadripartite rib-vault, transforming it into a star or even a labyrinth of ribs both curved and straight. Simultaneously, a consequence of the preceding remark, the outline of these vaults is lowered, nearing the horizontal, whereas increasingly heavy, moulded, and carved bosses hang from the summit.

Capitals disappear and the ribs of the vault run directly down into the support, gradually losing themselves in it; and sometimes this support is reduced to a simple column.

The interior elevation eventually becomes reduced to two storeys – nave arcades and clerestory – through the suppression of the triforium, a step already implied in the use of the pierced triforium.

There has been much discussion about the origin of these characteristics. Enlart once saw in them an importation from England, a consequence of the Hundred Years' War. But the curve and the counter-curve, the ribs penetrating into the pillar, appeared as early as the thirteenth century in southern Gothic architecture, above all in the work of Jean Deschamps. In reality we have to consider not particular forms, but the very spirit of Flamboyant Gothic. It is dominated by two factors:

(a) The perfection of a structural technique. Architects, certain of their skill, were attracted by virtuosity. There is no trace of decadence. The constructional quality is far from inferior; the buildings stand just as well. Preoccupation with logic was not even diminished, all the new elements can be justified.

(b) Prolific decoration, which exists primarily for its own sake; it is not functional or limited by constructional factors. As has been noticed, the history of architecture reveals a sort of rhythm – first a flowering of decoration, then its total elimination. Flamboyant Gothic is one of those periods in which the decorators had their revenge on the architects. The Baroque was to be another.

Examples of Flamboyant Gothic fill the fifteenth and even a good part of the sixteenth centuries, but we are now concerned with much less important buildings than previously. Numerous Parisian churches date from this time, a proof that religious fervour had not slackened – Saint-Laurent, Saint-Médard, Saint-Germain de Charonne, Saint-Nicolas-des-Champs, above all Saint-Germain l'Auxerrois, Saint-Étienne-du-Mont, and Saint-Séverin. The latter, masterpiece of Parisian Flamboyant art, also retains, like several of its sister churches, an echo of the cathedral of Paris, with its double-aisled plan, triangular vaulting of the ambulatory, and the persistence of the triforium. In Picardy, it is Saint-Riquier and Saint-Wulfram d'Abbeville; in Champagne, the fine church of Notre-Dame-de-l'Épine (1410–1524), a true cathedral in its spaciousness and worthy of Reims. In Lorraine there is Saint-Nicolas-du-Port; in the Lyons area, Saint-Nizier at Lyons; in the Bourbonnais, the cathedral of Moulins. In the Loire valley is the cathedral of Tours, also dating mainly from the fifteenth century.

Normandy is one of the richest provinces of France in Flamboyant works. Many keep the triforium. The key works are the church of Notre-Dame at Caudebec (begun in 1426), that of Saint-Maclou at Rouen (1436–1521), the choir of Mont-Saint-Michel, and the church of Notre-Dame at Alençon. Brittany completed at this time several of her great buildings begun at an earlier date: the cathedrals of Saint-Pol-de-Léon, of Tréguier, of Quimper, but with a time-lag so marked that Breton architecture of the fifteenth century is still 'Rayonnant', the Flamboyant appearing only in the sixteenth century.

v. The Sixteenth Century

Gothic architecture persisted throughout the sixteenth century and even longer. During this century were built on the one hand churches absolutely similar to those of the fifteenth century, thus prolonging the Flamboyant Gothic, and on the other hand churches which, though retaining the plan and the basis of Gothic structure (rib-vaults, flying buttresses) adopted several new elements of varying importance, but which, in the end, did not bring about a transformation of architecture, since this does not consist in a few new details here and there but in an ensemble of forms, and above all in a new spirit.

What are these details? First the supports: the substitution of the square pillar for the clustered column (Paris, Saint-Eustache) or the application of a pilaster to the column (Le Havre, church of Notre-Dame); in this way a flat surface is obtained which can be more conveniently decorated. Secondly, the vaults: the insertion of a horizontal ceiling between the ever more numerous ribs, which in no way implied a renunciation of the hanging keystone (Norman group); in the Loire region, the dome was substituted for the spire in the upper part of belfries. But these are only isolated details, scattered all over France, almost mere local variations.

Decoration offers more, so much so that those historians who give it as much importance as construction, if not more, can speak of a new style. Transformation began from without. From 1530 onwards, entire units, hallmarked by Italian or antique influence, were attached to Gothic buildings: internally, in the enclosures of choirs or chapels, the rood-screens, the furnishings, stalls, or stained glass; externally, in the portals. There is a revival of the round-headed arch as a frame for openings, a system of effects entirely based on the circle, which however does not always reject the heightening value of curves and counter-curves. Gradually, the geometry and schematization of the antique orders ousted the Gothic naturalism and the Italianizing effervescence; a pediment crowned the portals, suggesting the façade of a temple or a triumphal arch; figures of Fame or Victory strengthened this idea of triumph, which held such a large place in the sixteenth century that it was possible for the Renaissance to be defined as a reversal of moral values, by which the hero was substituted for the saint.

We may illustrate by a few examples from various parts of France these two aspects of religious architecture in the sixteenth century. It would be possible to consider first the tradition, and then the innovations; but to present them side by side in their regional setting will perhaps make the complexity and the slowness of their evolution more obvious.

Paris shows it most clearly. Tradition won the day easily with Saint-Merry, Saint-Gervais, Saint-Médard, the essential parts of Saint-Étienne-du-Mont and Saint-Nicolas-des-Champs. The innovations were represented in the rood-screen (now lost) of Saint-Germain-l'Auxerrois (1539–45), first product of the Lescot-Goujon collaboration, imitated half a century later in the rood-screen of the Cordeliers; by that of Saint-Étienne-du-Mont (mid sixteenth century), happily preserved; and above all by the fine side porch of Saint-Nicolas-des-Champs, already late in the century (1575), which reproduces a project of Philibert Delorme for a triumphal arch. To Delorme we owe even more – an entire building, Saint-Eustache, a Renaissance work of major importance; it was begun about 1530 on the initiative of François I, but work on it continued right through and considerably beyond the sixteenth century. The imitation of Notre-Dame in Paris is evident; not only in the plan with its double aisles and double ambulatory, but in the elevation, which revives the three storeys of Notre-Dame, though with an open triforium to give more light. The decorative motifs are new and pleasantly homogeneous. It is the very rare example of a church in which all the parts strive towards a new appearance – round-headed arches, pillars flanked by small pilasters in which the three antique orders, Doric, Ionic, and Corinthian-Composite, are superimposed; the bays of the triforium separated by fluted pilasters with capitals; fluting and capitals on the exterior buttresses; the ornamentation of the portals. But this new facing covers a completely Gothic skeleton of rib-vaults and flying buttresses.

The similarity of the decoration of Saint-Eustache to that of Saint-Maclou at Pontoise, the rebuilding of which seems to have been undertaken about the middle of the sixteenth century by Pierre Lemercier, has often resulted in the two works being attributed to the same architect. The district round Pontoise, the Vexin, was in the sixteenth century a centre of important research, led by the Lemercier and Grappin families; there are a crowd of little churches with doorways and belfries full of charming details. Against the buttresses of the towers of Chars and Maule are the three superimposed orders. The portals of Magny-en-Vexin, Chaumont-en-Vexin, and Vétheuil attempt to introduce the antique order, with column and pediment, into the medieval tympanum. Another more advanced group is nearer the Oise itself – Luzarches, l'Isle-Adam, Villiers-le-Bel, Sarcelles, Groslay, Goussainville, and above all Belloy; here the influence of Jean Bullant has been recognized, and the lovely porch of Belloy has even been attributed to him. This development was synthesized in the façade of the church of Saints Gervais and Protais at Gisors, unfortunately destroyed in 1940. With it we pass from the fifteenth century to François I, from François I to Henri II, in short from Flamboyant Gothic to the early Renaissance and finally to newly discovered antiquity. The lower part of the façade still had a tympanum; the upper part was treated like a triumphal arch; the decoration of the south tower consisted entirely of superimposed orders with friezes of triglyphs and metopes. But this is the only church of any importance which we can name; all the others are small and nothing similar can be seen in the cathedrals of Beauvais or Senlis, the very considerable transepts of which, begun under Louis XII, were to be completed in the middle of Henri II's reign.

In Normandy, neighbour to the Vexin, from the beginning of the century the cardinals of Amboise had made Gaillon a centre of the Renaissance. The lower chapel of the château, fortunately preserved, seems to be the prototype of the ribbed ceiling which we find again in the apse of Saint-Pierre at Caen, the work of Hector Sohier, and which is likewise crowded with decorative details singularly lively and abundant; in the chapel of Our Lady at the abbey church of Valmont (between 1525 and 1540); in the choir of Tillières (1534–46); in the three chapels built at Saint-Jacques at Dieppe by the ship-owner Ango, and even in the neighbouring province of Maine, at Notre-Dame-des-Marais at La Ferté-Bernard (Sarthe). As a purely decorative innovation may be mentioned the delightful wooden porch of Ry, which is covered with lively arabesques and small mythological figures, one of the most charming works of the early Renaissance, and the north portal of the church of Notre-Dame at Les Andelys, of a more classical taste with its four Ionic columns and its reliefs of Victories, which is directly related to the series of Vexin portals. But these are mere details by comparison with the great Flamboyant works begun or finished in the province in the sixteenth century: Saint-Ouen and Saint-Maclou at Rouen, even the main doorway of the cathedral, the choir of the church of Mont-Saint-Michel (completed in 1520) and the church of Notre-Dame at Caudebec.

We have already said that Brittany remained faithful to the Flamboyant. The decorative novelties appeared only at the end of the century and, no longer new, persisted under Louis XIII. The precocious appearance of a circular chapel must be mentioned; added in 1537 to the north side of the cathedral of Vannes, it was the whim of a canon who had lived for many years in Rome and wanted to re-create in his home-country a souvenir of the Farnese palace.

In Touraine we have spoken of another structural peculiarity, the dome which in 1507 replaced the spire on the north tower of the cathedral of Tours, the work of the brothers Martin and Bastien François – another prototype that can be traced to Saint-Antoine at Loches, to Bressuire and La Trinité at Angers; but care must be taken not to confuse these domes with the great classical domes of the following century; they are no more than details, and never the essential part of a composition. Almost all the churches and chapels of Touraine in the first half of the century have fine round-headed porches where the abundant decoration, with its exuberant fantasy, is comparable to that of the contemporary châteaux: the chapel of Ussé, the church of Montrésor, the chapel of Saint-Symphorien at Tours. To these are related the collegiate church of Oiron (Deux-Sèvres) in Poitou and Saint-Pierre at Loudon (Vienne).

To the east of Paris, in southern Champagne, Troyes has six churches of the sixteenth century, Saint-Nicolas, Saint-Pantaléon, Saint-Nizier, the Madeleine, Saint-Rémy, and

Saint-Martin. All belong, in their essentials, to Flamboyant Gothic, but a few façades must be specially noticed. The lower part of that of Saint-Nizier (church built in 1535) is conceived as a triumphal arch with its three unequal round-headed arches framed between columns with Ionic capitals. Saint-Nicolas (about 1555), with its two storeys, its super-imposed orders (on the ground floor there is a Doric frieze of triglyphs and metopes) and its four niches for statues, is already a Baroque pattern. Nor is the surrounding district to be forgotten – Saint-André-lez-Troyes (1549), Pont-Sainte-Marie (1553), Auxon (1535–40) – any more than the lovely façades of Bar-sur-Seine and Ricey-Bas. The north of the province is poorer. Yet Vouziers possessed a magnificent façade, twice destroyed, in 1914 and 1940. That of Rembercourt-aux-Pots (Meuse), to the east, suffered the same fate.

In Burgundy the Yonne valley – where the south transept of the cathedral of Sens was finished in Gothic style after 1500, while the north transept was begun in the same manner – offers us the façades of Villeneuve-sur-Yonne (1575) and of Saint-Pierre at Tonnerre (1562–90), both innovations. That of Saint-Michel at Dijon, with its three portals, remained faithful to the general traditional arrangement, in spite of its round-headed arches and tunnel-shaped and coffered porches; decorative detail is freer, not even hesitating to make use of the legend of Hercules (1537–51). The fine porch of Saint-Jean at Losne should also be mentioned. That of Saint-Nizier at Lyons is sometimes attributed to Philibert Delorme. On the contrary, in the Ain region, the church of Brou, begun by Jean Perréal in 1506, belongs entirely to Flamboyant Gothic.

In the south of France the greatest building of the sixteenth century is the cathedral of Sainte-Marie at Auch, rebuilt at that time, except for the façade, in Flamboyant Gothic, but with very original details, notably the design of the pillars and the triforium which, together with its elegant proportions, make it one of the most interesting Gothic buildings constructed according to the northern manner in the south of France. But the element of innovation is absent. It is to be found in a few church-porches in Toulouse, such as that of the Dalbade, and the outer porch of Saint-Sernin. Better still are small buildings such as the church of Assier (Lot), with a frieze (*litre**) running right round it, in which, with many references to antique mythology, are celebrated the exploits of Galiot de Genouillac, grand-master of the French artillery under François I. The charming church of Lonzac (Charente-Maritime), also built at the expense of Galiot, is similar; they must both be by the same architect, who is no longer believed to be Nicolas Bachelier of Toulouse.

*A *litre* is a band painted round a church as a memorial to the local seigneur. (*Trans.*)

CHAPTER TWO

CLASSICAL CHURCHES
(1550–1850)

THE Gothic formulas did not disappear even after 1550. Churches, even cathedrals, continued to be built with rib-vaults. That of Orleans was built by the Bourbons, from Henri IV to Louis XVI, and the greatest classical architects worked on it. In the second half of the nineteenth century there was a veritable Gothic revival. Nevertheless, for three centuries religious architecture gave preference to another type of church, that known sometimes as *Jesuit*, sometimes as *Baroque* (the fitness of these terms will be discussed later), which has its origin in the art of the Counter-Reformation.

¶ GENERAL CHARACTERISTICS

As we have done for the Middle Ages, let us first outline its general characteristics. The disdainful indifference which most often surrounds this art is combined with the view that all its examples are of the same kind, but they are in fact extremely varied, even more so than Gothic churches.

Plan. Western medieval art had finally reduced the various types admitted by Christian art of the early centuries to a single plan, that of the basilica. The most famous Gothic cathedrals, and even the principal Romanesque churches, are designed on the same lines. The aisleless nave of the south is no more than a local variant. Classical religious art offers almost as many plans as churches. We have to distinguish at least three types, linked by a common characteristic, a taste for great uninterrupted spaces. The medieval cathedral is a dense forest full of shade and mystery, where the eye is continually arrested by pillars. Classical art frees the field of vision to the greatest possible extent. Two conceptions of space are here contrasted; one has more poetry, the other more majesty.

A comparison of three Parisian buildings of the first quality (Saint-Paul, Saint-Sulpice, the Invalides) will enable us to grasp fully these differences of plan. They represent the three essential formulas, but leave aside many others (the Sorbonne, Val-de-Grâce, etc.).

(a) The church of Saint-Paul-Saint-Louis has a nave and no aisles, but has side chapels between the buttresses which project into the interior. In this a survival of southern Gothic can be recognized and later the intermediary stages will be seen. In Paris, the Carmelite Church, the Oratoire, and Notre-Dame-des-Victoires are of the same type; in the provinces other churches which will be named later.

(b) Saint-Sulpice has a basilican plan similar to that of the great northern Gothic cathedrals – nave and aisles, ambulatory and radiating chapels. This is also the plan of Saint-Roch, Saint-Nicolas-du-Chardonnet, Saint-Louis-en-l'Île, the cathedrals of Nancy and Versailles, etc.

(c) The domed church of the Invalides has a central plan. We know that this implies numerous variants – a Greek cross inscribed in a square (Invalides), a Greek cross alone (Panthéon), a circle or ellipse (chapel of the Collège Mazarin, church of the Assumption, etc.).

So, beside the basilican plan, the classical period took up the Catalan-Languedoc aisleless nave and re-established the importance of the central plan, laid aside since the Romanesque period.

Structure. This underwent a similar enrichment by similar means – a return to the past. In particular the three great formulas of the Romanesque vaults – barrel vaults, groined vaults, and domes – appear once more, though without the rib-vault being abandoned. In barrel vaulting the skill of the builders and the progress of stereotomy now allowed the placing of great lateral openings in the wall, practically perpendicular tunnels, penetrating deeply though not fully intersecting. These contained the windows, ensuring plentiful direct lighting for the nave. The dome reappeared over the crossing and often even over the side chapels. It differed greatly from its Byzantine and Romanesque prototypes, which were no more than half-spheres. The dome was now set on a circular drum with the pendentives below it. The whole was capped by a lantern. Sometimes, to increase its apparent height, the real dome of masonry was covered by a false one of timber (Val-de-Grâce, Invalides). The dome had reappeared in the sixteenth century in the chapel of the Château of Anet, by Philibert Delorme. The first example in Paris was at Saint-Joseph des Carmes (1613–20), here placed on pendentives and capped with a shell of wood and plaster on very simple lines, a half circle slightly raised and surmounted by a lantern. The upward movement continued in a crescendo, ending in the dome of the Panthéon.

For the abutment, flying buttresses and ordinary buttresses were still used. Only their profile was modified, the curve being frequently substituted for the straight line, as in the voluted screens on the façades.

The interior elevation often had only two divisions – windows above, nave arcades below. Sometimes, however, in the seventeenth century, a gallery or tribune was placed between the two. In the churches of basilican plan, the nave was separated from the aisles, in the seventeenth century, by square or rectangular piers like those of the Romanesque churches – robust flat-faced piers flanked with pilasters. The clustered columns on the Gothic pattern had disappeared. The simple column reappeared in the eighteenth century. In the aisleless churches the end of the buttress was also treated as a pier. The arcades always had round arches, as in the Romanesque period, and the windows too finished in a semi-circle.

Façades. The façade was often the outstanding part of the church. Here, too, several types must be distinguished – Saint-Jacques-du-Haut-Pas, Saint-Gervais, Sainte-Élisabeth, the Sorbonne, in seventeenth-century Paris alone. But here again a common feature is always found – the influence of the antique arrangement of columns or pilasters, with a pediment. It was not the Greek temple façade, since, except towards the end, the column was almost never weight-bearing or free-standing. It was mere ornament.

(a) The façade of Saint-Jacques-du-Haut-Pas was, or was meant to be, framed by two towers, but only one was built. This is a medieval type which, in fact, never disappeared. This example is of the seventeenth century (1675-84). It is not the only one: it is found even in Jesuit colleges such as that of Roanne. Towers were to be numerous in the eighteenth century – in Paris, at Saint-Sulpice and Saint-Eustache; in the provinces, in the cathedrals of Nancy, Auch, Langres, Arras, and elsewhere; in the nineteenth century, at Saint-Vincent-de-Paul.

(b) Saint-Gervais is the representative of the three-storey façade, each storey with a different order. These orders are here correctly superimposed – Doric, Ionic, Corinthian – as was already common in domestic architecture, for example in the courtyard of the palace of the Cancelleria in Rome or the entrance to the Château of Anet. In religious architecture, the sixteenth century had tried the formula on the storeys of a tower (Chars, Seine-et-Oise) or the interior elevation of a bay (Paris, Saint-Eustache). Its application to a façade was more difficult. Saint-Étienne-du-Mont was a hesitant attempt; Saint-Gervais, Saint-Paul, the chapel of the Collège d'Eu, realized it perfectly. But in spite of the fame of Saint-Gervais (1616-21; probably by Salomon de Brosse) this formula was not followed up.

(c) Two-storeyed façades were the rule: Sainte-Élisabeth at Paris offers one of the oldest surviving examples. In this case the origin is purely Italian. It is the façade of the Gesù – a ground floor with an upper storey, the two linked by volutes.

(d) The classical church generally calls for a dome. Too great an elevation of the façade (say three storeys) renders this invisible from outside. Even with two storeys and a long nave it cannot be seen well. By shortening the nave, and substituting the Greek for the Latin cross, the central plan for the basilican, the dome fits in naturally with the composition of the façade. It is towards this formula that French architecture strove constantly for two centuries. In Paris, the finest and most characteristic façades with domes are at the Sorbonne (over the courtyard), the Invalides, and the Panthéon.

Decoration. Here again there was a complete break with Gothic and the late Middle Ages, and in one respect a return to the Romanesque. All the elements of classical ornamental decoration could be found in the twelfth-century churches of Burgundy or Provence – Ionic or Corinthian capitals, fluted pilasters, pediments. But there the resemblance ends. Figure sculpture, notably in the round, was almost eliminated; façades now had only a few statues in niches – figures with no direct relation to the architecture, which could be placed in position or moved at will, or even omitted without the general lines of the building suffering in any way. Thus large-scale sculpture ceased to be a monumental art. In the interior, pulpits, stalls, organ-cases, where it is best seen, are by definition furniture. As in Romanesque art, vast wall surfaces offered painting an opportunity which it did not always neglect, as the frescoes by Mignard in the dome of the Val-de-Grâce, or those of La Fosse at the Invalides, bear witness.

¶ THE ORIGINS

The origins of the classical style are to be found in Rome. Perhaps, therefore, it should be called an imported art. But we need hardly be offended by this, since it was the same with medieval art, which came entirely from the East. And, as with medieval art, French architects quickly evolved a new style on which they impressed the national characteristics.

The two starting points were St Peter's – that at least of Bramante and Michelangelo – and particularly the Gesù. At the beginning of the sixteenth century Bramante had given Julius II the idea of a church dominated by an immense dome. After many hesitations, the dome, extolled again by Michelangelo and realized by him and Vignola, rose into the Roman skies at the end of the sixteenth century. Its memory and example dominated the two centuries to come.

The church of the Gesù provided still more – a ground-plan and a façade. A plan without aisles, with side-chapels between buttresses; a two-storeyed façade, the upper and narrower framed by two volutes. Yet Vignola, its author, had invented neither the one nor the other. The plan came from southern medieval art, probably transmitted to Rome by the Catalan church in the capital of Christendom, dedicated to Our Lady of Montserrat (1496). The façade had been conceived a little earlier by L. B. Alberti and realized by him at Sta Maria Novella in Florence. The Gesù was the mother church of the Society of Jesus. Such was its influence that an attempt has been made to call the new manner the 'Jesuit' style. This exaggerates its importance. The term is inadmissible because not all Jesuit churches are like the Gesù (in France, especially, the Society was the most zealous perpetuator of Gothic architecture), and because the plan and the façade of the Gesù are very far from setting the pattern for the churches of the seventeenth and eighteenth centuries, even in France – we have indeed just seen their variety.

A more general term is therefore needed. We cannot accept *Baroque* any more than Jesuit. The notion of Baroque art is complex, even confused. Historically, certain periods should be distinguished within it. True Baroque is not to be mistaken for the art of the Counter-Reformation which preceded it. The latter, originating from the decisions of the Council of Trent, attempted to bring religious art back to austerity and simplicity. The Gesù – Vignola's Gesù, for it has been altered – obeyed these directives. This was at the end of the sixteenth century. Italy broke from them very quickly. The Baroque is the art of Bernini and Borromini in the seventeenth century. With them religious architecture gave up austerity. It decided no longer to deny itself any pleasure. It sought it in caprice rather than logic, in imagination rather than reason; it appealed to the senses and the heart rather than to the mind and the will; in a whirl of curving lines, a triumphal and passionate décor which aimed only at moving, stirring, and carrying away the beholder. This style was to overrun Europe. As we have already said, France resisted it. The ways of the two countries parted from the moment when Italy passed beyond the Counter-Reformation.

The independence of France was doubtless incomplete. It has always been impossible to enclose French art and the French temperament within a single formula. But the most characteristic works, especially those which we have already mentioned, were inspired by another ideal – to maintain the predominance of reason and will over feeling, and also to return to the most austere and bare of antique forms. One of the elements of this resistance is doubtless the national trait already stressed in St Bernard – a dislike of showiness. There must be no ostentation; to make a display of wealth, not to mention power, seemed in bad taste. This tendency was to reappear in the seventeenth century with Jansenism. Avarice, some might call it – petty-bourgeois mentality. Be that as it may; our business is to describe, not to judge. The Mass is a drama, say the Italians; therefore the church is a theatre. The church is a place of prayer and meditation, reply the Cistercians and the Jansenists. Yet there is quite another side to French art, the side which opposed Suger to St Bernard. In the words of Suger, *Mens hebes ad verum pervenit per artem*. It is the *mind* of man that has to be raised towards God. The mind first. This affirmation of the primary of the intelligence does not contradict what has been said before. A single name – 'classical' – is applicable to both.

The Evolution of Classical Religious Art

In pleading the cause of this misrepresented art we have spoken of its variety and adaptation in France. We have now to show that it developed, that is to say that it was a *living* art.

What date can we take as our point of departure? In Italy the new architecture produced masterpieces as early as the sixteenth century. In France, we have to wait until the seventeenth. The second half of the sixteenth century, taken up in France by the wars of religion, was practically barren as far as religious art was concerned. There is one work, a clean breakaway from the Gothic, physically small but an important indication of what was to come – the chapel of the Château of Anet by Philibert Delorme. The central plan with a domed covering indicates the influence of Bramante's St Peter's, though the idea was probably borrowed directly from a project of Primaticcio's for a chapel of the Valois at Saint-Denis. It is also said that Philibert Delorme had thought of transforming the church of Saint-Nizier at Lyons into a circular building with dome and lantern. In this way classical religious art in France might have begun with the central plan. But although it returned to it later, in the meantime fashion had taken another course.

¶ THE COUNTER-REFORMATION

The policy of the Council of Trent bore fruit. With the return of peace, a great religious fervour took hold of France. The first half of the seventeenth century was a period of intense faith. Great saintly figures appear once more – St Vincent de Paul, St François de Sales. New orders were founded: the Eudists by St Jean Eudes, the Oratorians by the Cardinal de Bérulle, Saint-Sulpice by Olier. Heresies such as Jansenism and the vivacity of the quarrels they aroused show the place occupied by Christianity in intellectual life. In art the consequence was the revival of architectural activity. In Paris alone, between 1610 and 1660, forty religious houses were founded and twenty churches begun.

The Gesù was the model which imposed itself at first, because the Society of Jesus took the lead in architectural activity. Though its churches were varied in structure – as will be realized from a comparison of three of the finest, Paris, Rouen, and La Flèche – and a number of traditional elements are found in them, since local workmanship exerts an influence on the architects themselves and journeymen transmit the same methods from generation to generation, it is however true to say that many churches were inspired by the Gesù. The principal rôle in this diffusion was played by Father Étienne Martellange (1568–1641), who entered the Society in 1590 as a 'temporal coadjutor'. From 1590 to 1604 he stayed in Rome, studying Vignola. Back in France, he went about the country as a kind of inspector of buildings to the Society, almost always collaborating with a local architect. About 1635 he resigned these functions in favour of Father Turmel. It was mainly the ground-plan of the Gesù that the French Jesuit churches borrowed, at least its aisleless nave so suitable for ceremonial and preaching; but in regard to the structure and the façade there was no uniformity. In certain provinces – notably the north and Franche-Comté – the Jesuits were faithful perpetuators of the Gothic style.

In Paris the church of the professed Fathers, Saint-Paul-Saint-Louis by Martellange and Father Derand (1625–34) is the most important of the Society in France. It has the aisleless nave and lateral chapels of the Gesù, but differs therefrom by the transept which projects to form a Latin cross, a pattern which France has always favoured more than Rome, and by its three-tiered façade, derived from a neighbouring model, this time a French one, the façade of Saint-Gervais. The Jesuit church at Blois (now the church of Saint-Vincent-de-Paul) by Martellange and Turmel, begun at the same time, combines in the same way the aisleless plan and the three-storeyed façade (Turmel, 1634), in this case with the classical Doric-Ionic-Corinthian superimposition, not yet to be found in Paris. There was again an aisleless nave in the chapel at Avignon, also by Martellange (1620–55), now the Lycée chapel; but the façade follows the Roman pattern, as do those of the churches of the Society at Bordeaux (church of Saint-Paul, rather later, 1663–76) and at Caen (Notre-Dame-de-la-Gloriette, 1684). That of Roanne, now the Lycée chapel, is of an austere simplicity, with its great arch framed between two towers. At Rouen the Lycée chapel, begun in 1610 and completed in 1704, is one of the most original because of its fidelity to the rib-vault, the Flamboyant tracery of its pointed windows and its plan with polygonal arms to the transept. At La Flèche there are also rib-vaults, but combined with the ground-plan of the Gesù.

Many other churches erected under Louis XIII and during the minority of Louis XIV borrow the plan or the façade of the Gesù, and occasionally both. The adoption of the two-tiered façade, which may be called the Counter-Reformation type though it is considerably earlier, was not arrived at without hesitating experiments and modifications. The Jesuits were not even responsible for the introduction of the formula into France. One of the first experiments is at Le Havre, in the church of Notre-Dame (1605–8); free-standing columns have a shaft encircled with large rings, as in the Tuileries of Philibert Delorme and in the Luxembourg; the example was to be imitated at Harfleur. At Bordeaux, in Saint-Bruno, the church of the Carthusians (1611–20), the basic elements are searching for their proportions; the door seems suffocated between heavy composite pilasters; two small triumphal arches set vertically are bound to the centre of the façade by a little wall supporting a pyramid; the whole is inscribed within buttresses capped with triangular pediments. The precise and, so to speak, classical form is found in Paris in the Feuillants façade (1624 or 1629, by François Mansart; destroyed), at Sainte-Élisabeth (1631, church of the nuns of the Third Order of St Francis); and in the Visitation at Avignon (1632).

¶ CLASSICISM

The fidelity of seventeenth-century France to the prototypes of the Counter-Reformation, then abandoned in Italy, already represents a liberation from the Baroque. Subsequently France was to escape from the Counter-Reformation itself.

From the first half of the century some churches, rejecting the plan of the Gesù, tried out the central plan; such, for example, is the chapel of the Filles de la Visitation-Sainte-Marie, rue Saint-Antoine, in Paris (François Mansart, 1632–4); and it is often the case with the chapels of the confraternities of penitents, such as the delightful chapel of the Pénitents Noirs at Villefranche-de-Rouergue (1642).

Above all the four great Parisian parish churches begun after 1650, Saint-Roch, Saint-Sulpice, Saint-Nicolas-du-Chardonnet, and Saint-Louis-en-l'Île, were to return openly to the medieval plan, with a nave flanked by aisles, an ambulatory, and radiating chapels. The series began in 1653 with Saint-Roch, by Lemercier, who had already adopted the formula for the parish church of Richelieu. Saint-Sulpice, begun in 1655 on plans by Daniel Gittard, is the most characteristic. As large as a cathedral, it represents, together with Notre-Dame and Saint-Eustache, one of the three peaks of religious art in Paris. Saint-Roch and Saint-Sulpice passed for perfect master-pieces until the Romantics made them ashamed of their nobility and their clarity. They served as models for Saint-Nicolas-du-Chardonnet (1656), the plan of which, in spite of Blondel's statement, was not provided by Le Brun, and for Saint-Louis-en-l'Île (Le Vau, foundation stone laid in 1664). But the building of the four churches was a lengthy business, continuing for almost a century.

At the same time the formula of the two-tiered façade, only just attained, was transformed by the addition of a third storey, the dome, which came to take up a place in the façade. This also is a Parisian development, with the series of the four great domes of the Sorbonne, the Val-de-Grâce, the Quatre-Nations, and the Invalides. At the Sorbonne, about 1635–42, Lemercier built two façades, an external one, and another facing the courtyard. The external façade, with two storeys, Corinthian and Composite, is crowned by a dome which can be seen very well if one moves back a little. It was to obtain this viewpoint that Richelieu had the Place de la Sorbonne cleared. The courtyard façade is much more original. At the top of a broad flight of steps are ten magnificent Corinthian columns for a portico; above comes the end of the transept; above again, the dome, much freer than on the other façade, since the transept is shorter than the nave; it is a masterpiece of clarity in the division into tiers, of harmony brought about by exact proportions, of boldness in the almost vertical ascension of the dome. The façade of the Val-de-Grâce was built about 1660, but followed a much earlier project by François Mansart, slightly modified by Le Duc. From above the two storeys emerges the dome, the drum of which is raised by an attic and whose shell is more than hemispherical. Since the length of the nave was always the difficulty in this kind of composition, a conscious return to the central plan was to follow. In 1668, in the chapel of the college of the Quatre-Nations by Le Vau (now the Institut de France), we have a simple ellipse preceded by a portico and surmounted by a dome. The masterpiece of the type was finally realized by Hardouin-Mansart at the Invalides, about 1700 – a Greek cross plan, hence little or no nave, and a dome with two drums, so important that it accounts in itself for half the total height. The two storeys of the façade proper are no more than the pedestal. It has been pointed out that its design is similar to that of St Paul's in London, and also to a plan of François Mansart's for a chapel for the Bourbons at Saint-Denis, with which Wren, the creator of St Paul's, may have been acquainted. But it is not only the technical skill implied in the double drum which makes the beauty of the church of the Invalides; it is the relation of the dome to the building which it crowns, the majestic simplicity of the whole. Compare it with St Peter's in Rome, and the difference between the classical and the Baroque is immediately evident.

¶ THE FIRST PART OF THE EIGHTEENTH CENTURY

The eighteenth century is a great period in religious architecture, not only for its variety – it is perpetually renewing itself – but for its abundance. A much more religious century than one would suppose, especially between 1700 and 1760, there was considerable architectural activity. In Paris this activity was most often one of completion; in the provinces one of new undertakings; there is hardly any town which does not possess an eighteenth-century church.

The first period was the most original. To note only a few features:

(a) As regards the plans, the rejection of the aisleless nave was completed. The basilican or central plan was the rule. One of the foremost churches of the basilican type is the cathedral of Nancy, the foundation stone of which was laid in 1700, though work on it really began only in 1706 after new plans provided by Hardouin-Mansart; Boffrand supervised its completion. Also by Boffrand and by Héré is the church of Saint-Jacques at Lunéville (1730–47); at Pont-à-Mousson the church of the Premonstratensians (now a hospital) by the obscure Nicolas Poisson, a member of the Order, is an unknown masterpiece. In addition should be mentioned the church of the Madeleine at Besançon (Nicole, 1746) and at least two other cathedrals, those of Versailles (Hardouin-Mansart de Sagonne, 1752–54) and that of Arras (Contant d'Ivry, about 1755).

The central plan is represented by the church of the Madeleine at Lille, begun at the end of the seventeenth century (1675) and completed in 1713 – a rotunda surrounded with chapels and flanked by four arms giving the design as a whole the form of a Greek cross; by Notre-Dame-des-Ardilliers at Saumur (1695); by the elliptical church of the Oratory at Avignon (1717–41); especially by Soufflot's Sainte-Geneviève, now the Panthéon. The plan dates from 1757; building was finished only in 1789; it is a Greek cross with each arm divided into nave and two aisles.

(b) If these plans are not completely new, they are accompanied by important structural innovations; above all the return to the column, no longer an applied ornament but with the function of a support. This is the case at Nancy, at Lunéville, Pont-à-Mousson, and Arras, to limit the list to names already mentioned. The columns of Saint-Jacques at Lunéville have a curious entasis; those of Arras carry an architrave, not arcades. At Saint-Géry, Cambrai, the dome rests on four Corinthian columns. In the same way Soufflot wanted to set the dome of Sainte-Geneviève on eight columns. From the very first the boldness of this conception caused alarm. Patte strongly attacked Soufflot, and the Academy, on being consulted, hesitated to approve his idea. In fact cracks began to appear in 1778 and Soufflot died at the time of this failure, leaving the work unfinished. It was completed by Rondelet, but four sturdy piers of masonry were substituted for the columns of which Soufflot had dreamt.

(c) A few façades remain two-tiered, for example Saint-

Roch (Robert de Cotte, 1736), the Oratory, Saint-Thomas-d'Aquin, Notre-Dame-des-Victoires, all Parisian churches which represent, in the eighteenth century, the distant heritage of the Gesù; and some of them, like the Oratory, have a magnificent personality of their own. Others are three-storeyed like the Premonstratensian church of Pont-à-Mousson. The dome still often plays an essential part, as in the Panthéon. But the real innovations of the period are the façade with towers and the façade with portico, sometimes combined in the same building. Already at the end of the seventeenth century D. Gittard, the creator of Saint-Sulpice, had designed for Saint-Jacques-du-Haut-Pas a façade with two square towers, very simple and almost primitive. J. Hardouin-Mansart had used towers for the church of Notre-Dame at Versailles. Those of the eighteenth century were to be more complex. In a competition opened in 1731 for the completion of Saint-Sulpice, Servandoni was the winner, with a project based on just that combination of tower and two-tiered portico mentioned above. The design of the towers themselves was extremely complicated. It was abandoned for a simpler model by Maclaurin: a square storey topped by a circular one. Even then the north tower was rebuilt later by Chalgrin. Saint-Eustache in Paris and the cathedrals of Auch, Langres, Arras, Rennes, and Nancy were also given façades with towers.

The portico represents the victory of the column as an external element. It was already found on the lateral façade of the Sorbonne and in the Collège des Quatre-Nations; there the columns are no longer applied, as they are in Rome. The main examples of the eighteenth century are at Saint-Sulpice and the Panthéon; the first has two storeys, the second only one: twenty-two Corinthian columns, six of them on the façade; above that, eighteen isolated columns. The beauty of the whole, of the same kind as that of the Invalides, lies in the just relation of the mass of the dome to the monumental base, in which the portico is the essential element.

(d) The interior decoration of seventeenth-century churches was comparatively simple; sometimes it even went as far as austerity, as in Saint-Jacques-du-Haut-Pas, the architectural expression of Jansenism. The eighteenth century accepted the exuberance of the Baroque but, treating it with more familiarity and elegance, called it *Rococo*. The chapel of the Château of Versailles (Hardouin-Mansart and Robert de Cotte, 1699–1710) is already like a sigh of relief, a relaxation of the senses after the rigorous discipline of the Grand Siècle. Between 1708 and 1714, to carry out the vow made by Louis XIII, de Cotte, with the aid of Coysevox and his nephews the Coustou, carved an immense marble decoration, the greatest sculptural ensemble of the century, in Notre-Dame de Paris. Saint-Louis-en-l'Île is a richly gilt drawing room in which wealthy worshippers came to visit, almost as equals, a God whom they imagined as indulgent. The most bizarre fantasies are in Lorraine, at Nancy – a few in the cathedral, many in the Bon-Secours chapel in which King Stanislas Leszczinski tried to recapture something of his native Poland – stuccoes on the walls, wrought iron screens in the gallery, carving on the confessionals, painting on the ceiling – every virtuosity unfolds at its ease. We might feel ourselves transported into central Europe, were it not for the lightness of the execution, and the order which underlies this ensemble and subordinates each detail to the architecture as a whole. Though such a sparkling display is not to be found elsewhere, it is not rare for some piece of woodwork or wrought iron, pulpit or organ-case, even in the village churches, to show that eighteenth-century France was a country of incomparable craftsmen.

¶ NEO-CLASSICAL ART

In the reign of Louis XVI taste changed profoundly in religious art as in all else. Antiquity returned to fashion, archaism was prized above all else. In Greek decorative elements, preference was given to the Doric, the true Doric, that which was revealed at Paestum, where the shaft of the column rests directly on the ground without a base. For Roman patterns use was made of Etruscan sources; and for churches, the models were the early Christian basilicas, in which the elaborate combinations of stone covering were still unknown.

The two most characteristic works of this movement are, in Paris, Saint-Philippe-du-Roule, by Chalgrin and the Capuchin convent by Brongniart.

In Saint-Philippe-du-Roule (1774–84) Chalgrin attempted an adaptation of S. Paolo fuori le mura or of Sta Sabina. The church is but a mere rectangle divided into a nave and two aisles by two rows of columns and ended by a semi-circular apse; the painted wooden ceiling is an imitation of a stone barrel vault; the façade is a portico with Doric columns (with bases) supporting a pediment. In the Capuchin friary in the Chaussée-d'Antin (1781), the chapel of which is now the church of Saint-Louis-d'Antin and the cloister the courtyard of the Lycée Condorcet, Brongniart was stricter and more severe: in plan, a rectangle between two apses, with a single aisle, following the pattern of certain Franciscan churches; externally, a flat façade without decorations, merely a unit, and not even the central unit, in the façade of the convent.

The formula, once accepted, was to be exploited for half a century with variants, especially in the façade, but also in a different spirit, with less desire to keep only to essentials. In Paris it produced Notre-Dame-de-Lorette (Le Bas, 1823–36) and Saint-Vincent-de-Paul (1824–44), the most important church of the series and the most luxurious, though the timbering of the roof was left open. The church of Saint-Louis at Toulon is reminiscent of Saint-Philippe-du-Roule (1782–9) and followed closely after it.

Another archaeological whim showed itself in the Madeleine. This time the church was frankly conceived as an antique temple. The formula was in fashion. It served alike for theatre and market-hall, why not use it for a place of worship? A classical basilica, with a great dome, had been projected for the site at the end of the eighteenth century, but it was a temple that Napoleon wanted to raise there, a real temple to the glory of the soldiers of the Grande Armée. He imposed Vignon on the judges of the competition of 1806, because, he said, 'his project is the only one which fulfils my intentions. It was a temple I asked for, not a church.... By temple I meant a monument like those of Athens, such as does not exist in Paris.' Since it was a question of pastiche, Fontaine had proposed the Pantheon of Agrippa in Rome. 'A large circular building is more suitable than a nave for large assemblies.' Napoleon soon lost interest in the temple of Glory and the building was completed only under the July Monarchy (1842). Though restored to Catholic worship, it has nonetheless never had a cross, remaining in this a temple and not a church, according to the Emperor's wish. The interior with its built-up, windowless walls is very unsuitable for religious ceremony. The lighting is provided by four domes. Only the monumental peristyle has real importance, particularly the great portico of the façade, perched at the top of a flight of twenty-eight steps.

The Expiatory Chapel of Percier and Fontaine (1815–26) is in a class apart. The chapel itself is a small square, flanked on three sides by semi-circular apses, on the fourth by the entrance portico, and covered by a dome lined with coffering in imitation of the Pantheon in Rome. In front of it, between two cloister galleries, stretches a garden planted with roses, the favourite flowers of Marie Antoinette. The galleries are dedicated to the Swiss Guards who died on 10 August, 1792. They link the chapel with the vestibule, which is also of extreme simplicity. The whole, in its harmony of line, its discreet sensibility, and the purity of its taste, is without doubt the masterpiece both of neo-classical art and of its two authors, esteemed creators of a decorative style which they here voluntarily discarded.

¶ NEO-GOTHIC ART

Together with the neo-classical fashion we see the beginning of a Gothic renaissance. It was to take much longer to triumph in religious architecture, yet during the July Monarchy both shared the favour of the public – Sainte-Clotilde is contemporary with Saint-Vincent-de-Paul. It is often called the Romantic movement of architecture, though its most flourishing period was during the Second Empire and its origins in the eighteenth century. Neither Michelet nor Victor Hugo discovered Gothic.

Actually it had never disappeared. We have pointed out cases of persistence, as in the cathedral of Orleans and the Jesuit churches of certain provinces. The fire glowed beneath the ashes. But in the eighteenth century it began once more to throw out sparks. As early as 1741, in a dissertation to the Academy, Soufflot showed that the builders of the Middle Ages were superior to modern builders in science, boldness, and ingenuity. He declared that in the Panthéon he proposed to unite the lightness of Gothic construction with the magnificence of Greek architecture. Towered façades and the structural function of the column may be taken as indications of this return to the Middle Ages. We are also beginning to realize all that the medieval buildings owe to the Benedictines of Saint-Maur. The much quoted attacks against Gothic art did not originate among the architects; on this point the professionals were firmly decided. The opposition came from men of letters, admittedly illustrious, like Molière and Rousseau, and masters of their own art, but incompetent in the neighbouring discipline.

All the same, the classical architects considered that every age must have its own style; they never believed that their rôle ought to be limited to copying endlessly the cathedral of Paris. True architectural romanticism, on the contrary, exchanged the creative spirit for historical knowledge. It gave its best efforts to the upkeep of ancient buildings. When it built new ones, they were no more than pastiches.

The work of restoration was linked up with a new administrative organization, that of the Historical Monuments. In the space of a few years, without reason, some of the most illustrious buildings of the Middle Ages were demolished, among them the abbey of Cluny and the Romanesque cloisters of Toulouse. This vandalism spurred Montalembert and Victor Hugo to an eloquent press campaign, which was sanctioned by the law of classification in 1837. Two thousand churches were declared national patrimony. Neither the officials such as Merimée, nor the architects formed in the neo-classical school such as Duban and Caristie, who had seats on the Commission for Historical Monuments, were prepared for their task. The essential rôle fell on Lassus and Viollet-le-Duc.

Lassus, architect of Saint-Séverin and Saint-Germain-l'Auxerrois, who was commissioned in 1841 together with Duban to restore the Sainte-Chapelle, and later, with Viollet-le-Duc, the cathedral of Paris, was a great animating influence. His building-yard at Saint-Séverin was the training-ground of a great army of sculptors, stained-glass workers, smiths, joiners, and decorators of all kinds of whom Viollet-le-Duc was later to take command.

Viollet-le-Duc dominates French architecture from 1840 to 1870, both by his work as a restorer and by his books. Vézelay, Saint-Denis, Notre-Dame-de-Paris, Amiens, Chartres, Reims, Saint-Sernin at Toulouse, and later Carcassonne and Pierrefonds, almost all the great monuments of the Middle Ages, passed through his hands and in many cases were his victims. Nowadays we judge his restorations very severely, but not unjustly. In spite of his pretensions no mind was less historical, if by this we mean respectful of the past. He himself gave a famous definition of his practice: 'To restore a building ... is to re-establish it in a state of completion, which may never have existed at any given moment in the past.' In the first place this resulted in the disappearance of all the elements added after the Middle Ages; at Notre-Dame he demolished all the decoration in the choir by Hardouin-Mansart and Robert de Cotte, the admirable Vow of Louis XIII. This brought about the establishment of a fictitious, almost a scholastic unity – at Saint-Ouen at Rouen an authentic fifteenth-century façade was replaced by a pastiche of the fourteenth century because the interior was of that century. Yet the Middle Ages had never hesitated to place the work of different centuries side by side; the example of Saint-Ouen itself was proof of this, and many churches, from Cahors to Mont-Saint-Michel, have a Romanesque nave and a Gothic choir. Yet Merimée and the Commission for Historical Monuments from the first gave the architect quite different instructions. On sending him to Vézelay, they considered that 'there was no need to recommend that he should respect the ancient arrangement in all its details. If some parts had to be rebuilt this should only be where it was impossible to preserve them.' To these instructions he paid no attention, and neither Merimée nor any official protested; no-one except the archaeologists themselves; Didron speaks of the 'vandalism of completion'. As early as 1833 Montalembert had spoken of the 'vandalism of restoration'.

At the same time, as regards new buildings, French religious architecture entered on an era of pastiche from which she has only just emerged. At the most, the models were varied and a few combinations were tried out. As early as 1840 pure Gothic inspired the church of Notre-Dame-de-Bon-Secours, near Rouen; Viollet-le-Duc himself drew on it for the presbytery of Notre-Dame. In Paris it was to produce Gau's Sainte-Clotilde (1846) and Lassus's Saint-Jean-de-Belleville; in the provinces the church of the Sacré-Cœur at Moulins by Lassus and the church of Saint-Epvre at Nancy by Morey (1855–71). The exploitation of the Romanesque produced Saint-Ambroise and Notre-Dame-des-Champs; to the variety known as 'Romano-Byzantine' belongs the church of Auteuil and the cathedral of Marseilles by Vaudoyer, and the Sacré-Cœur of Montmartre by Abadie. And coming to the renaissance, we have Ballu's Trinité (1861–7).

CHAPTER THREE

MODERN CHURCH ARCHITECTURE

A COMPLETE change in the style of religious architecture is naturally impossible, since one of the basic elements of the building, its ground-plan, is fixed by unchangeable rules depending on the liturgy. But, apart from the traditional Gothic basilican plan, there is a varied series of central plans, virtually making possible an infinity of combinations on which, as we have just seen, the classical centuries largely drew; contemporary architects continue to seek inspiration from them. As regards structure and decoration, a transformation could be and has been attempted during the last century. The change was gradual at first because of the neo-Gothic tradition, but later became more marked.

Two new materials have been employed in the construction of churches: iron and reinforced concrete.

The use of iron, originally in the form of cast-iron, goes back much further in ecclesiastical building than is believed by those who think both France and religious art behind the times. As early as 1823, when the spire of the cathedral of Rouen collapsed, it was decided to rebuild it in cast-iron. Work began immediately, but was very slow; it was interrupted in 1848, and completed only in 1876. Nevertheless the initial date, 1823, remains. It must also be remembered as a fact, with no intention of praise or blame, that this cast-iron was treated in such a way that many were deceived by it and many fine words have been written on the subject of the 'stone lacework' of this spire.

A little later, under the Second Empire, at the time when Haussmann found four million francs to undertake the building of La Trinité (£160,000 in the nineteenth century, an enormous figure at that time) iron made its appearance in

Paris in two churches which are, perhaps unfairly, of very un-equal fame, Saint-Eugène and Saint-Augustin.

To-day few Parisians know the church of Saint-Eugène, on the corner of the rue Sainte-Cécile and the rue du Conserva-toire, which was the parish church of Corot. Built by Boileau between 1854 and 1855, it was the first church building in which the framework was of metal. The method was adopted for reasons of economy, since only 600,000 francs (£24,000) were available. This is not the first instance of a slender bud-get forcing an artist to make a new discovery. The rôle of creative poverty in the history of art could be studied with profit; it comes up again at Le Raincy. The nave and two aisles of the church of Saint-Eugène, equal in height, rest on slender columns of cast-iron, supporting metal ribbed vaults. The buttressing is sufficiently assured by the side chapels, which have transverse barrel vaults. There is no need for either flying buttresses or buttresses, which gives an impression of extreme lightness and spaciousness. The work is perfectly logical, exactly what might have been erected by medieval master builders had they had metal at their disposal, nor is there any decoration. It is not surprising that this building, over-bold for its time, should have been misunderstood; it is more so that a building so modern in spirit should not have been placed in the first rank by present-day architects.

The church of Saint-Augustin was built by Baltard between 1860 and 1871. In the centre of the new districts planned by Haussmann, it is symmetrical with La Trinité, on the other side of the Gare Saint-Lazare. Its appearance is not much more original. The same scholarly eclecticism here combines the dome of the cathedral of Florence with a Romanesque-Gothic façade: great rose-window and Gallery of Kings*. But the execution presents two innovations. In the first place, the plan, which is an ingenious association of the basilican and the compact plan, makes the most of a rectangular site. Saint-Augustin is a large square flanked on three sides by three apses and preceded on the fourth by a nave which gradually tapers towards the point of the triangle. As regards structure,

* i.e., sculptured images of kings. (*Trans.*)

it mingles, or rather juxtaposes, iron and stone. The lower part is a stone church of twelfth-century elevation: round-headed nave-arcade, galleries opening in three coupled bays below a relieving arch, and clerestory windows. But in front of these Romanesque pillars flanked with Corinthian columns are fixed columns of cast-iron carrying diaphragm arches which carry a depressed vault. The two elements are dissociated – the metallic framework seems a vast system of scaffolding. The same applies to the dome. It must be added that all this cast-iron is worked and treated like stone. It was the same at Rouen, but here the process is more questionable, since it applied to a new building.

Iron was to be used again very much later, this time quite boldly but perhaps no more successfully, by Astruc in 1899–1901 in the nave of Notre-Dame-du-Travail (Paris, XIVth *arrondissement*). The building, planned like a market-hall, loses all religious character. A church has not only a body but a soul, not only matter but spirit. The architect did not appreciate this.

The use of iron is no more than a brief episode in this history. It is reinforced concrete – without our yet being able to say how it will last – which represents, in religious architecture as elsewhere, the true modern material. It was even employed for this purpose earlier than anywhere else, in 1894, in the church of Saint-Jean-de-Montmartre (Paris, rue des Abbesses). The architect, Anatole de Baudot, disciple and collaborator of Viollet-le-Duc, instead of imitating the Gothic architects, adopted their method of reasoning or rather the method attributed to them by his master. He was therefore in the vital tradition which prolongs creative effort. Everything in his work is experiment: the plan, the structure, the decoration. A series of domes rest on a double intersection of great arches of reinforced concrete – two of these crossings for the nave, one for the apse. The arches also supply the basis of the décor – intertwined curves, internally on the balustrade of the gallery, externally along the brick walls – although, generally, concrete produces mainly straight lines. Finally, stained glass regains its importance, notably in the tracery of the apse, where there blazes a large Crucifixion. The façade is no more than a tall porch-belfry, weakened by the curves in which it ends. This abundance of curves betrays the 1900 period. But the effort is of great value. The master's pupils were right to emphasize its importance by the small commemorative monument which they set up in front of the work.

The originality of Saint-Jean-de-Montmartre can be measured by the time which lapsed before another architect made use of concrete. In Paris, before 1920, there was only one example, Saint-Dominique, rue de la Tombe-Issoire, a church begun in 1913 by Gaudibert and completed only in 1921. Historical influences can be felt in it. It is still only a matter of expressing old forms in a new material. The prototype is Byzantine, but the beauty of the central plan with the great dome flanked by four minor ones is fully grasped and the construction is logical and well-balanced.

On the contrary, the uses of concrete after 1920 were numerous, often faced with brick, sometimes left bare. First and foremost must be mentioned the church of Notre-Dame, Le Raincy, by the brothers Perret, not only for its date (1922–3), but because here, for the first time, we meet not only a new material but new forms. Concrete is used, we may say, in its pure state. All the consequences of this principle have been faced. It fulfils all needs – supports, vaults, trellis-like walls, called *claustra*, filled in with glass. It remains visible – there is no facing, not because of any aesthetic reason but for lack of money. The architects have succeeded in making us forget its poverty by the logical proportions of the parts and the harmony of the whole. The plan is very simple – a rectangular hall of 183 × 63 feet, with a slight curve in the rear façade stressing the apse. It is divided into nave and two aisles by slender columns 17 inches in diameter and 36 feet in height; the depressed vault, 2 inches thick, is placed longitudinally in the great nave, but there is a series of transverse barrel vaults over the aisles; in fact, as little material as possible is used. All is light in spirit, hence the comparison with the Sainte-Chapelle. The bell-tower itself, 140 feet high, is a mere grouping of pillars of the same section as those in the nave, but linked in fours or fives. The church of Le Raincy was admired throughout Europe and much imitated. The Perret brothers themselves used the pattern again in 1925–6, for Sainte-Thérèse at Montmagny. One of the finest works which can be related to it is the church of Saint-Antoine at Basle (K. Moser, 1930). In Saint-Christophe at Javel (1926–30), Besnard used concrete made not with the aid of shutters but with moulds, according to a new method. But these are still exceptions. More often only the framework is in concrete, with a brick facing.

Since religious architecture must keep to the traditional plans, the preference given to the compact plan and its corollary, the dome, must be emphasized. The churches built in France in the last twenty years are closer to the East than they have been since the tenth century. But only a few Byzantine buildings of the first quality had shown such boldness and such a strongly developed feeling for space. Saint-Louis at Vincennes (Droz and Marrast, 1924) is a great hall in the shape of a Greek cross, with a vault resting on four immense arches springing from the ends of the cross and intersecting two by two. In Paris, the church of the Saint-Esprit by P. Tournon (1930–5) is, like Sancta Sophia in Constantinople, a domed basilica; but few examples show better how the same general outline on paper can give rise to two entirely different works and how architecture is above all a conquest of space. This entirely modern expression of feeling, of great boldness and perfect harmony, was the result of a technique which was also essentially modern. At Sainte-Jeanne-d'Arc at Nice, Droz, one of the architects of Saint-Louis at Vincennes, designed great parabolic or ellipsoidal domes, an outline which is always a little surprising but of which Gaudi had shown the practical advantages at Barcelona. We must hasten to add that this attempt at innovation in religious architecture has not been unanimous, and that conservative architects are not lacking even among those to whom the greatest projects have been confided.

Immediately after the 1914 war, the devastated areas in the

north needed churches as well as houses. Here religious architecture was happier than its domestic counterpart. There were many experiments and some successes. The central plan was employed at Rouvroy-les-Mines by Duval and Gonse, at Rouges-Barres (Nord) by Vilain and Sérex, and in Sainte-Jeanne-d'Arc at Charleville by P. Chirol. Worthy of separate mention is Dom Bellot, a specialist in brick buildings, who has evolved new forms for this material, varying its appearance by different combinations of colour.

After 1930 the population of Paris reached five millions. The material nakedness of some suburbs and the spiritual nakedness of almost all was eloquently pointed out by Father Lhande (*Le Christ dans la banlieue*, 1927). Besides, a serious unemployment crisis was beginning. Cardinal Verdier opened 'The Cardinal's Workshops' at this time. New churches meant more work; but no architectural doctrine, nor even any aesthetic preference was imposed. The works produced as a result of this fine inspiration thus brought tradition together with innovation – tradition at Gentilly, the church of the Cité Universitaire (P. Paquet, 1936), innovation at Montrouge (E. Bagge), to mention only two works on almost neighbouring sites, both of great value but as unlike each other as possible. This crusade had been begun under the double ensign of faith and poverty; one of the most moving works from this point of view is the church of Saint-Antoine-de-Padoue (Azéma, 1936).

The renaissance of architecture was accompanied by a renewal of decoration – painting and mosaic, sculpture, liturgical furnishings – in so far as the resources available allowed any thought of decoration. Many buildings remained Cistercian through necessity: they are not always the least successful. Painting, where it was called upon, regained its monumental character – the frescoes of Saint-Louis at Vincennes and at the Saint-Esprit are among the finest productions of Maurice Denis. Sculpture has sometimes regained its place on the exterior – the façades of Saint-Pierre at Chaillot and Élisabeth-ville. Sarrabezolles, in the belfry of Villemomble, has even invented a new process – sculpture in concrete, while it is still wet.

CHAPTER FOUR

MONASTIC ARCHITECTURE

Monastic architecture is derived from both religious and domestic patterns, since the monastery is both a dwelling place and a place of prayer. But the monastery always lies in the shadow of the church. Moreover it is not only monks who live in community. In the Middle Ages, from the twelfth century onwards, cathedral canons also often lived in this way.

¶ THE MIDDLE AGES

The idea of monastic life was brought to the West from the East about the fifth century. Since then it has undergone many changes. The great religious Order of the West is that of the Benedictines, instituted in the sixth century by St Benedict. Their establishments in France were very numerous. One of them, Cluny (Saône-et-Loire), became of outstanding importance from the tenth century onwards. It set up daughter houses everywhere, and we have already seen its fundamental rôle in the evolution of Romanesque architecture. A little later, in 1113, under the fresh impetus of St Bernard, the Benedictine was modified into the stricter Cistercian rule. Like the Carthusians, founded in 1098 by St Bruno, both of these were cloistered Orders, generally set up outside the towns. They dedicated a part of their activities to the reclaiming of uncultivated land. In the thirteenth century appeared the mendicant Orders, Franciscans, Dominicans, and Carmelites (the last of more ancient origin but transformed at this time), who established themselves in the towns, where they threw all their energies into preaching against heresy. The Crusades produced military Orders, such as the Templars and the Knights Hospitallers of St John.

The architecture of monasteries is naturally very varied,

according to their setting (in town or country) and also according to their inmates' way of life. The monastery in its most complete form consists of two parts; one, the enclosure (*clausura*), reserved for monks who have taken the vow to live withdrawn from the world; the other intended for labourers, guests, and those monks permitted to remain in contact with the world outside. Each section is enclosed by a wall.

Let us give a quick sketch of a monastery. First comes the door of the outer court, with the porter's lodge; next to it, the almonry, where the needy were certain of receiving alms; and beyond the door, the guest's quarters or hospice. In some monasteries and at certain periods these quarters became of considerable importance, becoming almost the essential part of the monastery and giving it the character of a hospital or refuge. This was the case with certain establishments in the neighbourhood of the great sanctuaries or along the pilgrimage routes, such as that of Santiago. *The Pilgrim's Guide to Santiago de Compostela*, written about the middle of the twelfth century, mentions the three biggest hospices in the world, which were all three religious establishments. 'God has set up three pillars necessary for the support of His poor on earth: the hospice of Jerusalem; the hospice of the Great-St-Bernard; and the hospice of Somport. These hospices are hallowed places, houses of God for the comfort of holy pilgrims, the refreshment of the poor, the consolation of the sick, the salvation of the dead, and the succour of the living. Those who build these holy houses, whoever they may be, will without doubt enter into the Kingdom of God.' (*Guide du Pèlerin*, ed. J. Vielliard, p. 11). Powerful nobles sometimes had luxurious apartments made for their visits to the abbey. Also outside the enclosure were various store-houses: the cellars, the bakery, the wash-house, and so on; the infirmary, isolated in order to avoid contagion; the novices' quarters, the monastery school, if there was one, and, if necessary, the labourers' cottages.

Let us now pass to the other side of the second wall and into the clausura. The actual monastic buildings are ranged round the cloister, a central court surrounded by galleries.

The church overlooks one side, the refectory another, and on the other two are the chapter-house and the monks' living quarters (calefactory, dormitory, etc.). The cloister is thus the heart of the monastery. But it is not an element peculiar to the abbey. Most cathedral churches had one, and we can still see the Romanesque cloisters of the cathedrals of Elne, Le Puy, Vaison, Saint-Bertrand-de-Comminges or Saint-Lizier, and the Gothic cloisters of Bayonne, Saint-Dié, Noyon, and Tréguier cathedrals. It is a square or rectangular court, situated sometimes to the north, sometimes to the south of the church; to the north at Moissac, Beaulieu, Le Puy, etc.; to the south at Saint-Bertrand-de-Comminges, Saint-Trophime at Arles, Vézelay, etc. Sometimes these galleries are vaulted, with barrel vaults, groined vaults, or ribvaults; sometimes they have only an open timber roof. Even the arrangement of the arcades and the columns supporting them gives an opportunity for variety so that every cloister has its own individual character. Sometimes the arches are round-headed, sometimes they are pointed, sometimes they rest on a single column and sometimes on coupled columns; sometimes all the openings are the same and placed at equal intervals, sometimes they are grouped in twos, threes, or fours under a relieving arch, which in its turn may be fretted, and which rests on sturdy pillars; an arrangement often found in Cistercian monasteries. Among the sculptural masterpieces of the Romanesque period were the capitals of the cloisters at Elne, Moissac, and Saint-Trophime at Arles, and those of the cloisters of Saint-Sernin and of the cathedral in Toulouse which have disappeared. The cloister always has a fountain opposite the door of the refectory, so that the monks can wash their hands before meals. In Cistercian monasteries the fountain is often enclosed in what is virtually a small chapel. Sometimes there is only a simple basin (as at Daoulas, Finistère), sometimes, as at Fréjus, there is a well at the centre.

The chapter-house is the main hall of the monastery. It is here that the chapter or general assembly meets. Rectangular or square in shape, it is always vaulted and divided into several aisles by rows of columns. The chapter-houses attached to cathedrals were particularly important. One of the finest still preserved is that at Noyon (thirteenth century); it is divided into two aisles of five bays by a line of four slender columns. Among the finest chapter-houses we may mention those in the Cistercian houses at Fontenay, Fontfroide, etc., and those of the Augustinians and the Dominicans at Toulouse.

The refectory is always on the side of the cloister opposite the church. It is a long rectangular room, often vaulted, but sometimes with an open timber roof (Saint-Wandrille, twelfth century), and so like a church aisle that several examples have been converted into chapels (the Lycée Henri IV in Paris, formerly the abbey of Sainte-Geneviève). The refectory in Benedictine monasteries is generally built parallel to a gallery of the cloister, while in the Cistercian establishments the one is at right angles to the other. In the middle of one of the walls is the tribune or pulpit recess for meal-time readings. In Paris, in the old Benedictine monastery of Saint-Martin-des-Champs (now the Conservatoire des Arts et Métiers), we can still see one of the finest examples of a monastic refectory. It is now transformed into a library. It is a long hall, of more than 130 × 40 feet, with eight vaulted bays divided into two parts by a series of delicate columns – one of the most elegant works of the French Middle Ages, probably inspired by the refectory of the abbey of Saint-Germain-des-Prés by Pierre de Montereau. The pulpit is reached by steps cut in the thickness of the wall and the lectern well lit by three windows.

Opposite the church, in a corner of the cloister near the dormitory stairs, we often find the calefactory, with one or more large fire-places. This is the only room in which the Cistercian rule allowed fires to be lit; it served as a common-room and workshop for indoor occupations. The dormitory runs along one side of the cloister, often on the first floor; this again is a large hall, like the nave of a church. Only in Carthusian monasteries did each monk have the right to a cell of his own; elsewhere there is a common dormitory. The kitchen is sometimes next to the refectory, communicating with it through a hatch, and sometimes set apart to avoid the smell of cooking. There is a fine example preserved at Fontevrault.

The kitchens of the Lycée Henri IV in Paris are those of the old abbey of Saint-Geneviève and are still almost intact (twelfth century).

It is easy to discover here and there isolated examples of these parts – we have already described some of them. It is more difficult to make a study of complete monasteries. Most of the medieval buildings were restored in the seventeenth and eighteenth centuries; and even among these, many have suffered either from France's lack of respect for its architectural past, or from the laws suppressing the religious communities. In very few cases have the buildings survived their occupants. Mont-Saint-Michel is almost the only one to have been taken over by the State. Thus Cluny, most precious of all the Benedictine monasteries for the historian, has almost entirely disappeared. The Order is at least represented by Mont-Saint-Michel (materially restored by the Historical Monuments Commission though its soul has gone) which still rises up against the menace of the sea on the famous rock held fast between the two great promontories of Cotentin and Brittany. The abbey is said to have been founded in 996 by Richard I, Duke of Normandy. It was rebuilt several times, notably by Philip Augustus. The site dictated an arrangement of the various elements of the building which is found in no other instance. Not being able to spread out, Mont-Saint-Michel grew upwards to a height of three superimposed storeys: the top storey, called *la Merveille*, corresponding to the enclosure, the middle and lower parts being divided between the monks and their guests. Right at the bottom almost in the foundations are the almonry and wine-cellars. Above them is the hospice, built in 1215, which is over 115 feet long and divided into two aisles, and next to it the Knights' Room (1220) with four aisles, corresponding virtually to the chapter-house, or rather to the monks' *scriptorium*. Also on this level is the monks' cemetery, as well as a place for them to take exercise, and the church crypt. And finally, right at the top, is the church (Romanesque nave, 1122–35, and Gothic choir, 1450–1521) on the side of which the cloister and the refectory are built. The cloister, finished in 1228 but very much restored, is a small rectangle 82×46 feet, with a curious quincuncial arrangement of the columns (pl. 32b). The refectory (1217) is a large hall covered by an open timber roof, excellently lit by fifty-nine long, narrow windows. The kitchens were next to it, connected with the cellars by a lift.

Although France used to have a magnificent series of Cistercian monasteries, no surviving ensemble can be compared with Poblet or Santes-Creus in Catalonia. The most fortunate abbeys are the ones which were bought up for their own pleasure by private individuals who have kept them in repair and often skilfully restored and saved them. Fontenay, Pontigny, Fontfroide, Royaumont, and Vaux de Cernay are examples; in Provence, Le Thoronet, that exquisite gem, Silvacane, and Sénanque. But others have become prisons (Clairvaux) or schools (Noirlac), sometimes even factories (Ourscamp). Characteristic of them all is that desire for simple lines, which gave the Order's first churches their austere grandeur; a robust style, hostile to decoration, eliminating all superfluous detail. Thus, in the cloisters, there is no figure sculpture. Many interesting remnants survive here and there: the cellars at Vaux de Cernay, the infirmary at Ourscamp, wrongly called the Mortuary Chapel, which was probably only the hospice dormitory. For the examination as a whole of a single example, we shall take Fontenay, near Montbard (Côte d'Or), because of its association with St Bernard. The monastery, founded in 1130, was at the height of its prosperity in the first half of the twelfth century. After the sixteenth century it declined rapidly. When it was restored in 1907, the church and some important medieval remains were preserved. The cloister runs right along the south side of the church; like the latter, it is covered with barrel and groined vaults. Its round-headed arches are separated by strong square piers and each arcade is divided into two twin bays by coupled columns. The refectory, destroyed in 1745, was situated at right-angles to the gallery opposite the church; at its entrance was the lavabo in an aedicule projecting into the cloister court. The chapter-house, however, survives, a square room originally divided into nine bays (3×3). Here

rib-vaults, absent in church and cloister though all are more
or less contemporary, make their appearance. Beside it is the
monks' parlour, with its two aisles of six bays, also with rib-
vaults; at the end of the great hall is the infirmary, in this case
part of the clausura. Above, on the same side of the cloister,
was the wood-roofed dormitory (end of the fifteenth century).
Another rather interesting building, the smithy (end of the
twelfth century) has survived: a large stone construction
divided into four rooms.

The monastic architecture of the Carthusians is known to
us from several of their establishments, notably the Grande-
Chartreuse, Villeneuve-lès-Avignon, and Villefranche-de-
Rouergue. They are appreciably different from the previous
examples, since the rule of the Order allowed each monk to
live a private, isolated life. The Carthusian Father had a cell
divided into several small rooms. Even meals were communal
on Sundays only; the rest of the time each monk ate in his own
cell. Only the Brothers, of lower status than the Fathers,
shared a dormitory and refectory. These monasteries are
therefore on a much larger scale. In place of the monks' single
dormitory we have here a series of small apartments, generally
grouped round a second enclosure, forming a kind of second
cloister, the centre of which is occupied by the cemetery. The
small Charterhouse of Villefranche-de-Rouergue, much less
famous than some others, is perhaps more characteristic. It
was founded in 1450 to house seventeen monks, and is now a
hospice. The church is nothing but a simple chapel. There are
two cloisters. The first, very small, and as usual attached to
the chapel, is very fine Flamboyant Gothic. It is adjacent to
the refectory, the cellar, and the kitchen, it was here that, on
Sundays, the monks had permission to exchange a few
words after the meal. Beyond this classic group – church,
cloister, refectory – the great cloister, of much larger dimensions (220 × 133 feet) and very soberly decorated as was fitting
for a cemetery, was entirely surrounded by the monks' cells;
at the time of the Revolution they were no more than thirteen.
The Charterhouse of Villeneuve-lès-Avignon enjoys the prestige of having been founded by a Pope (Innocent VI, 1356)

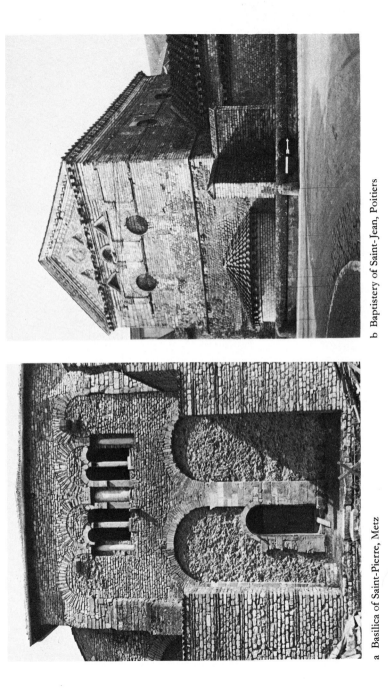

a Basilica of Saint-Pierre, Metz

b Baptistery of Saint-Jean, Poitiers

1 Merovingian architecture

b Germigny-des-Prés

a The Basse-Oeuvre, Beauvais

2 Carolingian architecture

a Saint-Michel-de-Cuixa

b Saint-Germain-des-Prés, Paris

3 Romanesque architecture: tower façades

b Abbaye-aux-Dames, Caen

a Abbaye-aux-Hommes, Caen

4 Romanesque architecture: façades with twin bell-towers

b Souillac (from a lithograph by Taylor and Nodier)

a Saint-Martin-du-Puits

5 Romanesque church interiors

a The Madeleine, Vézelay, nave

b Sainte-Foy, Conques, nave

6 Romanesque church interiors

b Coutances

a Chartres

7 Gothic cathedral façades

b Saint-Etienne, Laon

a Notre-Dame, Paris

8 Gothic cathedral façades

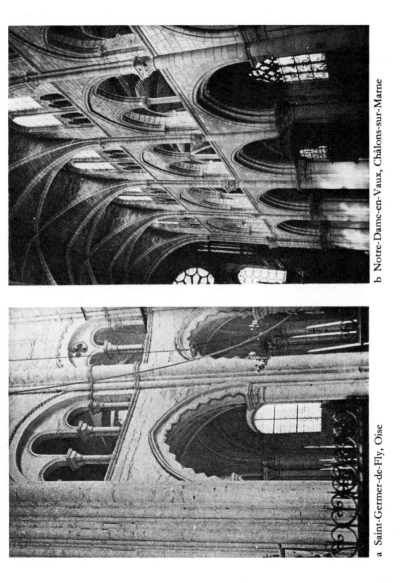

b Notre-Dame-en-Vaux, Châlons-sur-Marne

a Saint-Germer-de-Fly, Oise

9 Gothic church interiors

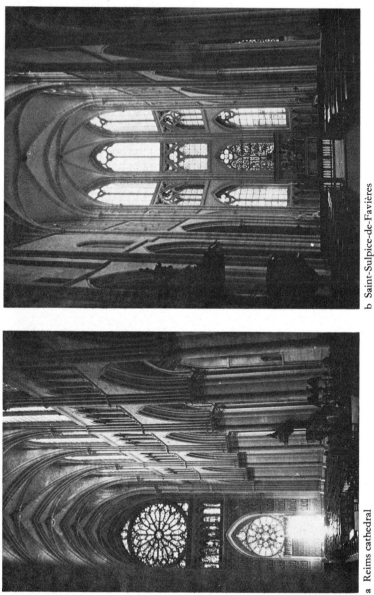

a Reims cathedral

b Saint-Sulpice-de-Favières

10 Gothic church interiors

a Saintes-Maries-de-la-Mer

b Rudelle, Lot

11 Fortified churches

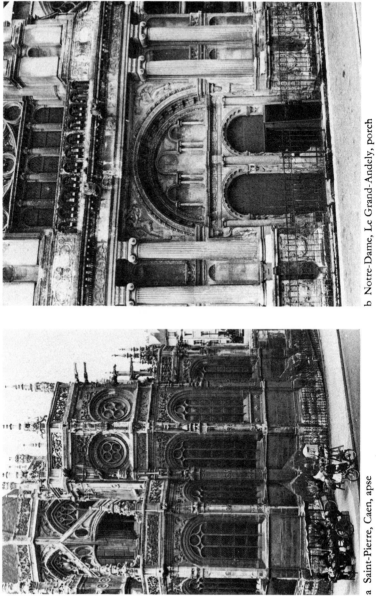

b Notre-Dame, Le Grand-Andely, porch

a Saint-Pierre, Caen, apse

12 Sixteenth-century architecture

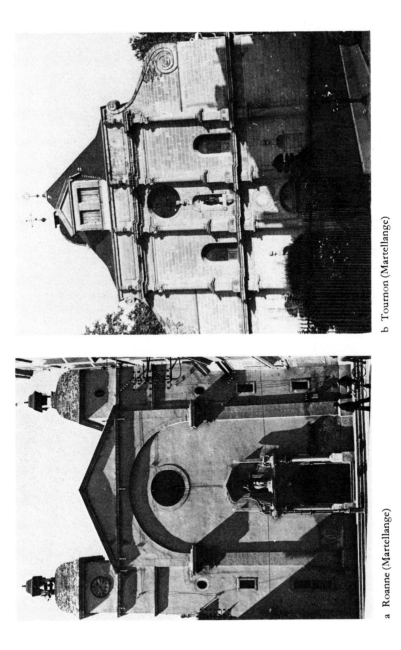

b Tournon (Martellange)

a Roanne (Martellange)

13 Seventeenth century: façades of Jesuit churches

b Saint-Paul, Paris (Derand)

a Saint-Vincent-de-Paul, Blois

14 Seventeenth century: façades of Jesuit churches

a Church of the Sorbonne, Paris (Jacques Lemercier)

b Church of the Val-de-Grâce, Paris (François Mansart)

15 Seventeenth and eighteenth centuries: façades with domes

b Sainte Geneviève, the Panthéon, Paris (Soufflot)

a Les Invalides, Paris (J.-H. Mansart)

16 Seventeenth and eighteenth centuries: façades with domes

b Saint-Sulpice, Paris (Servandoni)

a Montauban cathedral

17 Eighteenth century: façades with twin towers

a Saint-Philippe-du-Roule, Paris (Chalgrin)

b Palais de Justice, Blois

18 Eighteenth century: neo-classical façades

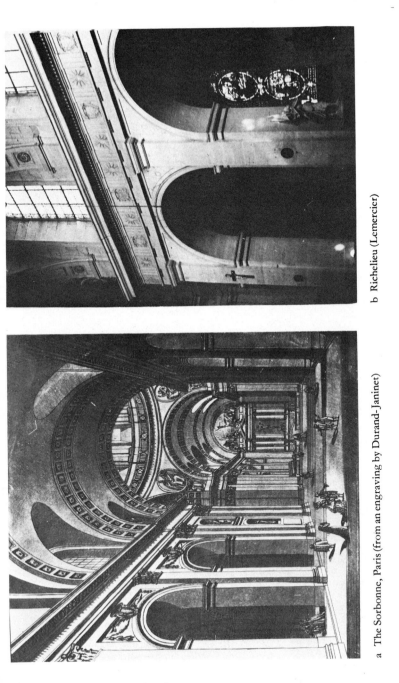

a The Sorbonne, Paris (from an engraving by Durand-Janinet)

b Richelieu (Lemercier)

19 Eighteenth-century church interiors

b Saint-Paul, Paris (Martellange)

a Former Jesuits' college, Avignon (Martellange)

20 Eighteenth-century church interiors

b Saint-Géry, Cambrai

a Saint-Jacques, Lunéville

21 Eighteenth-century church interiors

b Saint-Symphorien, Versailles

a Sainte-Madeleine, Besançon

22 Eighteenth-century church interiors

b Sacré-Coeur, Montmartre, Paris (Abadie)

a Saint-Augustin, Paris (Baltard)

23 Nineteenth-century churches

24 Twentieth-century churches: Notre-Dame, Le Raincy (Auguste Perret)

25 Post-1945 churches: Ronchamp (Le Corbusier)

a Audincourt

b Saint-Servan

26 Post-1945 churches

a Abbey of Saint-Michel

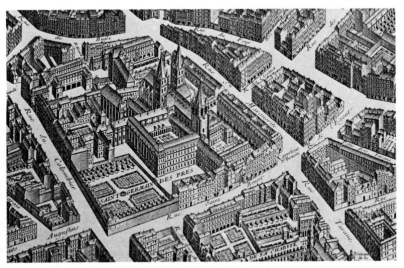

b Abbey of Saint-Germain-des-Prés, Paris (from a map by Turgot)

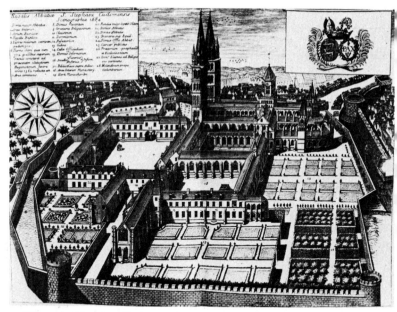

a Abbaye-aux-Hommes, Caen

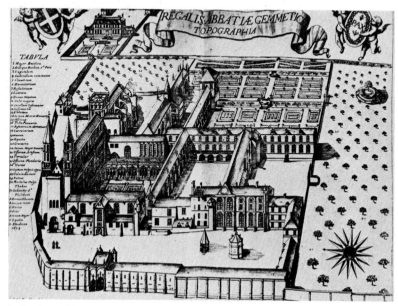

b Jumièges abbey

28 Monastic establishments: from *Monasticon gallicanum*

a Noirlac, cellar

b Mont-Saint-Michel, refectory

29 Conventual establishments

a Moissac

b Saint-Trophime, Arles

30 Romanesque cloisters

a Mont-Saint-Michel

b Fonfroide (Cistercian)

31 Gothic cloisters

a Lagrasse, cloister of the monastery

b Cloister of the Capuchin convent, Paris

32 Seventeenth- and eighteenth-century cloisters

a Angers castle

b William the Conqueror's castle at Caen: the keep, in 1974

33 Medieval castles

a Timbered house in rue François-Miron, Paris

b Stonebuilt Maison du Grand Fauconnier, Cordes

34 Medieval town halls

a Chambord

b Fontainebleau

35 Sixteenth-century châteaux

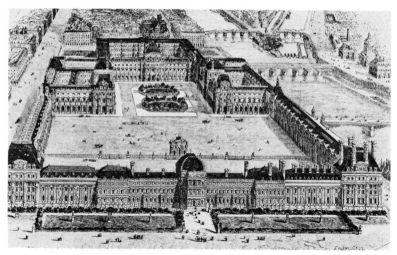

a The Louvre and the Tuileries, Paris

b The Louvre, Paris: colonnade

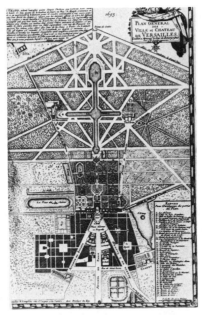

a Plan of the château and park (from an engraving by Israël Silvestre, 1693)

b Galerie des glaces

37 Versailles

a Versailles, colonnades

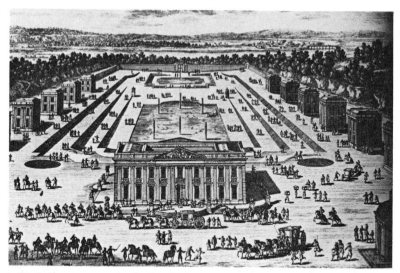

b Marly (from an engraving by Israël Silvestre, 1693)

a The peristyle of the Grand Trianon (Mansart)

b The Petit Trianon

39 Versailles

a Rotunda dedicated to Cupid (Mique)

b The Hameau (Mique)

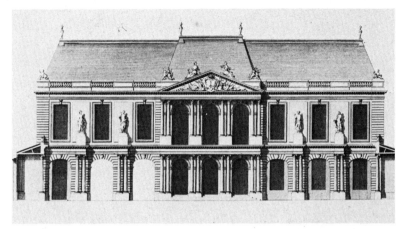

a Hôtel de Soubise (Delamair)

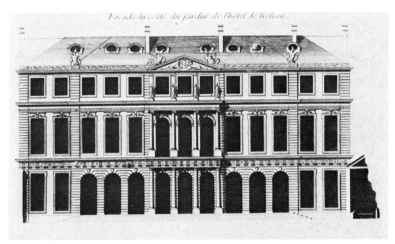

b Hôtel de Rohan (Delamair)

41 Parisian hotels: façades

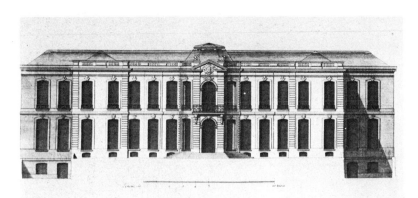

a Hôtel Matignon

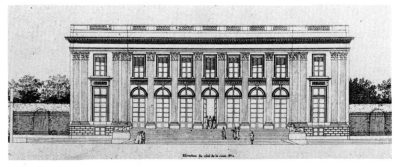

b Hôtel de Monaco

a Hôtel Lambert: Cabinet des Muses (engraving by Picart)

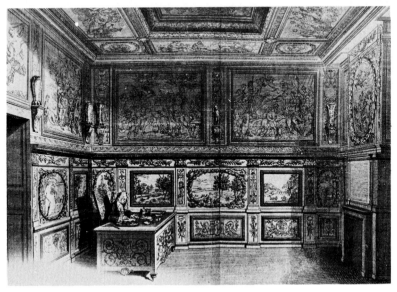

b Hôtel Lambert: Cabinet de l'Aurore (engraving by Picart)

43 Parisian hotels: seventeenth-century interiors

44 Parisian hotels: eighteenth-century interiors. Hôtel de Soubise, prince's salon (Boffrand)

a House of Mlle Guimard (Ledoux)

b Bagatelle, pavilion (Bélanger)

45 Eighteenth century

b House c. 1900, rue La Fontaine, Paris (Guimard)

a Second Empire house, Avenue de l'Opéra, Paris

a Marseilles apartment block (Le Corbusier)

b Le Havre apartment block (Auguste Perret)

a Pantin, apartment block

b Paris, apartment block in XVᵉ arrondissement

a The fourteenth-century Pont Valentré at Cahors (from Taylor and Nodier)

b Twentieth-century bridge at Tancarville

a Eighteenth century: Nancy (Héré)

b Twentieth century: Le Havre (Auguste Perret)

50 Town halls

a Eighteenth century: the Odéon, Paris (Peyre and de Wailly)

b Twentieth century: the Opéra, Paris (Charles Garnier)

a Fifteenth-century market hall at Lorris, Loiret

b Nineteenth century: Les Halles, Paris (Louis Baltard)

52 Covered market places

a gatehouse

b workshop

53 Eighteenth-century industrial building: the Chaux saltworks at Arc-et-Senans (Claude-Nicoles Ledoux)

a exterior

b interior

54 Railway stations: the Gare du Nord, Paris (Hittorff)

a exterior

b interior

55 Contemporary architecture: the Centre National des Industries Techniques, Paris

a outer section

b tower

56 Contemporary architecture: the Maison de la Radio, Paris (Bernard)

a radial plan: Bram, Aude, aerial view

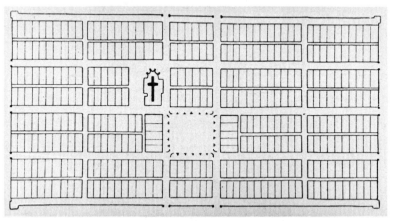

b rectangular plan: Montpazier

57 Town plans

a Montpazier

b Mirepoix

58 Medieval squares

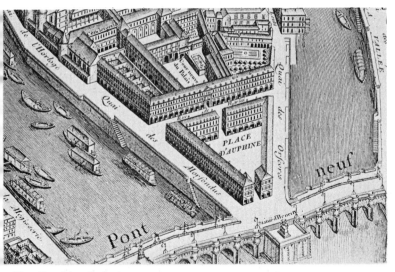

a Place Dauphine, **Paris**

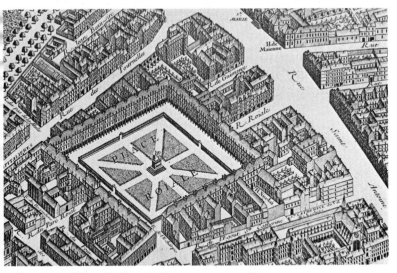

b Place Royale (Place des Vosges), Paris

59 Royal Squares of the seventeenth century (from maps by Turgot)

a Place des Victoires, Paris

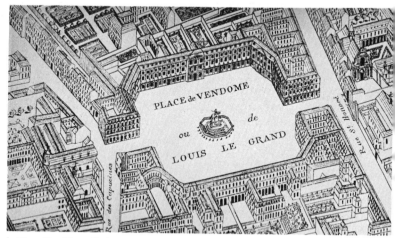

b Place Vendôme, Paris

60 Royal Squares of the seventeenth century (from maps by Turgot)

a Place Louis XV (Place de la Concorde), Paris

b Place Louis XV, Reims

a Arc de Triomphe de l'Etoile, Paris

b Boulevard de Sébastopol

a Buttes-Chaumont

b The lake of the Bois du Boulogne

63 Haussmann gardens in Paris (from Alphand's *Promenades de Paris*)

a Restoration at Saint-Malo (Arretche)

b New development at Le Havre (Auguste Perret)

and has also the distinction of having housed two of the most famous works of fifteenth-century French painting – the *Pietà* and the *Coronation of the Virgin*. Planned at first for a Prior and twelve monks, it was subsequently very much enlarged by the creation of a second group of cells set beside the first, within a common surrounding wall. The plan is therefore more complex, though each element is clearly recognizable. The original part, that of Pope Innocent VI, includes the church, the small and great cloisters, as at Villefranche-de-Rouergue, to which the second foundation added another great cloister for the new monks. Finally, the Grande-Chartreuse (Isère) is the most famous of all, both for the beauty of its site and because it was the work of Saint Bruno himself. But the majority of the buildings date back no further than the seventeenth century. Only a few older elements remain, above all the church (fifteenth century), the great cloister, built on a sloping site, in the form of an elongated trapezium cut through by two transverse galleries. The chapter-house used to contain copies of the *Life of Saint Bruno*, painted by Le Sueur for the Charterhouse in Paris. So, in spite of their deliberate search for simplicity, the Carthusians did not scorn art. To their Order belongs one of the most important monuments in the history of architecture, the Charterhouse of Pavia, near Milan, in the decoration of which all the early French Renaissance is potentially present.

The mendicant Orders, as we have seen, had settled in the towns, and urban evolution was particularly disastrous for their establishments. There is no architectural complex which we can compare with those of the Orders dealt with above – at least in France, for indeed one of the peaks of Italian art is the convent of St Francis at Assisi. In Paris, the old refectory of the Cordeliers (Franciscans), a vast, unvaulted hall of fourteen bays, last remnant of their huge monastery dating back to the thirteenth century, is now the Musée Dupuytren. In Toulouse, the Petit Lycée for boys shelters a few remains of the old Jacobin or Dominican monastery, founded in 1215 by Saint Dominic himself. The chapter-house (1301) and refectory (1303) are both worthy of note, and the chapel is particularly fine. Here we should remark a peculiarity of Dominican architecture: the plan of some of their churches. Like the great refectories of other Orders, they were sometimes divided into two parts by a central row of columns. The idea seems to have been connected with the desire to put layman and monk on the same footing, each in his own part of the building. The chapel at Toulouse is on this pattern. Its columns soar to a height of 90 feet; from the shaft of the last one springs a group of twenty-six ribs, which branch out again almost immediately, to fall back on all sides like a great bunch of palm leaves. This was also the plan of the Jacobins at Agen and their convent at Paris where the famous *Montagnard* club sat at the time of the Convention. But it was not generally adopted by the Order, which, like the Franciscans, seems to have preferred the aisleless church, which was more suitable for preaching.

We can see from these few pages the historical importance of monastic architecture in the Middle Ages. It constitutes our best source of information as regards housing conditions. The occupants of the monasteries led a very special kind of life; they also had greater resources at their disposal than the isolated individual. Their houses were not those of everyone. But nevertheless they do show us how houses were built, or, at least, how the resources of the architect were used for purposes other than those which were purely religious. These vast refectories and dormitories are works of great technical boldness and perfectly successful artistically. We even see them serving as a field for experiment, and as models for the churches. We have pointed out the similarities between refectories and two-naved churches. The aisleless churches with open timber roofs resting on thin arches, which flourished from the thirteenth century onwards in southern France and the Mediterranean basin, are variations of the great Cistercian dormitories.

¶ THE CLASSICAL PERIOD

With the sixteenth century new Orders made their appearance and the old ones radically changed. For the Jesuits, established in 1534, there was no question of leading a cloistered life; they had to work in the world in the defence of the faith. Their chief activity was education; their establishments were really colleges. In the seventeenth century the Benedictines adopted the reforms of Saint Maur. They left the country for the town. Their monasteries lost their rustic-fortress character. As town buildings, they could no longer spread so widely; they had to be reduced in area and increased in height. The buildings were ranged round several courtyards, but one of these still remained the open-arcaded cloister, nucleus of what may be called the monastic block: refectory, chapter-house, and dormitory. The superimposition of storeys presented new problems. Architects put all their knowledge of stone-cutting into perfecting the vaulting. The staircase became an essential element in the building. Naturally the style of the building itself depended on the development of taste in various periods. Forms changed: the round-headed took the place of the pointed arch as in the churches; the antique orders appeared, but only in the cloister; a triangular or curved pediment crowned the façade. But this kind of architecture did not forget the watchword of the Counter-Reformation, and all things considered it is this which best represents the movement's struggle for simplicity. Naturally it concentrated on beauty, not in the decoration, but in the rightness of proportion. And at the same time it had a strong sense of grandeur. Certain monasteries of the seventeenth and eighteenth centuries may be considered masterpieces of the architecture of their period just as much as, if not more than, the secular buildings. The names of the greatest architects are connected with them: Mansart, Robert de Cotte, Gabriel, Mique. As in the Middle Ages, the monastic architect profited by the innovations of domestic architecture and improved on them.

The monasteries of the various Orders differed less from one another than in the Middle Ages; it will therefore be sufficient to mention a few examples, chiefly to demonstrate the stylistic evolution, the general pattern being now firmly fixed. In Paris, the Val-de-Grâce, a convent not a church, still provides us with a good ensemble of monastic buildings of the time of Louis XIII. Founded by Anne of Austria in 1638, after the birth of Louis XIV, it was a convent for Benedictine nuns where the queen occasionally liked to go into retreat. Hence its semi-religious, semi-worldly character. The work was begun about 1655. The credit for it is due to François Mansart, who was responsible for the plan, and to Le Duc. The buildings are still set round a cloister, but the arrangement is different from the medieval one: here cloister and church are not adjoining but are separated by the nuns' choir, which forms a small church at right-angles to the large one (the chapel of St Louis). Thus the monastic block, with its four façades, appears as a complete and isolated unit. The elevation of the cloister included two storeys of superimposed galleries (ground and first floor), a storey without galleries, and a top storey with dormer windows surmounted by small triangular pediments. It is adjoined by the refectory, which reaches to the height of the second gallery, the chapter-house, the kitchen, and, above, the dormitories and cells. Four pavilions stand at the corners. One of these was reserved for the queen. The exterior façade of the refectory is pierced by windows with pointed arches, separated by buttresses, so that its appearance is still medieval. In contrast, the cloister itself, with its pilasters, its groined vaults resulting from the intersection of two elliptical barrel vaults, and its semi-circular arches open right to the ground, is extremely classical. The finest exterior façade is the one opposite the refectory, overlooking a large garden. It has two storeys and dormer windows over the ground floor; one of the two pavilions projecting from the corners was the queen's; in the centre is a large double door, crowned by a balcony and curved pediment decorated with coats-of-arms. It is a refined type of classical beauty, at once simple and powerful.

For the study of the monastic architecture of the congregation of Saint-Maur it is sufficient to go through the beautiful collection of plates in the *Monasticon Gallicanum*. In the seventeenth century we still find classical structures side by side with the medieval; but gradually the former gained the ascendancy. In Saint-Denis, Robert de Cotte separated (1708 onwards) cloister and church as in the Val-de-Grâce. After his death, Jacques Gabriel supervised the construction of the buildings which are models of architectural nobility. At Caen, in 1704, Father Guillaume de La Tremblaye undertook the restoration of all the abbey buildings of William the Conqueror in the Abbaye-aux-Hommes. The plan here is more elaborate with three closed courts; but only one of them has arcades and remains the actual cloister, set between church, refectory, dormitory, and store-houses. The cloister is decorated with Doric pilasters; the refectory with fine wood carvings; the stairs with magnificent wrought-iron banisters. The great block forming the exterior façade both of the cloister and the court beside it, with its great façade and two storeys over the ground floor, is a work of powerful simplicity, its rhythm skilfully set by the projection of the two corner pavilions and a central one, all with accentuated decoration; unadorned pediments at the corners, central pediment over the clock, decorated with two figures placed back to back, and capped with a small lantern.

Throughout France there are many such examples, which, collected together, would form a group comparable with the colleges of Oxford and Cambridge. However, their history has not been adequately investigated and many of them have not even been registered as historical monuments. For while some of them are known to everyone, such as those mentioned above, or Saint-Ouen at Rouen, Prémontré in the Aisne region, etc., others are much less familiar. Few people have visited the Lycée Henri IV in Paris (formerly the monastery of the canons of Sainte-Geneviève) to see not only the cloister but also the rooms of the library, now converted into dormitories, with a fine central rotunda (eighteenth century) decorated with a fresco by Restout; and not many have ever cast a glance at the courtyard of the Récollets' (Franciscan) monastery (seventeenth century), now the Villemin military hospital. In the provinces, the abbey of Lagrasse, securely hidden away behind its mountains, the old abbey of the Premonstratensians at Pont-à-Mousson (rebuilt after 1711), though more accessible, are hardly ever visited. And completely unknown in the very heart of Rennes is the prodigious façade of the old abbey of Saint-Georges, rebuilt in 1670 by the Abbess Magdeleine de La Fayette, whose name is proudly displayed there in large iron letters; few works disprove more convincingly the fallacy of always associating the idea of French art with the graceful, the pretty, the measured, something like the Attic miracle, perfect but small. Here only one epithet is possible: colossal.

While all these works, most of them large, were austere, in the course of the eighteenth century we find creeping in here and there the profane luxuriance of the Rococo. The Abbey of Prémontré is very much in the Louis XV spirit; at Châalis (Jean Aubert, after 1737) it is easier to imagine a marquis's red heels than the habit of St Bernard. But the end of the century brought back an atmosphere of severity; monastic architecture became neo-classical. Here we must mention Richard Mique, one of the least-known names of the eighteenth century, though he was First Architect to the King and the last to have borne that title. To him we owe both the chapel of the Carmelite convent at Saint-Denis founded by one of Louis XV's daughters, and, more important, the old 'queen's convent' at Versailles, founded by Marie Leszczinski – the Val-de-Grâce of the eighteenth century. Yet what a difference there is between the pomp of Mansart with his triumphal cupola and these flattened domes, this graceful portico with the slender Ionic columns, and the slightly chill delicacy of the whole building: it is the difference between Bernini and Palladio. This retrogression, characteristic of the period, is still more evident in the Capuchin convent of the Chaussée d'Antin (Brongniart, 1780); the columns in the cloister (now the court of the Lycée Condorcet) are without bases, repeating the Doric of Paestum; the portico is the same as that before which David was to place the heroic action of his *Horaces*.

PART THREE

Secular Architecture

*

The problems of secular architecture are many and very different from those of religious architecture, although the same materials are used for their solution, and they are subject to the same historical influences. This kind of architecture comprises domestic buildings (castles, town houses, and country houses), public buildings, town planning, and landscape gardening.

*

CHAPTER ONE

DOMESTIC ARCHITECTURE

O F all the problems with which the historian is faced, that of domestic architecture is the most complex. The differences in men's dwellings appear not only in relation to the period, but also according to the site, and to the rank of their occupants. A house is not only a historical record, it is the expression of a geographical and social background. The town house is not the same as the country house; the home of royalty or of the wealthy differs from the house of the ordinary man. These categories must be kept in mind in our account. We shall therefore study in turn the château (both in the country and, in the case of the royal palaces, in the town); the private town house (*hôtel particulier*), the apartment house, and the country cottage. But it must be admitted at once that our knowledge is incomplete. We are well informed about the dwellings of the nobility, but know little of the houses of the middle and lower classes. This is largely due to the fact that the former, for which more money was available, were better built and have therefore lasted better. They were also the object of greater artistic effort which impressed contemporaries and consequently descriptions and engravings supply information where buildings are lacking.

1. Castle and Palace

¶ THE MEDIEVAL CASTLE

Fortification was the first architectural expression of social power. In the Middle Ages the home of the noble was his stronghold. This is not the place to go into its connexions with either the fortifications raised by the Romans or the

villa rustica, the country dwelling of the Gallo-Roman aristocracy. It must be remembered simply that at the height of the
Middle Ages the castle served a triple function: it housed the
lord of the estate, it was an element in the defence of the town
or village where it stood, and it was a refuge for the population of the neighbourhood. Many castles are linked to a group
of houses, either as part of the original fortifications (inside
them, as at Carcassonne, or outside them, as at Boulogne) or
because the villages built in their shadow have sometimes
developed into towns. In place-names the word *château*, as
prefix or suffix, indicates this feudal origin, e.g. Châteaudun,
Château-Thierry, Châtellerault, Coucy-le-Château, or Sévérac-
le-Château.

The castle occupied a considerable space and was made up
of several parts, corresponding to each of the functions mentioned above. It was built on an easily defensible site, either
an isolated hill (*motte*) or the bend of a river, the neck of which
was barred by a moat or trench. After natural resources, its
safety depended on the solidity and the defensive equipment of
its great surrounding walls – thick walls with few openings,
loop-holes or arrow-slits, narrow windows splayed inwards,
and just wide enough for a bow. The wall parapet was the
most important part, because it was from there that the
defender dominated the attacker. It was battlemented with
'crenels', or low units, alternating with 'merlons', or high
units. To command the foot of the wall and look down on the
enemy, overhanging galleries called 'hoardings' were made.
The hoarding was made of timber. Later a gallery carried on
stone corbels was built, with openings called 'machicolations'
which allowed missiles to be dropped vertically. At intervals
the wall was reinforced by towers. All these principles of
defence are common to both fortified towns and castles.

The castle was surrounded by several curtain walls; but its
essential element was a tower bigger than the others, the
'keep'. The curtain walls are called the 'revetments' of the
keep. Sometimes there is no keep, or it may stand alone. The
first keeps, in the Merovingian or Carolingian periods, must
have been of timber. Nothing of them remains. The eleventh-

century keeps were square or rectangular buildings with very thick walls. Powerful buttresses flanked the corners. There are fine examples at Langeais and Beaugency. The entrance was placed above ground level and could be reached by light ladders, easily removed or destroyed in case of attack. The keep of Beaugency has four storeys and is 116 feet high with a large room on each floor. With the twelfth century the form of the keep changed. There were some polygonal keeps (Gisors, Provins), then some round ones, especially in the north, whereas in the Midi the square kind prevailed.

Examples of completely preserved castles date only from the thirteenth century, but the Bayeux tapestry shows us, though naively, the castles of the late Carolingian period and the eleventh century. They are perched on high ground and reached by wooden ramps; the entrance is closed by a wooden postern and the square keep, with crenellated platform at the top, is also in wood. The Crusades brought decisive innovations to castle architecture and defence. Here again the West learned from the East, and this time it applied its new knowledge on the spot, as is shown by the magnificent and perfectly preserved Frankish fortresses of the Holy Land, above all Krak des Chevaliers, the finest of them all, with its two curtain walls.

In France there are only remains, in consequence of Richelieu's order of *c.* 1630 to dismantle all the feudal fortresses and transform them into country seats. The remains of Château-Gaillard, near Les Andelys, are at the same time magnificent and famous. Situated high above a bend in the river, they dominate the valley of the Seine. The castle, built by Richard the Lion Heart in 1196, was completed by Philip Augustus, when he took possession of it after a memorable siege (1204), keeping in mind, it is said, the lessons of the Holy Land. In fact, like Krak des Chevaliers, it had two concentric curtain walls with the keep, an enormous circular block, straddling the smaller. The defensive system was reinforced by an independent structure, triangular in shape, at the head of the bend. The occupants also had at their disposal subterranean rooms dug out of the rock. Najac (Aveyron), rebuilt almost entirely from 1253 onwards, is, perhaps, though almost unknown, the very finest of French feudal ruins. It was sold for twelve francs during the Revolution. Set in the same way on a bend – in this case of the Aveyron, over which it towers from a height of nearly 328 feet – it dominates the complete circle of the horizon. From the bottom of the valley the effect is overwhelming. It had three curtain walls, two of which – they can still be clearly discerned – join together on the north front. One of them must have served as a refuge for the inhabitants of the nearby village. The inner wall formed a courtyard surrounded by buildings. A large round tower, projecting outside, was called the keep; it seems to have had chiefly a military rôle, since the lord's quarters were installed in a more spacious square tower built in the area of the court itself.

The castle of Coucy (Aisne) was the masterpiece of this architecture. Unfortunately nothing remains of it, even its ruins having been destroyed by the Germans in 1917. But it is at least extremely well known through old surveys and an engraving of Androuet Du Cerceau of 1576. It was built between 1225 and 1240 and altered at the end of the fourteenth century. On the edge of a plateau, it dominated the valley of the Aisne from a steep cliff 150 feet or so high. Its arrangement was essentially different from those of the two previous examples: there were indeed two curtain walls, but contiguous, no longer concentric. One, the lower bailey (basecourt), well defended towards the south, the most vulnerable side, by semicircular towers, probably gave shelter to the people of the neighbouring town; to this end it was equipped with living quarters, a chapel, and a well. The other was the castle proper, an irregular quadrilateral with round towers at the corners. All along the curtain wall, and leaning against it, were the two-storeyed buildings making up the owner's quarters, and including the chapel and the two great halls called the Hall of the Nine Worthies and the Hall of the Nine Noble Ladies, rebuilt in the last quarter of the fourteenth century. The keep, linking the inner and the outer walls, was a high round tower, the biggest in the world, 105 feet in diameter and 178 feet high, with walls 25 feet thick at the base. Inside there were three rooms, one on each storey, with an average diameter of 52 feet and a height of 42 feet, vaulted by twelve ribs radiating from a central boss. Communication from floor to floor was provided by a spiral staircase within the thickness of the wall, which also led to the crowning platform. One of the rooms did service as a cellar; a well ensured the provision of water. Underground passages linked up all parts of the castle.

As the Middle Ages developed, the castle changed its character. It gradually became no more than a strongly fortified residence. The transition was shown by the great royal castles of the fourteenth century. In Paris, royalty had first settled in the Île de la Cité, in the shelter of the Gallo-Roman wall. The Palais, rebuilt by St Louis and Philip the Fair, surrounded by the great walls shown in the *Très Riches Heures* of the Duc de Berry, was burnt in 1610. Only three of its lower rooms survive in the present Palais de Justice, beside the Seine; they probably go back to the beginning of the fourteenth century and have at once a feudal and a monastic air. A little later Charles V left the Cité. The Louvre, built by Philip Augustus outside the new walls of Paris, was hardly more than a keep surrounded by a moat and protected by a great curtain wall. Charles V and his architect, Raymond du Temple, turned it into a comfortable, sumptuous palace. Tall buildings were linked together in the courtyard by an external spiral staircase like that of Jacques Cœur's house at Bourges. Long rooms, paved with glazed tiles and covered by 'ceilings' painted to look like rafters, were decorated with frescoes. They were heated from fireplaces 15 feet wide. The private apartment of the king included a state room, a bedroom, an oratory, and a bathroom. The library was placed in the keep. At Vincennes it was again a keep (built by Philippe VI, 1336) which Charles V surrounded with a curtain wall within which the nobles of the court were to reside and which formed a little town in itself. The king reserved the keep as his own quarters; on the ground floor were the kitchens, on the first floor the royal chamber, in which the rib-vaults rested on a delicately worked pillar. A reconstruction would include a hooded fireplace, panelled walls, and tapestry hangings; a main staircase led from it to a similar room above. The Louvre, the Palais de la Cité, and Vincennes appear in the *Très Riches Heures* of the Duc de Berry, no longer as fortresses which could be lived in but as fortified houses.

The finest remaining example is the Palace of the Popes at Avignon, an enormous mass, covering an area of almost seventy thousand square feet, overlooking the Rhône, defended by its sturdy walls and high towers, several of which are over 160 feet high; in reality it consists of two palaces, that of Pope Benedict XII (1334–42) and that of Clement VI (1342–52), and encloses two courtyards. Here too the character is half feudal, half monastic: there are large rooms for the conclave, the papal audiences, and the tribunal; two chapels; and more comfortable apartments, especially in the Wardrobe Tower. Painting provided the decoration. Those in the Wardrobe Tower are of fishing, hunting, and bathing scenes, and are most astonishing because of their secular character, their freedom of expression, and their delightful colouring.

In the very last years of the fourteenth century must also be mentioned the castle of Pierrefonds, not far from Compiègne, built between 1390 and 1420 by Louis of Orleans. Being both a strong fortress and a comfortable house it was well able, after its all-too-complete restoration by Viollet-le-Duc under the Second Empire, to serve as a residence for Napoleon III. It is an irregular quadrilateral with towers at the angles and half-way along the sides. The keep is on the inside, projecting on to the court and occupying a part of it. It served as the owner's house; on the first floor were the reception room and the bedroom; on the second, the knights' room. It was in direct communication with the chapel installed in one of the towers. But it no longer had any special provision for defence; only the height and solidity of the walls could count as such.

The complete transformation of military tactics at the end of the fifteenth century, particularly the progress in artillery, was to hasten this evolution. To defend the castle completely against cannon, would involve measures that would make it uninhabitable. Therefore the old elements of defence, now useless, gradually disappeared. Yet they survived for more than half a century in a purely decorative character, whereas the house lost its forbidding appearance and opened up more and more to the outside. At Langeais, at the beginning of the reign of Louis XI (1465–70), the exterior appearance was still formidable; but the garden façade was already much less severe. At Ussé about 1475, in spite of an imposing military design with machicolated towers, keep, and wall passages, the towers had dormer windows with large and small chimneys. The castle of Chaumont (1473), seen from a distance, could pass for a fortress, with great round towers at the angles and the entrance; a drawbridge leading to a postern, and crenellation and machicolation. But the façade between the towers is pierced by windows affording a broad view over the river and surrounding country; the high pointed roof has many dormer windows; a frieze of initials forms a band round the walls; and as for the inner court, with its galleries over depressed arcades, its turreted staircases with sculptured buttresses, it has lost all military character. Large circular towers were still found as late as Chambord and pepper-pot turrets as late as Azay-le-Rideau, already a long way into the sixteenth century. Entirely new, on the other hand, at the end of the fifteenth, is the château which Louis XI had built at Plessis-les-Tours between 1463 and 1472. It had nothing in common with the sombre fortress of romantic historians – a country house with a pleasant, gay look about it, numerous windows with stone casements, and dormer windows surmounted by pointed, crocketed, or pinnacled gables. Here we already have the true Renaissance château, whose occupants no longer dreamed of battle but desired rather to devote themselves entirely to enjoying life.

¶ RENAISSANCE CHÂTEAUX

The distinction between the two periods of the Renaissance was indicated above: the early Renaissance, which was subject chiefly to Italian influence and dominated by the memory of the decorative fantasies of the Certosa of Pavia, and the high or late Renaissance more directly inspired by antiquity.

The great châteaux of the early Renaissance are in the Loire valley (Blois, Amboise, Chambord, Chenonceaux, Azay-le-Rideau) and in Normandy, at Gaillon. Here their general characteristics can only be outlined and a few examples briefly studied. During the reign of Louis XII preference was given to combinations of stone and brick; later stone was used by itself. The roofs remained pitched according to French tradition; the great halls remained covered with rib-vaults, the smaller with coffered wooden ceilings. The buildings, as in the feudal castle, were grouped more or less regularly round a courtyard which was often provided with open arcades on one or more sides. The various storeys communicated with one another by means of a spiral staircase, generally enclosed in a small tower projecting externally. There was still much decoration, as in Flamboyant Gothic, and it was of more importance in the upper than the lower parts of the building; but the elements of this decoration had changed. Flemish influence decreased and new motifs were borrowed from Italy. They include, cut in very low relief, foliated scrolls with or without medallions, details such as ribbons attached to a ring which run the length of the panel and link up various motifs, or *candelabra* (superimposed broad-rimmed goblets with extremely fanciful small figures seated on them); here and there were acanthus leaves borrowed from the Corinthian capital. Without modifying the principles of construction, the Italian influence worked towards an even more extensive opening up of the house to the outside by arcaded galleries or loggias, either on one of the floors or at the top of the building. In the interior the coffered ceiling was occasionally introduced. Most important of all, that indispensable adjunct, the pleasure garden, was associated with the château.

All the innovations – even the foreign ones – were applied by architects of French nationality but of so little renown (such as Colin Biart, Pierre Fain, Gilles le Breton) that historians long hesitated to see in them more than mere master-masons, to whom an Italian draughtsman brought plans and models which they were merely charged to execute. Yet the documents hardly ever mention anyone else and we are forced to surrender to this evidence.

So it was these almost unknown masters who transformed Amboise under Charles VIII, who introduced Lombard decoration at Blois under Louis XII while still keeping the general lines of the construction within the national tradition. It was they who created at Gaillon in Normandy, for the Cardinals of Amboise, one of the marvels of the Renaissance of which almost nothing remains to-day and which is known chiefly through engravings, notably the fine set by Du Cerceau. Italy, apart from a few decorators, as yet provided only the prototypes for the gardens and doubtless also the furniture.

With François I, after 1515, her influence became more pressing. At Blois again, the wing of François I with a loggia on its exterior façade introduced the rhythmic *travée*, as conceived by Bramante, into France; and the spiral staircase opens on to the courtyard like a gallery or a box at the theatre. These are old castles remodelled, in which symmetry and regularity are still lacking in the whole. Chambord, begun in 1519 in the heart of the forest, was a new undertaking, one of the first for which a vast symmetrical plan was conceived. The general appearance remained feudal, but the addition of a terraced roof allowed the ladies to follow the progress of the hunt; this terrace supports what amounts to a little village with great sloping roofs, highly decorated, in this case with a high proportion of elements borrowed from antiquity. The châteaux of the nobility at Chenonceaux (first part 1515–22) and Azay-le-Rideau (1518–25) also showed an innovation: two straight parallel flights of steps replaced the spiral staircase.

About 1528 François I abandoned the Loire for the region around Paris. Here he first built and then altered the Châteaux of Madrid, Fontainebleau, and Saint-Germain. The château of Madrid (begun in 1528, to-day completely destroyed) in which

Girolamo della Robbia seems to have played a leading part, marked a decisive development because of its exclusively Italian character – the rigid symmetry of the façade, two storeys of open arcaded galleries, pilasters, terracotta medallions. At Saint-Germain-en-Laye, altered from 1539 onwards by Pierre Chambiges, the great innovation was the flat terrace, this time open to the sky; but it rests on Gothic vaulting and, in spite of the admiration which it aroused, was not imitated. Fontainebleau is less interesting for its architecture (a collection of ill-assorted buildings, in which Gilles le Breton nevertheless gave proof of a simplicity which is in itself a novelty for this period) than for its interior decoration, due to Italian artists summoned by the king, chief among them Primaticcio and Rosso. This decoration is based on a combination of painting and stucco, the model of which had been provided by Raphael and his pupil Giulio Romano in the Vatican Loggie at Rome and the Palazzo del Tè at Mantua; to this is added a very fine decoration in woodwork, probably by French or Flemish carvers. The appearance of the Long Gallery must be noted; it was to become the perfect reception room for two centuries; we find it in the Louvre, at Versailles, and in the town houses of seventeenth-century Paris. The Italian architect Serlio, who was called to Fontainebleau but does not seem to have worked there much, has left at least one fine example of his style in France, the Château of Ancy-le-Franc (Côte d'Or), one of the first buildings of the classical Renaissance.

French architects of the first half of the sixteenth century were still partly masons, but this was certainly not the case in the years following. They became scholars and artists. Pierre Lescot (c. 1510–78), the architect of the Louvre, was a distinguished humanist, Lord of Clagny, counsellor and almoner in ordinary to the king. Philibert Delorme (c. 1515–70), whom we shall meet again at the Tuileries, Chenonceaux, and Anet, had made the journey to Rome and measured the monuments of antiquity on the spot; he wrote various books, notably a *Traité d'architecture* (1567); and moreover, by family tradition, he was as well versed in the practice as in the theory of his trade. Jean Bullant (*c.* 1510–78), who was to be architect to the Montmorency family, was also a scholar and a writer (*Règle d'architecture des cinq manières de colonnes*, 1563.) The same can be said of the members of the Du Cerceau dynasty, and we have already mentioned several times the standard work of Jacques Androuet Du Cerceau, *Les plus excellents Bâtiments de France*, 1576–9.

From these new minds was born a new architecture. In many respects it remained faithful to the national tradition, refusing in particular to substitute the Italian flat roof for the pitched roof; it accepted only the dome, which was later to be developed so successfully in France. The essential innovation was the use of the antique orders, on which all decoration was based. The principles of Vitruvius, widely known through Jean Martin's translation, a first-hand acquaintance with the Roman monuments, and, shortly after, the first great Italian treatises, particularly those of Serlio and Vignola, who had both been to France, were to become the dogmas of the new art. Sometimes each storey had its order, the same for the entire elevation or varied according to its position; in this case supreme perfection was reached by the superimposition of the three orders, Doric, Ionic, and Corinthian, placed in that order from the base upwards; very rarely this order was inverted (Assier). Elsewhere, one colossal single order dominated the whole height of the façade, linking up its horizontal divisions by a single vertical line. Philibert Delorme gave one of the finest examples of superimposed orders at Anet, while Jean Bullant preferred the single or 'colossal' order. We even find French architects endeavouring to add a fifth order to those of Vitruvius and Serlio. Philibert Delorme devised the French order, in which the shaft of the column is encircled by heavy rings of stone; it was hardly successful, but the idea of a national order was taken up again at Versailles in the seventeenth century.

Some of the major works of this second Renaissance period must now be studied. The artistic centre from now on was the Seine valley. In Paris itself, François I decided on the reconstruction of the Louvre and entrusted it to Lescot, who worked on it for thirty-two years, most probably with the technical advice of Jean Goujon. Lescot's Louvre at first took in only the rectangular building which forms the south part of the west wing of the present square court. At right-angles to this he added a similar building. The entire south-west corner of the court of the Louvre thus goes back to the sixteenth century and its history may be traced on its façades in the monograms of Henri II and Charles IX. The work is characterized by its symmetry, by the regular distribution of its windows with alternate triangular and curved pediments, by the pilasters which separate the windows, by the super-imposition of different orders, and by the substitution of an attic for the dormer windows; but also by its great tradition-ally pitched roof and by the decoration which remains abun-dant in the upper part. This time it consisted in great bas-reliefs of allegorical figures, produced by Jean Goujon and his workshop. It is possible that Lescot had greater projects in mind, for example the fourfold multiplication of the square court, but this is unlikely.

Twenty years later, in 1564, Catherine de' Medici under-took, some distance away and outside the city walls, the con-struction of the Tuileries, for which she employed Philibert Delorme and Jean Bullant. The Tuileries, burnt down in 1871 by the Commune, were the major achievement of French architecture in the second half of the sixteenth century. It represented the new ideal of architecture at its best, in which sculptural decoration (ornament or sculptural figures) was eliminated and in which all the beauty lay in the general accuracy of the proportions and the correct use of the antique orders. Its loss too often prevents our realizing its importance to-day. The central part (Delorme) was dominated by a four-sided dome, the first to be seen in Paris, set on two super-imposed orders, Ionic and Corinthian respectively. To it Philibert Delorme had applied his invention of the French order. To right and left two rather lower galleries, roofed by a terrace, linked up with the side pavilions of Jean Bullant. These were characterized by the use of a colossal order. Tuileries and Louvre were extended in the Grande Galerie

(Galerie du Bord-de-l'Eau) and in the Petite Galerie (Galerie d'Apollon) to join up with each other.

Together with the Tuileries must be mentioned also the Château of Anet, the masterpiece of French Renaissance architecture built by Philibert Delorme for Diane de Poitiers. The entrance of the main façade, with its regular superimposition of the three orders, Doric, Ionic, and Corinthian, was long to remain a prototype for both religious and domestic architecture. To-day it stands in Paris in the court of the École des Beaux-Arts next to the portico from Gaillon. Each of them is the perfect expression of one of the great moments of the Renaissance and in comparing them it is easy to measure the advance made by French art in the space of fifty years. Another equally telling comparison is that between the two main blocks of Chenonceaux. On the one hand the building of the early Renaissance of which we have spoken still blossoms with Flamboyant niceties; on the other, the severe, bare Long Gallery, which Philibert Delorme threw over the Cher like a bridge at the request of Diane de Poitiers, is stripped of all ornament.

The art of Bullant is perhaps even more classical, at least more Roman. At Fère-en-Tardenois (1552–62) over a 65-foot deep ravine he built six arcades to support a two-storey construction; the now ruined complex resembled one of those grandiose enterprises conjured up by Piranesi. At Écouen his portals with their giant columns recall the temple of Jupiter Stator.

Besides these royal or semi-royal undertakings, some space should be given to the more modest or less famous houses of the aristocracy, which also reflect the evolution we have just sketched. Mesnières (Seine-Inférieure), Fontaine-Henri (Calvados), Assier (Lot), the north wing of Bournazel (Aveyron) belong for the most part to the buildings of the early Renaissance and are in many ways reminiscent of the Blois of François I. La Rochefoucauld (Charente) is a perfect unity with a triple arcaded gallery over the inner courtyard, and is perhaps the masterpiece of this Italianate architecture. Classicism is represented by the château of Bailleul (Seine-Inférieure), unfortunately little-known, the façade of which is the realization as early as 1543 of a very precocious and correct superimposition of the orders; by the east gallery of Bournazel; by the Grand-Jardin at Joinville (Haute-Marne), etc. The extraordinary château of the Tour d'Aigues, in Provence, derives directly from the Roman monuments; but the gap was bridged by the Romanesque art of Provence, which had itself been a Renaissance.

¶ THE SEVENTEENTH AND EIGHTEENTH
   CENTURIES

The châteaux of the seventeenth and eighteenth centuries, with the exception of Versailles, are not as popular as those of the Renaissance. Yet they are neither less numerous nor less attractive. Here little can be said of anything apart from the royal houses, but in what other country could the history of architecture offer such a list of aristocratic homes as this in the space of two centuries: Richelieu (Lemercier, 1631); Maisons (François Mansart, 1642); Vaux-le-Vicomte (Le Vau, 1656); Champs (Pierre Bullet, beginning of the eighteenth century); Champlâtreux (Chevotet, 1733); Ménars (Gabriel and Soufflot, c. 1760); Benouville (Ledoux, 1767)? Even among the royal houses we must limit ourselves to the three main ones, the Louvre, Versailles, and Marly, and leave aside the Luxembourg, Saint-Cloud, Meudon, Clagny, and Compiègne.

The Louvre. The history of the Louvre in the seventeenth century is, in the words of R. Josephson, one of the most dramatic and from certain points of view the most decisive episodes in the history of European art. At the death of Henri IV in 1610, the Louvre was no more than two buildings raised at right-angles by Lescot at the south-west corner of the present square court. They were linked with the Tuileries by the Grande Galerie and the Petite Galerie, which at this time were only just completed. The interior was so dilapidated that when Marie de' Medici arrived in France in 1601 she thought she was being made fun of by being taken to visit an

uninhabitable palace. She preferred to build another, the
Luxembourg. In 1624 Louis XIII carried on the work. He
undertook to complete the square of Lescot's buildings, so
as to enclose the courtyard. First of all Lemercier prolonged
Lescot's wing on the west to double its original length; the
Clock Pavilion, higher than the rest, capped by a dome supported on eight caryatids, stressed the centre of the new façade.
Then the north wing was begun, still repeating the sixteenth-
century elevation. As for the apartments, they were to have
been decorated, like Fontainebleau, with a combination of
stucco and painting, for which Poussin was called back from
Italy. The project was only realized during the minority of
Louis XIV, when Anne of Austria came back to Paris after
the Fronde in 1652. Poussin was dead, and the winter quarters
of the queen were entrusted to Le Brun and Le Sueur. For her
summer quarters, which mark the summit of the Italianate
style in France, stucco work by the brothers Anguier framed
great frescoes by the Florentine Romanelli, inspired by the
Pitti Palace.

After 1661 Le Vau finished the three remaining sides of the
court on the pattern of the west side, composed of the extended Lescot pavilion and the Clock Pavilion. By 1664 the square
was closed in; but the three new sides had as yet only two
storeys, their completion being combined with that of the
façades as seen from the outer side. When it was decided to
give these a terraced roof, the corresponding interior façades
were covered in the same way.

For these exterior façades an outstanding effort was felt
to be necessary. The palace of the king in Paris, the capital of
France, had to be something special. This caused some hesitation. About 1663 Le Vau built a preliminary façade on the
south, along the Seine. It repeated, with a few variants, the
western interior façade by Lescot and Lemercier, and had a
central dome based on that of the Clock Pavilion, though more
ponderous. Le Vau also produced a plan for the façade towards Saint-Germain-l'Auxerrois. Colbert asked François
Mansart for another, but he refused to provide a design. At
this point Colbert decided to turn to Italian architects, in par-

ticular Bernini. Four masters of Italian architecture were approached in 1665 – Candiani, Rainaldi, Pietro da Cortona, and Bernini. After some correspondence Bernini was summoned to Paris, welcomed with royal honours, and lodged in the Palais Mazarin where he drew up a final project. We know it chiefly through the engravings of Jean Marot, which are probably not altogether faithful to the real conception of the artist, better expressed in models. Although until then Bernini's style had been very extravagant, he provided a completely bare, almost cubist project, with no striving after elegance in the detail but merely an effect of mass. On a stone foundation forming the basement stood a roughly faced ground floor, two storeys linked by a colossal Corinthian order, and a terraced roof with a balustrade decorated with statues. These ideas were accepted in principle. On 17 October 1665, the foundation stone of the façade towards Saint-Germain-l'Auxerrois was laid; on 20 October Bernini started back to Italy, leaving the head of his studio to oversee the works. For at least a year he continued to deal with it from Rome, but the work was never completed. The coalition of French architects, momentarily swept aside, was to profit from his absence by taking over the direction of the Louvre and bringing it to its completion on quite different lines. There was never an open break between Bernini and the French, but the project was none the less a failure which marked the end of Italian influence in France.

In 1667, eighteen months after Bernini's departure, Le Vau, Le Brun, and Perrault were commissioned to go ahead with another plan. This was the present Colonnade, executed from 1668 onwards. Posterity has given all the merit to Perrault. Actually it was the outcome of a collaboration. It was only when Le Vau was completely engrossed in Versailles, in 1668, that Perrault took charge of the work and modified the plan elaborated in common. The result is well known: a ground floor with tall windows forming an immense base, a great storey with a free-standing Corinthian colonnade in front of it, and a flat roof. The effect of grandeur is undeniable and the colonnade of the Louvre was to be imitated many times.

Its defects are no less obvious: the decoration was applied without relation to the rest of the building, the apartments which open on to the colonnade instead of the street are not sufficiently well lit, and in addition a flat roof is more suitable for the Italian than the French climate, since its line has to be broken by a host of chimneys. The other three façades were later built in harmony with that opposite Saint-Germain-l'Auxerrois, but with no colonnade, only with a colossal order running through two storeys. No hesitation was felt in demolishing the façade over the Seine, previously built by Le Vau, and replacing it by a new one in harmony with the whole.

One last thing remained to be done before the Louvre could be considered finished – the establishment of a link with the Tuileries to the north, towards the rue Saint-Honoré, symmetrical with that on the south along the Seine provided by the Grande Galerie. Bernini, Perrault, and others had had ideas for doing this, but it was not executed until the nineteenth century under the two Napoleons.

Versailles. The history of Versailles is at least as complicated as that of the Louvre. It can be divided into five periods – the Versailles of Louis XIII, the three Versailles of Louis XIV, and the Versailles of Louis XV.

(i) The first royal château of Versailles was built by Louis XIII from 1624 onwards. The king often went there to hunt. It was a small building of brick and stone with a great slate roof, such as could be seen at the time in Paris in the Place des Vosges. It had a very simple plan, which was to become the general model and may have been so already: a main rectangular block, framed to the right and left by two wings linked at their other extremities by a low covered arcade. The same is found at the Luxembourg. The court enclosed in this way, known as the Cour de Marbre, still exists. The essential part of these buildings, except the arcaded gallery, also remains, for Louis XIV would never allow them to be touched. On the other side were gardens with flower beds laid out like embroidery. This early Versailles was perhaps designed by Salomon de Brosse, the architect of the

Luxembourg; or perhaps only by the master-mason Le Roy.

(ii) In 1661, as soon as Louis XIV came to power and insisted on ruling personally after the death of Mazarin, his name was linked with that of Versailles. This first Versailles of the *Grand Monarque* was as yet not much more than the Versailles of Louis XIII, with a few new decorative innovations by Le Vau. The most important was the transformation of the garden. Le Nôtre presented a new design, the basic pattern of which, in spite of modifications in detail, has never been altered: a great vista flanked by two shrubberies and following the axis of the palace, with symmetrical arrangements of lawns and flowers on either side of this line: statues everywhere; an orangery built by Le Vau; and a menagerie for rare animals. This was the Versailles of Louis XIV's youth, where Molière came to act his first plays; the Versailles of the king's love-affair with Mlle de La Vallière.

(iii) The second Versailles of Louis XIV was that of Mme de Montespan. Louis XIII's château, said Mme de Scudéry, was only 'the little house of the greatest king on earth'. In 1668 the transformation was decided upon. To avoid a 'patched-up' result Colbert suggested complete reconstruction. The king set himself obstinately against this, declaring 'with some feeling, that they could demolish every bit of it and he would have it rebuilt just as it was without changing a thing' (Perrault). Finally it was decided to preserve the original château, enveloping it on three sides. Only the façade on to the Cour de Marbre remained intact. The new building which enclosed the old was conceived by Le Vau and realized between 1668 and 1671. Towards the entrance, the Cour de Marbre was lengthened by two elegant wings ending in porticos of six columns, and with flat roofs. Towards the gardens appeared the central block of the present palace, a vast rectangular building with an arcaded ground floor forming a massive basement, a *piano nobile*, an attic, and a flat roof. But in the middle of the façade the main storey and the attic receded, leaving over the ground floor a terrace paved with marble and decorated with a fountain. Simultaneously, the complete transformation of the interior was carried out under the direction of Le Brun. One of its finest parts, no longer extant, in one of the new galleries prolonging the Cour de Marbre, was the Ambassadors' staircase, a mixture of noble and familiar styles, a combination of real architecture and illusory perspectives. On the first storey, painted courtiers seemed to press between columns over the balustrade of a great loggia to watch the ambassadors ascend the stairs; further up again there was a similar optical illusion, though this time the spectators were the animals of the menagerie. These two names, Le Vau and Le Brun, to which that of Le Nôtre should be added, sum up the effort achieved at Versailles before the arrival of Hardouin-Mansart. Bernini had only just returned home. The art of Le Vau and Le Brun still shows the subjection of France to the influence of Italy. It may be labelled Baroque, for it must be remembered that among the most outstanding characteristics of the Baroque style is a persistent search for movement and turbulent composition, which Le Vau favoured. His Versailles, from whatever angle we consider it, either from the entrance, with its ever narrowing courts, or from the garden, with the immense central recess in the façade, is movement throughout. We can say the same for Le Brun – his opulence, his sense of perspective, his desire to astonish, as they appear in the Ambassadors' staircase, all remain very close to the Italian spirit.

(iv) Jules Hardouin-Mansart, nephew of François Mansart, came on the scene in 1678 for the third Versailles of Louis XIV. He had just built Clagny for Mme de Montespan. His art, at least at the beginning, was intellectual rather than sensual, or at any rate much less sensual than that of Le Vau and Le Brun. He was closer to his uncle, whose designs he had inherited.

The Versailles of Le Vau, begun about 1668, did not last ten years. It had seen the triumph of Mme de Montespan. In 1678, after the Peace of Nijmegen, at the very moment when the favourite was definitely discredited in the Poison affair, a new transformation was being contemplated. But Hardouin-Mansart, born in 1646, was then little more than thirty years old; he was not to have free scope until 1683 after the death of

Le Brun, a survivor from the previous generation. In the Cour de Marbre where Le Vau had accumulated graceful but small-scale decoration, emphasizing the restriction of the space and the closeness of the walls, Hardouin-Mansart transformed everything to arrive at the present result. The change is much more obviously felt on the garden side. He removed the great terrace over the ground floor which characterized the work of Le Vau. The two wings were linked in a straight line and the terrace replaced by a gallery. The elevation remained the same, but the effect was completely changed: no more contrast, fantasy, or movement – nothing but one great horizontal, along the whole length of which are superimposed basement, *piano nobile*, and attic; no more strong projections, only some very slight ones supporting coupled columns; hardly any attempt at variety, apart from the contrast between the round-headed windows of the first floor and the square bays of the mezzanines. There is no longer any question of the Baroque, only of the Classical style, meaning by this calm majesty, magnificence, and richness of line, and with a horizontal rather than a vertical emphasis. In addition logic and reason govern the whole structure, since this exterior transformation was bound up with changes in the interior, notably the creation of the Galerie des Glaces.

Mansart planned on an even greater scale. The new façade became only the central element in a much vaster complex; two wings, slightly set back, frame it: the South or Princes' Wing (1679–82) and the North Wing (begun 1684) bring the total extension of the palace to 550 yards of façade. Here is another opportunity for stressing that characteristic so often denied to French art – the colossal.

Internally the new Galerie des Glaces owes as much to Le Brun as to Mansart. As at Clagny, it extends between two rooms: the Salon de la Guerre and the Salon de la Paix. Over it is a vast painted ceiling, on the walls between the windows and between the large mirrors is a rhythmical succession of marble pilasters. Until then only Italy had been capable of creating décor dependent on mirrors. Colbert wanted to show the world what the new French factories were capable of.

The size of French plate glass was much larger than the Italian, but still far from that of the present day, since at Versailles each mirror was composed of eighteen bevelled-edged plates, joined together by chased and gilded brass. The columns and pilasters separating the mirrors and the windows bore capitals in metal designed by Le Brun, which he called the *French order* – a background of palm fronds with a *fleur-de-lys* in the centre, a sun at the top and two cocks beating their wings in the upper corners. The lily, sun, and cocks were three symbols, standing for the monarchy, Louis XIV, and France. A little later on Hardouin-Mansart was to complete his work at Versailles with the new Orangerie (1684–6) on the site of the south flower beds, several shrubberies decorating the garden, and, above all, the construction of the Trianon and the chapel.

The chapel, begun after 1699, at the very end of the century, already belongs to another style. It owes as much to Robert de Cotte as to Hardouin-Mansart. The plan belongs to the tradition of the Palace chapels without aisles and with an internal division into two storeys. The building itself, much higher than the other parts of the palace, no longer complied with the rigorous discipline of a unified plan. The exterior decoration, very exuberant, also breaks with the desire for simplicity stressed up to that time by all the façades.

(v) All this very nearly disappeared under Louis XV, who, with less respect for family souvenirs than his great-grandfather, had accepted a plan for a complete renovation presented by Ange-Jacques Gabriel (1742). Funds failed, except for destroying Le Vau's right wing over the entrance court, the very one where the Ambassadors' staircase was. In its place Gabriel erected the present building, in which the colonnade topped by a pediment is an echo of the Louvre and the palaces in the Place de la Concorde (1772). With Louis XIV on the left and Louis XV on the right, the result was rather lopsided. Louis-Philippe re-established the symmetry by demolishing the left wing and rebuilding it on the pattern of the Gabriel block. Thus it is Louis XV who now receives the visitor on his arrival.

Of the Versailles of the eighteenth century, the admirable decoration of the private apartments of Louis XV, designed by Gabriel, is still preserved – white woodwork carved by Verbeckt and Rousseau. A little later Mique provided a symmetrical element in the small apartments of Marie-Antoinette (after 1782). With what remains of the Versailles of Louis XIV (above all, the Galerie des Glaces, the Salons de la Guerre and de la Paix, the king's bedroom), we can follow, in a single building, three aspects of royal life during a century and a half. This royal art was to serve as the example for private individuals; we shall find it in Paris also, but obviously on another scale.

The palace should not be considered apart from the Trianons, where the sovereigns, one after another, sought to escape from court etiquette. The same three periods are represented. The Grand Trianon, built from 1687 onwards by Hardouin-Mansart and Robert de Cotte, is a reduced version of the main palace: a simple all-marble ground floor with a flat roof, in the middle an open colonnade with coupled columns, allowing of free circulation. This replaced the porcelain Trianon, so called because it was decorated with plaques of blue, white, and yellow porcelain; with its roofs of gilded lead, it was a picturesque and colourful ensemble typical of Le Vau's taste; actually it was only a simple little pleasure pavilion which Louis XIV had had built in the park, after 1670, for intimate afternoon refreshments.

Some distance away, at the end of Louis XV's reign, Ange-Jacques Gabriel built the Petit Trianon (1751) for Mme Du Barry; it is perhaps, of all French architecture, the work which best merits the epithet 'Attic'. Further off still, Richard Mique conceived the charming and fragile décor of the Hameau (including the master's house, the dairy, and the mill) for Marie-Antoinette, where the ill-fated queen amused herself by playing shepherdess, in the years of innocent happiness for which she was to pay so dearly.

Marly. Marly was the only great palace both planned and wholly realized during the reign of Louis XIV. Nothing of it remains to-day. The king sought in it not solitude or even intimacy, but a more limited setting to which only a few privileged persons should be admitted, so that an invitation to Marly became the most envied of favours. The setting, planned by Hardouin-Mansart, was admirable (pl. 37a). Twelve small pavilions faced each other across a stretch of water; at the end, there was a larger pavilion for the king: symbols of the sun and the twelve months of the year. Le Brun provided the exterior decoration, which was sumptuous and full of optical illusions. The group stood against a background of gardens and waterfalls, smaller but no less rich than that at Versailles. The work, which was begun in 1679, was – we can fairly say – never finished; the expense, in 1703, outstripped that of Versailles itself.

11. The Town House

There are two principal types of town house, the apartment house and the private house.

¶ MEDIEVAL TOWN HOUSES

Some are in timber, others in stone. Viollet-le-Duc held that the former, in the north, were the result of the Germanic invasions, the others, in the south, a survival of Roman domination. Nothing could be more incorrect. At a time when transport was difficult for the ordinary citizen, materials were not chosen; those found on the spot were used without question. What is more, there are timber houses in the south (Languedoc) as well as in the north, and we now know that they existed in Gaul long before the invasions.

Timber houses were the more numerous. Generally the ground floor was of stone, or at least a base of stone or brick was provided to prevent the timber from coming into direct contact with the soil. In France, the system of building on piles, as practised in mountain regions (Switzerland and the Tyrol), is not known. The units are set either vertically (posts) or horizontally (cross-pieces) and are bound together by oblique units. In this way the timber forms a casing, filled in with quarry stones, bricks, or earth mortar. There are several variants of this basic arrangement; sometimes the vertical posts are the same length as the height of the house (this was the oldest system, which called for very tall timber and disappeared towards the fifteenth century), sometimes their length corresponds only to the height of one storey. Other more special arrangements characterize certain regions.

Often the second system (short timber) does not require the upper storeys to be placed exactly above the same area as the lower ones: space is gained over the street. This overhanging system tends to reduce the lighting of the public thoroughfares, and municipal councils have never ceased to fight against it. The abundance of documents on the subject demonstrates their slight efficacy. Many very narrow streets were turned almost into covered passages by this method; people in opposite houses could easily link hands. And what is more, most of these houses, built on narrow sites, which went very little distance back, had their gables facing the street. This lasted until the end of the sixteenth century, giving the towns a very different appearance from that of to-day, and a picturesqueness which enraptured the Romantics.

The interior arrangement of such houses was generally very simple; on the ground floor, a shop open to the street, a kitchen at the back, a side passage leading into a court with a spiral staircase; on the first floor, a room or chamber; on the upper floors, bedrooms. Sometimes there was a second building at the end of the court, joined to the first by a gallery.

Many examples of these timber houses still survive in old French towns but they generally do not date back further than the fifteenth century. Normandy had a wealth of them, particularly at Rouen and Lisieux, though many have been allowed, or made, to disappear. The majority were very plain, free from any decoration. Ornament appeared only after the second half of the fifteenth century – Gothic first of all, then Italianate, and progressively more complex. The so-called house of Diane de Poitiers at Rouen (about 1525) has a façade decked out like a shrine – sculptured brackets, medal-

lions, friezes, arabesques, and shells in the manner of the early
Renaissance. In Paris, the house at number 3, rue Volta,
four-storeyed and timber-framed, probably goes back to the
fourteenth century. The south of France also has many
wooden houses, notably at Albi. The many miniatures in
manuscripts or the paintings of the fifteenth century help to
give us a more complete idea of these houses, both inside
and out.

Stone houses, like those in timber, were found in north and
south alike. But we have older examples of them, of the thirteenth century and even of the twelfth. Their evolution is
easy to follow from the arrangement of the windows. In its
simplest form the window was a rectangular opening capped
by a lintel; the length of the latter determined the width of the
window. Often, as in church porches, the lintel was strengthened by a relieving arch. In the twelfth century the arch was
round-headed; later pointed, finally depressed. Sometimes
twin openings separated by small columns were set under a
single arch. From the thirteenth century the window was
divided up into two parts by a horizontal transom; from the
fourteenth century into four, an upright support, the mullion,
being added to the horizontal.

The Four du Chapitre at Rouen (rue Saint-Romain) is of
the thirteenth century. In Paris, the so-called house of Nicolas
Flamel, 51 rue Montmorency, is of 1407. The south of France
is richer. At Saint-Antonin (Tarn-et-Garonne), the Town
Hall occupies a twelfth-century house. A small town such as
Cordes (Tarn) is a veritable museum of medieval domestic
architecture, with the houses of the Grand Falconer, the
Grand Master of the Hounds, the Grand Equerry, etc. (fourteenth century).

1. THE PRIVATE HOUSE (*Hôtel*). Some of the houses
which we have just mentioned, perhaps almost all of them,
were the residences of one family only. All the same, we reserve the term private house (*hôtel*) for a more important
complex, characterized by the grouping of buildings round a
court, and in which the main residential block does not over-

look the street. This is the adaptation, the urban transposition, of the nobleman's castle or the feudal country house.

The house of the archbishops of Sens, in Paris, is of the late fifteenth century. Older and more characteristic is the house of Jacques Cœur at Bourges (1442–53). The court is still very irregular and surrounded by arcades (this kind of vague pentagon was later to become a perfect square or rectangle and the arcades disappeared). Here, the ground floor is given up to the servants' quarters and offices. On the first floor is the main reception room, the great hall; together with this are the chapel and apartments, consisting of bedrooms and dressing rooms. The vertical link is provided by spiral staircases, three of which are encased in charming little turrets, projecting into the court. A light, attractive abode, with nothing feudal or military about it, with its owner's personality clearly stamped on it, and his name and coat-of-arms set up in a number of places. The period – we are still in the Middle Ages – is revealed in the disdain for symmetry and the right-angle, as well as by the decoration, especially abundant on the upper part, consisting of coupled arches and little bas-reliefs of very varied themes ranging from the illustration of a love romance to the familiar representation of a kitchen interior. But the clear, easily decipherable disposition of the units must also be noted, particularly in the façade to the street, where we find the three classic divisions (basement, main storey, roof with dormer windows) clearly separated. Although it has not yet the proportions of François Mansart, it already has his clarity.

In the sixteenth century various houses throughout the country present a similar arrangement. They differ from each other chiefly in the decoration, ranging from Flamboyant Gothic in the buildings of older design such as the Hôtel de Cluny in Paris (1498) to the most clearly defined classicism in the Hôtel d'Assézat at Toulouse (1555). There are also many regional variations. In the Loire valley and in Normandy, in the Hôtel d'Écoville at Caen, in the fine aristocratic houses of Blois, Tours, and Angers, can be felt the direct echo of the art of the royal palaces. Elsewhere, there is a direct passage from the medieval to the Baroque, missing out the classical period

– at Dijon, Hugues Sambin (probably born about 1520), architect and woodcarver, treated the façades of private houses as a cabinet-maker would (Maison Milsant, Hôtel Le Compasseur) decorating them in a flamboyant way so that antique motifs are interspersed with lions' heads, grotesque masks, and even garlands of rosettes of ribbons. At Toulouse, the series is complete – early Renaissance in the Hôtel de Pins; classicism in the Hôtel d'Assézat; precocious Baroque in the Hôtel de Bagis and the Hôtel du Vieux-Raisin. The name of Nicolas Bachelier (about 1500–56) dominates all the others and for many years his hand was seen everywhere; it is certainly not present in the Hôtel d'Assézat, except perhaps in the detail of one door. Bachelier was really a sculptor and his expressive manner can be clearly recognized in the Caryatids of the Hôtel du Vieux-Raisin and the Atlantes of the Hôtel de Bagis.

Yet it was in Paris, towards the end of the sixteenth century, that the typical classical hôtel was evolved; its type was dominant through two whole centuries, while a constant evolution took place in its plan and decoration – a particularly significant evolution, because it corresponds to the changes in French society itself. This type of hôtel arose with this society at the close of the Wars of Religion; it was at first the background of a powerful, exuberant life at the time of Mme de Rambouillet and the heroines of the Fronde; it finished in the eighteenth century in the most elegant and enchanting dwelling which has ever been created in France.

In Paris itself* – examples are also found in the provinces – it is worth noting that the hôtels of each period are concentrated in a particular quarter. Under Richelieu, it was the area around the Louvre and the Palais Cardinal (now Palais-Royal); under Mazarin and during the minority of Louis XIV, the Marais and the area around the Place des Vosges; later, the Île Saint-Louis. At the beginning of the eighteenth century, the fashion was for the Faubourg Saint-Germain, then right in the country; the end of the century takes us to the Chaussée d'Antin and north of the boulevards. The site-condi-

*See Appendix for the principal hôtels of Paris, arranged by streets.

tions differed in the various quarters and would have been enough to introduce differences of structure. Land was limited and dear in the Île Saint-Louis; on the left bank, along the rue de Grenelle, expansion was unlimited. Other differences depended on the rank of the occupants – the same thing would not do for the Princesse de Bourbon and the wig-maker Peyrenc de Moras.

Though there are almost as many kinds of plan as there are houses, we can recognize certain general characteristics.

The living quarters were set between court and garden, so that they did not face the street (one exception – the Hôtel de Beauvais, rue François-Miron. The main block is at the end of the court. In the seventeenth century two wings of the same dimensions projected from it towards the street; this is the so-called 'half H' (i.e. ⊓) plan (Hôtel Tubeuf, Hôtel de Sully); in the eighteenth century these wings were no more than lateral projections (Hôtel Matignon, Hôtel de Moras). To compensate for this, the depth of the main building is doubled; it has two series of rooms, one facing the court, the other facing the garden. The court itself, square at first, was rounded off at the corners opposite the house (Hôtel de Hollande, Hôtel de Rohan, Hôtel Matignon). The outhouses, particularly the stables and manure heap, were a drawback; so a second courtyard (the base court) was added at the back, or even a side court for the servants, the forecourt becoming the court of honour (*cour d'honneur*).

What was the internal arrangement? The present fundamental distinction between reception rooms and living rooms was not established all at once. The work by P. Le Muet, *Manière de bâtir pour toutes sortes de gens* (first edition, 1623), which includes all sorts of plans for sites of all sizes, makes hardly any mention, even in the most sumptuous examples, of anything but the hall and, more important, the bedroom with its closet and dressing-room. For the master and mistress of the house often received in their bedroom, and even from the bed. In her state bedroom Mme de Rambouillet discoursed on the *Carte du Tendre* with the *Précieuses*, and lackeys placed around her 'the necessities of conversation' (chairs). About

1650 appeared the alcoves, perhaps a Spanish idea, but one for which Tallemant des Réaux gives the credit to Mme de Rambouillet herself. The marquise's house and her Blue Bedroom have disappeared, but we can see alcoves of the period in the Hôtels Lambert and Lauzun. In the adjacent dressing-room slept the maid or valet, for servants were no more separated from the life of the family than reception from living quarters. Molière's plays are commentary enough on this custom.

Gradually, however, there was more specialization. The dining-room, the drawing-room, made their appearance, the hall disappeared, but not always the bedroom in which guests were received, and still less frequently the ante-rooms. The vestibule and monumental staircase were also essentials. The finest reception room was the gallery, doubtless only a transformation of the great hall of the medieval castle. We have seen it in the royal palaces, at Fontainebleau (François I gallery), in the Louvre (the Apollo gallery), and at Versailles (the Galerie des Glaces). It exists in certain seventeenth-century hôtels, in the Luxembourg (the famous gallery decorated by Rubens), in the Hôtel Mazarin (now the Bibliothèque Nationale), the Mazarin Gallery, in the Hôtel de La Vrillière (now the Bank of France), in the Hôtel Lambert – all large houses; and sometimes also in the smaller ones, such as the charming miniature gallery of the Hôtel de Hollande (47 rue Vieille-du-Temple). The gallery disappeared in the eighteenth century when the drawing-room became the real state-room.

The living-rooms, for their part, were split up into apartments, each with a bedroom, sometimes an ante-room, also a closet, a dressing-room and, more and more frequently, 'amenities'. In 1722, at the Hôtel de Bourbon, we find 'bathing apartments'; in 1728, at the Hôtel Moras 'petits lieux'. Corridors and interior staircases made each apartment independent. The Hôtel de Bourbon (by Giardini) is said to be the first example of this. At the most it marks the culmination of prolonged attempts. During the lifetime of Louis XIV, the Hôtel de Rothelin (1704, by Lassurance) or the Hôtel Amelot de Gournay (1695 or 1712, by Boffrand) were very ingeniously planned. French architects of the eighteenth century often placed the reception rooms in the centre of the house, framing them with the living rooms. They were soon recognized throughout Europe as true masters in this art.

There are no longer those enfilades of rooms which the seventeenth century loved. The disadvantages of a system in which all the rooms open one upon the other then seemed slight beside the long vistas, the impression of space given by open doors all in line with one another. It was the affirmation of a point of view which did not mind a little bodily inconvenience and a few draughts for the sake of triumphant appearances. Mme de Maintenon said of her royal husband, 'With him only grandeur, magnificence, symmetry matter; it is infinitely worth while enduring all the draughts which sweep under the doors if only these can be arranged facing each other. ... We must perish in symmetry.' It is not that the eighteenth century scorned long vistas; but it procured them in another way, and more cheaply, by mirrors in which the illusion of a succession of rooms all on the same pattern was reflected.

In decoration period variations are even more obvious. In exterior decoration sculpture, at least of figures, was gradually eliminated. It still persisted over the whole façade in the sixteenth century and at the beginning of the seventeenth (the Seasons on the Hôtel Carnavalet and Hôtel de Sully). Then only the pediment remained, sometimes with symbolic figures lying above it. Finally it was reduced to a few ornamental keystones over doors and windows and fine balconies of wrought iron (exceptions, the Seasons on the Hôtel de Soubise, 1710; the Horses of the Sun on the Rohan stables, about 1735). The orders were sometimes superimposed and sometimes simple, in the latter case generally Corinthian, running through the whole height of the façade. They were, says Blondel, 'the court dress of French architecture'; but not everyone wore it. At the end of the eighteenth century, at the time of the neo-classical movement, sculpture was found again, often in long narrow reliefs applied as a frieze to the upper part of the house (Hôtel de Salm, now the palace of the Légion d'Honneur, rue de Solférino). Clodion produced some charming examples of this type.

In France the major efforts of the decorator have always been concerned with the inside of the house. But the spirit, the very technique of decoration changed constantly in these three centuries. The seventeenth century was the century of painters. Some, like Rubens and Romanelli, came from abroad. Simon Vouet, trained in Italy, brought the Venetian manner to France in 1627 and for fifteen years, together with his pupils, monopolized all commissions. His work has almost entirely disappeared; but it would do him no small honour to have left us simply Le Sueur and Le Brun. These paintings are not always large historical compositions with figures. A very large part is left to 'grotesques' and 'ornament'. The name of the former derives from the 'grottoes', subterranean rooms of the Thermae of Titmus, of which the very broken-up decoration, with its figures of human beings or animals set amid arabesques, scrolls, and strapwork, was taken up with great success from the sixteenth century onwards. In 1550 and 1565 respectively, Du Cerceau published his two collections of *Petites* and *Grandes Grotesques*. Later came the grotesques of Le Sueur and Vouet. The specialists in ornamental motifs are Jean Le Pautre, Jean Marot, and Jean Berain the Elder.

In the eighteenth century, painting was confined to a few panels over doorways. Boucher was summoned to the Hôtel de Soubise; Fragonard to the Hôtel Matignon. Sometimes, too, some works of fantasy were admitted, *chinoiseries* or *singeries* (cf. the *singeries* of Huet at the Hôtel de Rohan, 1740). But the essential element was the panelling. Carved wood or plaster outlined panels along the walls. On one wall, the mantelpiece, reduced to modest dimensions, became the support for a tall mirror. The very forms of the panelling changed constantly. In the beginning, with 'Rococo', curve and counter-curve triumphed, with the 'serpentine', 'chicory', and 'orfèvre' motifs, against which, in 1754, Cochin addressed to French decorators an eloquent *Supplication*, begging them to revert to simplicity. In fact, stiffer and even straight lines and right-angles made their reappearance. Under Louis XVI the decorative vocabulary drew on Pompeian, Egyptian, and Etruscan sources, revealed by recent archaeological discoveries, and to continue in vogue throughout the Empire.

We must now illustrate the outline of this evolution with a few names and dates. We shall mention nothing which cannot still be examined at first hand, though we have, alas, only the fragments of an incomparable history. Many masterpieces have been destroyed or spoilt for ever. Only the great compilations of Blondel or Mariette remain to give an idea of this wealth. A few examples at least could be saved or reconstructed, as contributions to a Museum of the French House.

The sixteenth century is hardly represented save by the Hôtel Carnavalet (rue de Sévigné). A likely enough tradition sees in it the work of Pierre Lescot. Though it was altered a century later by François Mansart and again in the nineteenth century when the museum was installed, it preserves the main part of its court of honour, its façade, formerly linked with the street by two arcaded wings, its statues of the Seasons, in which the inspiration of Jean Goujon is perhaps not lacking, and its great entrance. The Hôtel de Sully (62 rue Saint-Antoine) begun in 1624 by Jean Du Cerceau the Elder, is a later replica of it; but the interior provides a fine souvenir in the bedroom of Sully (further decoration of the same period is preserved in the Bibliothèque de l'Arsénal).

One hesitates to place between those two names that of the Hôtel Lamoignon (24 rue Pavée) which is said to have been built in 1580 for Diane de France, Duchess of Angoulême. It fits more naturally in the reign of Louis XIII, to which period some fine remains in the interior seem to belong. But if the traditional dating is correct we must acknowledge it as a work of capital importance: the first application of the classical orders to a private house and the oldest remains of the colossal order in Paris.

The childhood and adolescence of Louis XIV are perfectly represented in the Île Saint-Louis by the hôtels Lambert and Lauzun. The first is a work of Le Vau's youth begun about 1640. The decoration of the Hercules Gallery, in which frescoes by Le Brun are combined with stuccoes by Van Obstal (1648), remains; but only the engravings of Picart tell us what the Cabinet des Muses and the Cabinet de l'Amour were like. However the Hôtel Lauzun (Le Vau, 1655–7), now a municipal museum, has preserved its decoration almost intact.

To the old age of the Roi Soleil belong the Hôtel de Soubise and the Hôtel de Rohan, in the Marais, both by Delamair (1705) but decorated much later; the oval drawing rooms by Boffrand (about 1730), in the former, constitute a major Rococo work (pl. 42a). More or less contemporary are the first hôtels of the Faubourg Saint-Germain – the Hôtel Amelot de Gournay (Boffrand, 1695 or 1712; 1 rue Saint-Dominique), the Hôtel de Rothelin (Lassurance, 1700–4; 101 rue de Grenelle, now the Ministry of Commerce), the Hôtel d'Estrées (Robert de Cotte, 1713; 79 rue de Grenelle, Russian Embassy). They belong already to the series most clearly represented by the Hôtel Matignon (Courtonne, 1726; 57 rue de Varenne, Presidency of the Council of Ministers) or especially by the Hôtel Biron (Gabriel and Aubert, 1728; now the Musée Rodin) where we immediately appreciate the simplicity of line, the appropriateness of the interior arrangement and the fine gardens which were restored a few years ago. The Hôtel de Bourbon (Giardini and Lassurance, now the Palais-Bourbon), much more sumptuous as was fitting for a prince of the blood, is also less characteristic.

At the end of the century the main works of Ledoux and Bélanger received particularly rough treatment. We have to go to the Bois de Boulogne, to Bagatelle, to become acquainted with the graceful art of Bélanger. As for Ledoux, how can one guess at his sense of grandeur, his Doric austerity, in the now pitiful hall of the Hôtel d'Hallwyl (1765; 28 rue Michelle-Comte), though it might respond to a cleaning. Chalgrin may be represented by the Hôtel de La Vrillière (1767; rue Saint-Florentin); Brongniart by the Hôtel Masserano (1787–8; 11 rue Masseran). The Hôtel de Bourrienne (58 rue d'Hauteville) for the Empire – failing the Hôtel de Beauharnais, before the war the German Embassy – and the Hôtel de Bony (32 rue de Trévise) for the Restoration may suffice to complete this outline.

II. THE RENTED HOUSE. The house divided up inside to be let off to different people is an economic and social fact too often unrelated to architecture. The religious orders – Franciscans and Carmelites – were among the first to exploit their land in this way. The houses of the seventeenth century – like those in Paris near the church of Saint-Gervais in the rue François-Miron – those of the eighteenth century – Place Saint-Sulpice, or rue Saint-Honoré in Paris, houses in Rennes, Bordeaux, and Nantes – often have finely designed façades, and some even have an enchanting quality of proportion, gracefulness and sobriety of décor. But those of the nineteenth century, the expression of a demographic revolution which ended in the overpopulation of the big towns, were mostly undertaken only for profit and are lamentable episodes in the history of building. We must, however, make exception for a few names and buildings: during the first Empire, for Percier and Fontaine and their façades on the rue de Rivoli; under the Second Empire, for Charles Garnier, who, while applying to his façades the eclecticism of the period, was the first to face the problem of the distribution of the interior and to create the formula of the modern flat with a clear distinction between reception and living rooms, perhaps sacrificing the second to the first. At the beginning of the twentieth century Charles Plumet applied to luxury flats the florid style of the post-1900 period, and after 1914 Roux-Spitz introduced contemporary geometrical forms.

It must be remembered that building is restricted by regulations which limit, at least in Paris and the large towns, the height and size of habitations. In Paris, nothing may exceed a height of 65 feet (20 metres) above the street, unless the additional height is progressively set back from the street line, like a stepped pyramid. Sauvage produced the first example of this in his blocks of flats in the rue Vavin and the rue des Amiraux. The highest houses in France, at Villeurbanne (Rhône) and in the great agglomerations of the suburbs of

Paris (Drancy, Châtenay-Malabry), called, as if in irony, garden cities, do not exceed fifteen storeys or so; they cannot therefore rival the American sky-scrapers.

III. The Rural House

The style of the rural house depends primarily on the area in which it is built. But often its aptness and sober elegance make it also architecture of the first order, although this was not its creators' aim. The historical factor is much less important, so that an evolution of styles corresponding to a succession of periods cannot be discerned. Like all things popular, it has an unchanging character, or at least its transformations in time are less perceptible than those of the town house. In the mid sixteenth century, in the sixth Book of his *Architecture*, Serlio gave plans for rural houses which are still of value to-day; he pointed out the difference between France and Italy, notably in the roofing, and recognized French characteristics.

It should however be noted that certain features correspond to particular populations and can only be explained historically, not geographically – such as the Basque house, or the Spanish influences which still persist in the countryside of Franche-Comté; and that the continual improvement in means of transport, making available to the rural community a large number of materials for construction, permitted a degree of choice and gradually abolished local differences. Here, as in the architecture of the town house, the trend in modern times has been gradually towards uniformity. The geographical factor implies that the rural house is bound to the soil and, consequently, varies from region to region. The variety of French landscape is such that it has been possible to call France 'the land of a hundred types of houses' (J. Brunhes).

Four factors may link the rural dwelling to the region in which it is built:

(a) The nature of the soil, which determines the materials used for building. As a general rule these were materials found on the spot, very often the simple earth transformed into cob by mixing it with straw and setting it up within a wooden frame. Even in such an area as Picardy, whose wealth of hard materials has been mentioned earlier in this book, the peasant did not, at a time when there were no good roads, go to the trouble or expense of looking in the quarries for solid stone or plaster. So we still see many houses built of earth today. The round pebbles of the river-beds, the shingle of the beaches, and the flints of the cliffs often give them, as in the Caux region, a greater solidity and a certain variety of surface. Then brick kilns were set up when it became possible to transport coal, and the use of bricks spread everywhere. The appearance of houses thus became very similar over larger areas. It was only when stone was very near at hand, as in the Soissonnais, Valois, Touraine, the Sénonais, and Périgord, that it was exploited – some houses in these areas could pass for palaces. Elsewhere, in wooded country (Argonne, the Alps), timber was the material preferred. But it too gave place to stone and brick. The importance of geography thus tends to be eliminated and the materials of which the walls of the house are made do not always carry its mark. The same applies to the covering. In the grain and straw producing regions thatch was ready to hand. It also had intrinsic qualities – giving warmth, for example, as nothing else can do. Nevertheless, though cottages are still plentiful, they no longer have thatched roofs. The danger of fire and the very high premiums charged by insurance companies on houses with thatched roofs means that tiles and slates are now used almost exclusively.

(b) The influence of climate is less easily avoided. It determines the form of the roof, its slope, and the level to which it comes down. In some regions the roof reaches almost to the soil, as in the Basque country. In areas where the winter is very hard a steep pitch is used to prevent the snow remaining on it and crushing it. On the other hand, on the Mediterranean coast a terrace roof is adequate. Wind and damp also have to be counteracted. Rows of cypresses are planted in the Rhône valley and rows of beeches in the Caux district for this purpose, or, as in the Ardennes, a facing of planks or tiles is applied to the part of the house which is most exposed. Sometimes a coat of lime-wash is given to it, much as a boat is tarred.

Yet here again not only geographical influences are involved. J. Brunhes has drawn up a map showing how French roofs fall into two traditional types: the north and west have steeply sloping pointed roofs covered either with slates or flat tiles, with thatch, or even small panels of stone or wood; the south, especially the Mediterranean district, has a low roof very slightly pitched and covered with curved hollow tiles. The dividing line is rather vague and no absolute contrast between north and south can be found. There are some outstanding irregularities such as that the roofs of the Limousin and Auvergne, although in Languedoc, correspond to the north, and in Lorraine there is a correspondence with the south. The climatic influence is not unaffected by the historical. And all local differences tend gradually to decrease with the development of transport.

(c) The influence of the subsoil can be seen in the grouping or scattering of the buildings. Just as there are some parishes which seem to have no centre but are divided up into isolated farms, and some which are concentrated, so the buildings of a farmstead will sometimes be grouped together in a single, or at least coherent, block within a farm-yard, or scattered over a large meadow. In dry country and on a permeable soil the houses are generally crowded close to one another. But a scarcity of water adds greatly to the danger of fire. This perhaps explains why the farm buildings of the Caux region are scattered, since the wells are some 325 feet deep and surface water is preserved only in a few precious ponds.

(d) A final geographical influence, of an economic rather than a physical order (if the two can be separated), depends on the nature of the crops. The rural house is not only a shelter for man, it is also the place where he works. Besides him and his family it has to shelter his animals, his tools, his crops and stores. Hence it varies according to the use made of the soil. The vine-grower does not live in the same house as the stock-breeder, nor the latter in the same as a wheat-grower. It varies also according to the landholding system and the size of the property, whether it is a large, medium, or small farm.

We cannot attempt to study here the 'hundred' types of French country house. We shall confine ourselves to a few examples corresponding to the four basic types distinguished by A. Demangeon.

(a) 'The simplest and most economical plan is that which groups all the essential parts of the dwelling under the same roof.' This basic plan may be realized in two ways: by spreading in width or in depth.

The house built breadthwise is common in all parts of France. We find it in certain regions of the north (the Ardennes, Argonne, Thiérache, Hainaut, Cambrésis, etc.), in the Paris basin (the Champagne section of Brie, Morvan, Nivernais, Loiret), in Central France, and in the south. It is also the Provençal *mas*. With a long façade, this includes, on the ground floor, besides the main room used in common by master and servants, the stable for mules and goats, the cart-shed, the rabbit-hutch and fowl-house. The bedrooms are on the first floor, often reached by an outside staircase. Openings are few, for a cool temperature is appreciated. To this rather schematic description may be added a great red roof with two slightly inclined sides, the rose-coloured, ochre, or yellow plaster or rough-cast of the façade, the vine or the flowers shading it, and a stone bench accentuating the horizontal line.

(b) In contrast, the Lorraine house, also in one block, is placed with its narrowest side overlooking the road. A corridor separates the part reserved for the human dwellers from that for the livestock and crops; the former has a small door and the latter a high square one. Everything is on the ground floor, surmounted only by a granary under a great two-sided roof of slight inclination but projecting far out from the walls. The living rooms are squeezed into a narrow strip and the kitchen between two bedrooms, one facing the road, the other facing the court. Into this narrow framework many elements of rural life cannot be accommodated, for example the manure, firewood and timber, and the carts; they are stored out in the street, which in this way serves as the collective courtyard of the village.

(c) In other plans the house is separated from the road by an enclosure, a wall or hedge; its buildings give on to a court. There are two possible variants – sometimes they are grouped together, sometimes scattered. The farms of Picardy or the Brie region are perfect examples of the former type. In these regions farms are large concerns. The complex is enclosed by solid, even impressive walls, with few openings to the outside, to which a small tower sometimes gives the feeling of a peasant fortress. The cart door, the main opening, is framed by a depressed arch, sometimes capped with a roof of its own. In the centre of the court are the pond and the well. On one side is the house, consisting of a ground floor only with granary over it; it comprises at least a large kitchen, sometimes a dining-room, and two bedrooms. To right and left are the sheds, stables, byres, almost all with granaries above them. Each house, though similar to its neighbours, differs from it in height, mass, and arrangement of the openings; but generally the fine quality of the materials gives not only nobility but unity to the whole.

(d) The 'scattered' plan is exemplified by the farms of Caux. In the farmyard, a great meadow planted with apple trees, are scattered the various dwellings and farm buildings. Here we often find examples of half-timber and thatch, but they are gradually giving way to brick and slate.

Some of these rural dwellings are charming and even picturesque. Most of them are merely convenient – exactly fitting the needs they have to satisfy, and in perfect harmony with their geographical setting. But architecturally the house is sometimes less interesting than some of the buildings attached to it. On the whole, the peasant, especially in the northern regions, is content with strict necessities, especially in the north; less so in the south, in the vine-growing country, where we find those small luxuries, those superfluities, which place art above craft.

The animals and the crops are sometimes better served.

Very remarkable, although very primitive, are the sheep shelters to be found scattered over the Quercy plateaux: small round constructions covered with a corbelled dome. The technique is at once so simple and so perfect that it has been considered the prototype of certain church domes later classed as historical monuments. Barns or dovecots also are often real works of art. The most outstanding example of this rural architecture is not really architecture proper. It is the corn-rick, of which the two forms, round and square, reflect differences of soil and builder, and whose compact, harmonious mass translates, over and above the vicissitudes of daily life and the seasons, the ideas of permanence, duration, and plenitude, of that poetry which springs from the earth.

CHAPTER TWO

PUBLIC BUILDINGS

SOME kinds of public building are purely modern in conception, but there are others which have been in existence since the Middle Ages, when they were centres, some of religious, others of civic or civil life.

1. Town Halls, Market Halls, and Guildhalls

These three must of necessity be grouped together. Their historical origins are very closely related, often even identical. Municipal life is, in principle, an economic as much as a political fact. As J. Calmette has explained, the idea of mutual assistance developed a great deal in the second half of the Middle Ages. The insecurity caused by the invasions made people turn to the protection of the lords, whence arose the feudal régime. But the inadequacy of feudal protection and the abuses which it involved led the merchants, craftsmen, and people of a single city to group together to defend their common interests. The merchants' association was the first to appear. Towards the end of the Carolingian period commerce had become a perilous enterprise; to make long journeys by road men had to form caravans, that is, to assemble their goods under a leader. Back in the towns, such associations continued as guild, Hanse, or charity. Its headquarters, the *market hall*, was at once a meeting-place and a warehouse. The craftsmen's association was the corporation; this too had its headquarters. The communal organization is often an extension of the merchant association; in countries where commercial life is very intense, as in Flanders, England, or the north of France, market hall and town hall are one and the same building. This is the case at Ypres; in London the 'town hall' still bears the name of 'Guildhall'.

Let us examine some examples of each kind and trace their development.

¶ TOWN HALLS

In France the communal association generally began by buying a private house, which it adapted to its needs as best it could. The oldest French town hall, that of Saint-Antonin (Tarn-et-Garonne), was the house of a local nobleman called Archambauld – an interesting type of twelfth-century house in stone with sculptures of King Solomon and Adam and Eve tempted by the serpent – nothing, in fact, to indicate its character of a public service. The municipal council bought it in the thirteenth century and settled there. In the same way at Paris the council bought the Maison aux Piliers, in the Place de Grève, a house with its façade resting on arcades. At Beaugency the council settled in an inn as late as the sixteenth century. However, in most cases, special buildings, often of considerable size and luxury, were built in the end. The most famous are in Italy and Flanders; but there are some extremely interesting ones in France too.

A town hall has at least one meeting room for the aldermen or councillors and a balcony from which proclamations to the people can be made. Also, especially in the north, as in Italy, there was often a belfry, symbolizing the building's importance. The belfry was a square tower which in small communities could itself serve as the town hall. Its summit carried the bells, symbol of municipal authority; from the fourteenth century onwards a clock was put on it, sometimes with figures to strike the hours on the bells; popular figures, personifications of the city, such as Martin and Martine at Cambrai; at Dijon, Jacquemart and his wife, who were taken prisoner by Philip the Bold on the battlefield at Courtrai, to which they had been brought, and carried away as trophies. In large town halls there was also a chapel and sometimes even kitchens (Amiens, late fourteenth century), for elections gave occasion for great banquets.

The finest French town halls of the late Middle Ages were

in the north, at Arras, Bailleul, Bapaume, Compiègne, Douai, Noyon, Saint-Omer, Saint-Quentin, Valenciennes. Most of them were seriously damaged in the 1914 war. The most typical is perhaps that of Arras, which runs along one side of the Petite Place. It was rebuilt in the sixteenth century (1511–17), in imitation of that of Saint-Quentin; the great hall, with its balconied windows, took up the whole of the first floor; the belfry, 280 feet high, dominated the building, the square, and the city. Also to be noted are a few more modest, but extremely charming, town halls of the Loire valley – Lorris, Orleans, Angers, Saumur.

Towards the middle of the sixteenth century, in 1533, at the suggestion of François I, Paris decided to build itself a town hall in the fashion of the day. The work was long drawn-out, interrupted from 1551 to 1605, and completed only in 1628. This town hall was burned down in 1871 during the rising of the Commune. The identity of its author started one of the most violent polemics known in the history of art; some gave it to a French architect, others to an Italian. It now seems unquestionable that the plans and the design of the façade (modified in the upper parts) were provided by Domenico da Cortona, an Italian impregnated with the French spirit after staying forty years in France. It was the first building in Paris to be liberated from the Gothic style, and it represents also the first intervention of the monarchy in Parisian architecture.

Subsequently the classical period included among town halls some of its most interesting works, often by the greatest architects. That of La Rochelle, rebuilt between 1595 and 1606, is one of the most characteristic secular buildings of the reign of Henri IV. Puget carved the medallion of Louis XIV for the façade of the town hall of Marseilles and heavy, sumptuous caryatids for that of Toulon (1656). Jules Hardouin-Mansart rebuilt, after 1674, the town hall of Lyons and perhaps provided the plans for that of Arles, in which the vault of the vestibule is admirably cut.

In the eighteenth century, the great movement for the embellishment of cities led quite naturally to the construction of new town halls. Sometimes they were simply bourgeois dwellings on the same pattern as the rest but more ornate (Avallon, Saulieu, Noyers in Burgundy). But elsewhere they fit into a grander plan, bordering on great open spaces. At Beauvais (1752), at Aire-sur-la-Lys, they form the principal motif in the main square; at Metz, the town hall (Jacques-François Blondel, 1766) faces the cathedral, on the other side of the new Place d'Armes; at Rennes (Jacques Gabriel, 1744), at Nancy (Héré), and at Toulouse (Cammas, 1760) the town hall is part of a royal square, of the architectural framework designed for a statue of the sovereign. They are broad buildings of three storeys – basement, *piano nobile*, and attic – and with finely proportioned façades marked by classical order and majesty.

In the nineteenth century the turning of church property to secular uses furnished many municipalities with vast premises at slight cost. The municipal headquarters of Bordeaux were set up in the old Archbishop's Palace and those of Rouen in the Abbey of Saint-Ouen. But in the twentieth century the period between the two wars saw a growth of new town halls, especially in the cities in which there was a rapid increase in population, as in the suburbs of Paris and Lyons. Their purpose, too, has been considerably extended since the Middle Ages. It is no longer simply a question of providing halls for council meetings and accommodation for a few clerks. From the nineteenth century the introduction of civil registration has made a marriage hall obligatory, sometimes combined with a banquet and entertainment hall. To-day many public services are conducted from the town hall, and offices for the staff, waiting rooms, enquiry desks, etc., for the public are therefore necessary; sometimes the public library is annexed to the town hall, and sometimes also the local police court and the police station with its gaol. The most typical example is perhaps the new town hall of Boulogne-Billancourt (Tony Garnier and Debat-Ponsan, 1934), strictly formal, exploiting to the utmost the resources of reinforced concrete, a vast trellis-work, in which the only solids are the pillars. The penalty for this design – penalty in the strict sense of the word

– is paid by the taxpayer in the heavy coal or fuel-oil bill which the heating of these glass-houses involves.

¶ GUILDHALLS

Although in Belgium and England there are many examples of the fine buildings of the professional guilds, hardly any are found in French architecture. Nothing remains from the sixteenth century; the seventeenth-century classical façade of the Drapers' Hall (Jean Marot) has been transferred to the Musée Carnavalet. The trade-union movement of the late nineteenth and early twentieth centuries has given us no major works. In Paris, the Cercle de la Librairie, by Charles Garnier, is worthy of note for its staircase, as if it were meant only for a series of social receptions.

We can, however, attach to this group – to avoid almost a complete lack of examples – the Loge de Mer at Perpignan, a sort of commercial Exchange of the kind found at that time throughout Catalonia, fine examples of which survive in Barcelona and Palma de Majorca – a building designed to be at once a place of business and a warehouse for merchandise. Begun in 1397, it has unhappily been so altered inside and out that it has lost all significance.

Hurrying through the centuries we can mention here Soufflot's Loge des Changes (1747–9) in Lyons, and the Bourse des Valeurs (Brongniart, 1808) in Paris. The latter bears the mark of another period, more preoccupied with appearance than with satisfying practical needs. Its appearance is that of an antique temple. The Bourse is the temple of money. Napoleon wanted it to be 'noble and magnificent'. With its sixty-four Corinthian columns, fourteen of them on the façade, it is one of the largest buildings of the imperial capital, but is in no way appropriate to its purpose.

¶ COVERED MARKET PLACES

France has no market halls comparable to that of Ypres. Their purpose in France was more modest, to give shelter from the rain to tradesmen who would otherwise have had to remain in the street. Sometimes they are no more than galleries leaning against a church (Bar-sur-Aube, church of Saint-Pierre). Even in a more complete form they are only covered buildings like large sheds, but without walls. The oldest which have survived have merely a timber roof supported by wooden posts, or piers built in stone. At the most some of them have a gable of masonry, the other walls remaining open, as at Crémieu (Isère), Saint-Pierre-sur-Dives (Calvados), or Egreville (Seine-et-Marne). But the market hall of Crémieu (fifteenth century) seems like a real triple-aisled cathedral. In southern France, at Montréjeau for example, the central and upper part of the hall, built in the Place de la Bastide, is reserved for the municipal administration.

In this rudimentary form these buildings could hardly interest the masters of architecture. But much later, towards the end of the eighteenth century, there was a change of spirit. From 1770 onwards the Académie d'Architecture included projects for market halls in its competitions. In 1792, on the eve of its dissolution, it set as subject a public market, with the following comment – the competitors 'will mark on the plan easy approaches by various streets; this market 'will be divided into several parts for the sale of different articles, bread, meat, fish, vegetables, fruit, etc.' Jacques-François Blondel made a special study of the subject in his *Cours d'Architecture* (1771; vol. II, chapter ix).

Moreover we soon find the conflict between progressive and traditional architecture starting up, over the Halle aux Blés. This market, built between 1763 and 1767 on the site of the old Hôtel de Soissons, was a rotunda, with arcades surrounding an open court. As early as 1783 it had been suggested that this central part should be covered in. Bélanger and Deumier had proposed a dome on wrought iron trusses, covered with sheets of copper. Molinos and Legrand prevailed with a dome in light wood. The building was burnt in 1802 and the problem arose once more. Five plans were presented, including that of Bélanger, still upholding the use of metal. A

commission of architects with Monge as its president declared
that 'everything combines to make us reject this kind of para-
sitic construction', and proposed a stone dome. It needed
the intervention of the Minister and the Emperor to decide on
an iron skeleton covered with tin-plated copper. An imperial
decree of 4 September, 1807, also appointed Bélanger as the
architect. And yet the Bourse is exactly contemporary, which
proves that the period did not regard its bread and its money
in the same light.

It was again over a market, the Central Markets (Halles
Centrales) that the first great battle over iron construction
raged, under Napoleon III. As early as 1842, under Louis
Philippe, the prefect Rambuteau had decided on its replacement. Baltard had planned it and had it accepted as a great
stone market. The first pavilion, built and inaugurated in
1853, aroused violent criticism. So heavy was it in aspect that
it was nicknamed 'le Fort de la Halle' (a pun on the name given
to market porters). The Emperor intervened, had it all
demolished and decided that the new markets should be in
iron and cast-iron. A very interesting study had been completed by the architect Horeau, now undeservedly forgotten,
who played the part of a pioneer throughout this period.
Horeau brought about the triumph of metal, but not of his
own plans, for Haussmann succeeded in keeping Baltard as
architect. The latter treated metal in a traditionalist spirit;
cast-iron columns with capitals supporting arcades decorated
with a frieze of palmettes. At least the general plan, with its
trusses of wrought iron spanning passages 100 feet wide and
its immense cellars, was highly appropriate for its purpose.
Ten pavilions out of the dozen that had been proposed were
built under the Second Empire, from 1854 onwards. The city
of Paris undertook the last two in 1934. In spite of a few not
too sweeping criticisms (the pavilions were compared to
umbrellas), the Halles were very much admired at the time.
Viollet-le-Duc praises them in his *Entretiens sur l'architecture*
(1872). 'The city of Paris', he says, 'can only congratulate itself
on having engaged one of its most renowned architects to
carry out the ideas and projects of an engineer for the central

markets.' Only the site chosen, which brought a confusion of traffic and untidiness to the centre of the city, merited all the criticism brought against it; but that is a problem of another order, of town planning, and not of architecture, and we shall come back to it later.

The period from 1870 to 1920 was the iron age for markets. Then reinforced concrete made its appearance. One of its first results, and among the most interesting in France, is the market hall of Reims by Maigrot (1930), with fine feeling for space, skilfully realized in the 130-foot wide nave without interior supports, and an ingenuity demonstrated in numerous matters of detail.

One plan, essentially modern and one of the best contemporary ideas derived from this general principle, is that of the department store. One could, indeed, trace its ancestry back to the late eighteenth century in the Portiques du Temple, praised by Legrand and Landon in their *Description de Paris*, or the Cour Batave, which they also mention, and which survived until Haussmann's day. But it was under the Second Empire that the vogue began. Zola described it in his novel *Au Bonheur des Dames*. The oldest store is the *Bon Marché*, built by Boileau in 1876. Iron plays an important part in its construction. The first application of the present formula, with the great hall rising straight from ground floor to roof, was the *Printemps* of Paul Sédille (1881–9). It is basically the same, though executed by other means for another end, as the great hall of the Opéra by Garnier. In 1905 Binet elaborated the idea, developing the hall further and creating open façades in the new stores of the *Printemps*, burnt down in 1921. The building which replaced them (Plumet and Selmersheim) may pass as a masterpiece of its kind in the logic and simplicity of its arrangement, the admirable clarity of the plan which can be taken in at a glance, and its magnificent spaciousness. In the meantime, at the *Samaritaine*, Frantz Jourdain (1905), hindered by the necessity of integrating several small new buildings with the main block as they were bought up, was taking on a thankless task. The building is of value chiefly as an example of the decoration in vogue between 1900 and 1910.

The French provinces saw one of the boldest experiments in the Decré stores at Nantes (Sauvage, 1931), with the outer walls made entirely of glass.

II. Hospitals and Educational Establishments

Hospitals and schools are here grouped together because both derive in principle from monastic architecture. Until 1789, teaching and social service were among the duties of the clergy, just as were religious services. The actual buildings of hospitals and schools were for a long time no more than monastic buildings adapted for a special function. The principle of the plan we have seen already – rooms grouped round a court, often surrounded by arcades like a cloister.

¶ HOSPITALS AND ALMSHOUSES

While the monastic organization was in existence, it afforded assistance to the sick, the needy, even the ordinary traveller without shelter. We have spoken of the hospice of the convent. In addition to this, since charity is one of the primary duties of the Christian, houses were very soon set up outside the monasteries to care for the suffering. The origin of these great town hospitals is very old. The Hôtel-Dieu in Paris seems to go back to the seventh century, when, in about 651, Bishop Landry had a house built near his own, in which sick priests were cared for by 'their brothers, the canons'. It has in fact always remained under the wing of the cathedral church.

The number of these hospital buildings increased all the more quickly since many people, when dying, bequeathed their homes, together with a perpetual income for their upkeep, to the Church for the accommodation of the sick. On other occasions the income was bequeathed without a house. The result was a great many hospitals, some of them very small. Towards the end of the Middle Ages an effort was made to amalgamate them, several bequests being put together for the upkeep of one house.

The main development was from the private house converted into a hospital to buildings erected expressly to serve as hospitals. Since the service was entrusted to religious communities, the buildings were naturally inspired by the monastic lay-out – a court, usually enclosed by galleries, on to which opened the wards, the service buildings (kitchen, pharmacy, laundry) and the lodgings for the religious.

The new element here was the ward. It was generally planned like a church, in that the dimensions were sometimes the same – 250 to 300 feet long by 65 feet wide – and the same problems arose over the covering. It was sometimes vaulted and sometimes had an open timber roof. Both types are found in France. The hospital at Angers, founded in 1153, still has a great hall planned like one of the local churches, divided by two rows of columns into three aisles and covered by dome-shaped rib-vaults. The hospital of Tonnerre, founded in 1293 by Marguerite of Burgundy, wife of Charles of Anjou the brother of Saint Louis, has another (330 feet long and 60 feet wide), covered by a magnificent open timber roof with king-posts and tie-beams. One end of the room was often converted into a chapel, without a separating screen, so that the altar could be seen from all the beds. Generally it was not possible to give every patient a bed to himself; often there were two in each, less frequently three.

Few remains of medieval hospitals have survived in France, and the French are perhaps less fortunate than their neighbours of Belgium, Italy, and Spain, which have the Saint-Jean hospital in Bruges, the Innocenti in Florence, and the great Catalan hospitals, less picturesque and less famous but more typical, of Vich and Barcelona. We have, however, the great wards of Angers and Tonnerre, mentioned before; and even more important is the Hôtel-Dieu at Beaune, founded in 1443 by Nicolas Rolin, chancellor of Burgundy, and inaugurated in 1451, which offers a complete fifteenth-century complex, still in use under the same religious order which undertook to care for it from the first. Rolin, in his foundation charter, declares that it is established on the model of that at Valenciennes. A charming courtyard, surrounded by wooden arcades with a wooden gallery on the first floor, is flanked by the Great

Ward for the sick, covered by a huge wooden roof, like an upturned keel. The windows are set high up, so as to allow ample ventilation without harming the patients. The hall measures 235 × 45 feet, and almost half of it is given up to the chapel. Rolin had planned for thirty beds. We know that in 1501 there were thirty-one with two patients in each. Also overlooking the court are the kitchen, with its great hooded chimney and its turn-spit worked by a small mechanical figure, the pharmacy, and the council room.

From the seventeenth to the nineteenth century the application and elaboration of this plan can be followed, naturally with the differences of style introduced by each period in the structure and furnishing of the buildings: the Hôpital Saint-Louis, the Salpêtrière, and the Invalides in Paris in the seventeenth century; the Hospice de la Charité at Mâcon, the Hôtel-Dieu at Lyons (façade by Soufflot), the Hôpital Beaujon in Paris, etc., in the eighteenth. Only two examples need be examined, corresponding to the two possible methods of developing the system – the placing of the elements side by side or their amalgamation.

The Hôpital Saint-Louis, built between 1607 and 1612 after the plans of Claude Chastillon as an annexe of the Hôtel-Dieu in Paris for contagious diseases, is a perfect technical success. The problem, which was to avoid all contagion, and hence all communication between the patients and the outside world, was very ingeniously resolved. The hospital is made up of a series of buildings enclosed one within the other, housing successively, from the centre outwards, the patients, the nursing staff, and the catering services. The central court, a square of about 330 feet a side, is completely enclosed by the four great blocks for the patients. It is surrounded at a distance of 100 feet by a second wall, against which are the staff quarters, the stores, the wash-houses and storerooms. Finally, 150 feet further on, there is the last wall, enclosing within the hospital precincts the kitchen and bakehouse, which have to be supplied from outside, but which themselves have no access to the inner quarters, the provisions being passed through a revolving hatch. The chapel straddles the outer wall and is built in such a way that people from without can have access to the nave only, and those from within only to the choir, without intercommunication being possible.

The other method, in which the courts are placed side by side, is perfectly demonstrated in the Invalides, a hospice designed for aged disabled soldiers who had been previously lodged in monasteries. Its erection was first decided upon on 24 May, 1670, the foundation stone laid on 30 November, 1671, the inmates installed in 1676. The architect was Libéral Bruant and the building is self-contained together with its chapel, the Soldiers' Church. The Dome Church, behind it, was subsequently added by Jules Hardouin-Mansart (1679–1706). The plan as a whole, which is reminiscent of the Escorial, includes in the entrance axis a central court surrounded by a two-storeyed covered colonnade framing the façade of the chapel at the end. On either side are two series of courts separated by rectilinear buildings. The whole is highly appropriate to its function. Its architecture is solemn, even severe. The main façade, which stretches for more than 650 feet, remains perfectly clear, though it is more complicated than the normal arrangement of the classical centuries – ground floor, three storeys, and a roof with dormer windows, in all five divisions. A greater height was needed to balance such a width. The only decorative motif, the central pavilion, higher than the rest, is dominated by a great curved pediment which once framed the equestrian statue of Louis XIV by Guillaume Coustou. The court of honour is finer still. The elevation is simpler, with only two superimposed colonnades and the great roof with dormer windows; in the middle of each side a slight projection with triangular pediment clearly marks the central axis. There are no antique orders, except in the portal of the chapel; and battle trophies decorate the dormer windows. Of monastic and military severity, it is the true expression of the spirit of a period which was all nobility and self-control.

The eighteenth century, while making a contribution to hospital architecture and taking into account the progress of hygiene, did not modify these plans. Only the façades and decoration changed with the taste of the period; archaeological whims are evident in the Cochin hospital (1780), in the Doric portal of Antoine's Charité, and in the Beaujon hospital (1784).

Of modern hospitals only two need be mentioned, representing the two formulas between which the hospital architect hesitates to-day. The Boucicaut hospital, built in the last years of the nineteenth century, is made up of bungalow pavilions scattered over a large area. It is a garden-hospital, spreading sideways rather than up. The new Beaujon hospital at Clichy (Walter, 1934) with its twelve storeys is, on the contrary, the skyscraper hospital. An advantage is facility of service; the possible drawbacks, particularly the danger of contagion, are reduced to a minimum by modern isolation technique.

¶ EDUCATIONAL ESTABLISHMENTS

Although we have a fair knowledge of university organization and sometimes even of student life in the Middle Ages, the architectural setting has almost always disappeared. The colleges of the University of Paris, even the Sorbonne, are now no more than names. Of the fifteen or more colleges, founded in the fourteenth and fifteenth centuries, mainly for poor students, which made up the University of Toulouse, only the Collège Saint-Raymond remains standing, and even this was rebuilt by Louis XII and restored by Viollet-le-Duc to serve as a museum. The buildings of the University of Orleans were demolished in the mid nineteenth century, except for a reading room, traditionally but incorrectly known as the Salle des Thèses; it is divided into two spacious aisles by a row of three columns, but has no features characteristic of its function. For the Renaissance we are no better off. There is nothing comparable to the riches of Oxford and Cambridge.

A history of scholastic architecture in France would begin only with the seventeenth century, when Henri IV authorized the work of the Jesuit fathers (1603). The Society then proceeded to erect numerous colleges throughout the country, many of them the work of its temporal coadjutor, Father Étienne Martellange (1569–1641). Most of them are still in use as high schools (*lycées*) or secondary schools. The buildings were grouped round several courts. At La Flèche, for instance, there were the classroom court, the boarders' court, and the Fathers' or masters' court. In 1629 Richelieu began the re-building of the Sorbonne by his architect Lemercier; only the chapel and the arrangement of the buildings round the court of honour remain. Mazarin left instructions in his will for a building which would be the architectural reply to Riche-lieu's Sorbonne. This became the Collège des Quatre-Nations (now the Institut de France, pl. 23), designed to house and instruct sixty young men from the provinces acquired by the Treaties of Westphalia and the Pyrenees (Artois, Franche-Comté, Roussillon, Pignerol). The college is one of the great works of Le Vau (1662–70). The ground plan was difficult to lay out, since the site was long and narrow. Here the buildings are grouped round two courts, but the great achievement lies in the court of honour, one side of which, as at the Sorbonne, is formed by the lateral façade of the chapel, balanced on the opposite side by that of the Library (Bibliothèque Mazarine). On the exterior of this nar-row group Le Vau applied a façade with the chapel at its centre, but a large portion of this was set up with almost nothing behind it, without even a moral relation to the College since shops were set up there.

From the seventeenth century again comes the Paris Observatory by Perrault (1668–72), an institution of scientific research if not of actual instruction, in which the architect concentrated more on the façade than on its functional use, despite the protests of the director, Cassini.

The eighteenth century would deserve a place of honour in this history by virtue of two buildings alone, which were care-fully planned with a view to their function; the École Militaire and the École de Chirurgie. The programme of the École Militaire, intended for five hundred cadets plus a staff of instructors, had been set forth in a long and very remarkable report by the financier and statesman Pâris-Duverney. The architect Gabriel worked on the basis of this report from 1750. All details were provided for, even the hygienic arrangements, which was rare at the time. 'It would not be possible,' read the text, 'to put so many people into a single building, and even were it possible, it should be avoided by reason of the discomforts and inconveniences which are inseparable from all houses where the inhabitants are, so to speak, piled on top of one another. We cannot be too pre-occupied with maintaining pure air in such a house and keeping away from it everything which might become noxious, because its function must be to mould the character together with the mind and heart. This then is our conception of the ordering and distribution of the buildings which are to make up the college.' There follows an extremely detailed study in which are considered successively the apartments of the staff and administrator, the class-rooms and all the rooms to be used for instruction, the great hall where the cadets deposited their weapons after the daily exercise, the refectories and kitchens, the rooms of the cadets, private rooms, since, says the report, 'it is absolutely necessary to avoid communal rooms in an establishment of this kind. The rooms of the cadets will be large enough to allow them ten to twelve feet square or twelve feet long by ten wide.' An officer's room to the right and left of every ten rooms ensured discipline. Then there were the chapel, the infirmaries, the riding school, the stables, and all the annexes. The work, begun in 1751, was slow; the roofs were not laid until 1771; the chapel was finished even later. The whole group is, moreover, comparable in size to the Invalides. It is the masterpiece of Gabriel, both for its simple, clear lay-out and the beauty of its architecture. The façade to the Champ-de-Mars, with its central pavilion capped by a four-sided dome, is the best known; unfortunately, its proportions were spoilt later by new blocks which lengthened it too much. The interior façade to the great court is the most perfect. The two superimposed colonnades of the Invalides are met with once more, but only on one side, for the court is open, the central block being prolonged by two lower wings. The stairs, the chapel, the so-called Marshals' Hall are the parts most generally admired.

L'Académie de Chirurgie (the former Guild of the Barber-Surgeons) commissioned Gondoin in 1769 to undertake the building of the École de Chirurgie at about the same time that Soufflot was beginning the École de Droit (1771) opposite the Panthéon. The more specialized plan of the École de Chirurgie included a dissecting theatre. It was a period of great enthusiasm for the archaic, Roman and even Etruscan, and Gondoin's imagination, fired by the word *amphitheatre*, conjured up the memory of the Colosseum. From it he took the passages and exits. The façade over the court is a less severe portico with six Corinthian columns and the inscription justifying the building's purpose: *Ad caedes hominum prisca amphitheatra patebant* – it was for the death of men that the ancients erected their amphitheatres.

The nineteenth century was for a long time content to draw on the very rich architectural resources bequeathed by the religious communities. Many *lycées* were housed in secularized monasteries – the Lycée Malherbe at Caen is the old Abbaye-aux-Hommes, the Lycée Henri IV in Paris is the Abbey of Sainte-Geneviève, etc.

It was really only with the Third Republic that new buildings for all grades of education were begun. It is possible to give only a few examples – for primary education the charming *École Maternelle* in Paris by Louis Bonnier (1911); for the high schools, the Lycée Buffon by Vaudremer (1889); for the University Faculties, the new Sorbonne by Nénot (1900); three works as different in purpose as in spirit. After 1914 increasing use was made of concrete for the skeletons of buildings, generally hidden beneath a brick facing. The influence of contemporary Dutch architecture is often considerable. In Paris the School of Infant Welfare in the Boulevard Brune, in Lyons the new Faculty of Medicine, are among the most characteristic works, aiming above all at simplicity of form and a design appropriate to the function they are to fulfil.

To school buildings may be added libraries. In Paris the Bibliothèque Sainte-Geneviève by Labrouste (1850) is one of the first buildings in which iron and cast-iron were used on a large scale, hidden in the lower part by a simple, powerful stone façade. The erection of the storehouses at Versailles for the Bibliothèque Nationale (Roux-Spitz, 1932–4) was made possible only by reinforced concrete.

III. Theatres

The modern theatre plan, a semi-circular hall and stage set within a closed and covered building, did not appear in France until the second half of the eighteenth century. Jacques François Blondel, in his *Cours d'Architecture* (1771), deplores French inferiority in this sphere: 'M. de Voltaire has expressed it well: the ancient Romans produced architectural marvels in which to fight wild beasts, and for a century now we have had no reasonable hall in which to present the masterpieces of the human mind. The Comédie-Française is the national theatre; there is no one who does not feel the necessity of a theatre for this company.' The prototypes were in Italy, particularly since Palladio and the theatre of Vicenza. About 1750, the chevalier de Chaumont was commissioned to 'make a survey at the King's expense of the various theatres in Italy'.

In 1763 the Paris Opéra in the Palais-Royal was burnt. Soufflot and Gabriel were commissioned to build a temporary hall in the Tuileries, adapting the former Salle des Machines used under Louis XIV for ballet. Inaugurated in 1764, it had little success, despite the reputation of its architects. The spectators complained that they could not see anything. At the same time Gabriel was working alone on the Opera House at Versailles (1753–70). For the traditional horseshoe plan he substituted the more logical U-form; the visibility and acoustics were praised unanimously; in addition the decoration itself was a marvel of taste and style which is still universally admired to-day.

But in these two cases the theatre was only one element in a greater architectural whole. The problem of the independent theatre, of the building devoted exclusively to stage representations, was faced and solved at Bordeaux by Louis (1773–80). This included not only the stage and hall for the audience, but a whole section set aside for reception – the vestibule, the foyer, the great double-flighted staircase. As to the building itself, Louis had the idea of surrounding it with a colonnade, so that it would have had the appearance of an antique peripteral temple. This was the classical period; the same formula served for the theatre, the church (the Madeleine), and the market (the Bourse). Louis's classicism is florid. That of Peyre and Wailly at the Odéon in Paris (1779–82; originally the Comédie-Française) is more severe. Then a number of theatres appeared simultaneously – at Besançon (Ledoux, 1777); at Nantes (Crucy, 1778); at Amiens (Rousseau, 1778–80). The antique hall-mark may be reduced to a façade, sometimes simply to a portico of four columns (in Paris, the Variétés, 1807, and later, the Gymnase).

The Opéra at Versailles and the theatre at Bordeaux are major works and representative of the eighteenth century. The Paris Opéra is their equivalent in the nineteenth century, the Théâtre des Champs-Elysées in the twentieth. In the Paris Opéra (1861–75) Charles Garnier merely amplified the programme outlined by Louis, but transformed the exterior appearance and adopted a new decorative style. The work is, indeed, characterized by the following factors:

(a) its precise adaptation to a given purpose – a place of official and social gatherings to which people go as much to be seen as to see. A hall lined with boxes in which visits can be paid and received; an enclosure with a foyer for those who have reserved seats for the season (Foyer de la Danse); an immense entrance hall for the reception of the public and the movement of official processions; vast corridors, the great foyer for the audience running the whole length of the façade, a staircase in the hall reaching from the ground floor to the very top of the building, giving a view of all the hall at one glance;

(b) the appearance of the exterior, which is modelled on the internal plan; the freedom of arrangement which clearly outlines and distinguishes the various parts of the building, instead of enveloping them in an indiscriminate cloak;

(c) a luxurious decoration which now perhaps seems in bad taste because it is no longer fashionable, but which has a historical value, for it was peculiar not only to a single architect but to a whole society; a wealth of materials almost attaining vulgarity (marble, porphyry, bronze, gilt plaster); a confusion of ornaments borrowed from every period (antefixae, palmettes, antique caryatids) but above all from the Venetian Renaissance, that is, eclecticism. And for this decoration Garnier called on the greatest names of the period, notably Baudry and Carpeaux.

The Théâtre des Champs-Elysées (1911–13), the work of the brothers Perret, inaugurated on the eve of the First World War, is the first theatre in which concrete was used for the skeleton, though it is faced with very fine marble. Its simplicity of line astonished a period accustomed to greater exuberance. There was talk of imitation of foreign art. Forain called it 'the Zeppelin of the Avenue Montaigne'. In reality the work has a great deal of decoration and nothing of manifest 'functionalism'. It is simply a work of good sense and good taste in the French tradition. A. Perret had entrusted the decoration of the façade to the sculptor Bourdelle and that of the interior to the painters Maurice Denis, Vuillard, and Roussel. The innovation lies in the plan and the structure. There are three stages set one over the other – an opera hall, which keeps and even accentuates the customary semi-circular outline (93 feet 6 inches in diameter, 2,100 seats), a theatre hall (750 seats), and a small theatre (studio) originally intended as an exhibition room, later used as an experimental theatre (250 seats). Technically, the keynote of the whole is four groups of four concrete piers, 80 feet high.

IV. International Exhibitions

There are many other types of public building, both traditional (law courts, prisons, cemeteries, public baths, etc.) and new (railway stations, aerodromes, post offices, banks, factories, etc.). There is not space to do more than mention them, but we must examine in a little more detail the buildings of the great international exhibitions. Though many of them lasted only a short time, they have frequently served as models or demonstrated new principles, and they have always expressed the tendencies of their period. In no other group can we so easily follow the evolution of French architecture within the last hundred years.

The three exhibitions of 1855, 1867, and 1889 were first and foremost three great proclamations of the victory of metal construction. For that of 1855 the emperor wanted a palace 'based on the plan of the Crystal Palace in London', which had housed the Great Exhibition of 1851. So Arderin built the Palais de l'Industrie, after plans by Alexis Barrault and designs by Viel – a vast parallelogram 820 feet long and 350 feet wide, covering, with its four annexed pavilions, an area of 13½ acres. In the centre, an aisle 540 feet long, 160 feet wide, and 115 feet high was covered by semi-circular trusses with a span of 80 feet, resting on columns of cast-iron. The effect was very fine. Unfortunately, the metal was clad in a shell of masonry in the heaviest of styles and the building was badly situated, bordering the Champs-Elysées and completely blocking the view of the Invalides. It was demolished in 1900.

The Exhibition of 1867 was situated in the Champ-de-Mars, a vast metal construction made up of concentric galleries cut through by radiating galleries. Each circle was assigned to a particular branch of industry (machines, raw materials, clothing, furniture, the liberal arts, etc.); the radiating passages separating the sections assigned to the different countries. This admirable plan had been conceived by F. Le Play, general organizer of the Exhibition. The actual building, due to Krantz and Eiffel, used iron almost exclusively. From this work Eiffel gathered the data for his famous memorandum on the elasticity of assembled pieces of metal.

Finally, the Exhibition of 1889 brought the Galerie des Machines and the Eiffel Tower. The site of the former, again badly chosen, ran parallel to the École Militaire, at the end of the Champ-de-Mars, hiding it completely from view. But technically it was a perfect success – its immense aisle, 380 feet wide, 150 feet high, and 1,400 feet long, covered by great metal girders, met with general admiration. The tower was to make the name of Eiffel famous. It was erected between 28 January, 1887, and 31 March, 1889. Its 980 feet constituted for a long time the record height achieved by a human construction. The project brought protests from a group of artists and writers, to whom Eiffel replied. But its success with the public was immediate and the Tower, which is still standing, has neither dwarfed nor humiliated the traditional monuments of Paris.

The Exhibition of 1900 marked a turning-point in French and a new phase in modern architecture, which in fact came to be called the style of the nineteen-hundreds. Iron was abandoned either for stone in buildings intended to last (the Grand and the Petit Palais) or for stucco and plaster, light, cheap materials, for temporary erections. But the essential characteristic was the triumph of a very exuberant decoration, as exuberant as Flamboyant Gothic or the Baroque, with elements borrowed from the vegetable world. Normally decoration derives from construction. In 1900 this was reversed: architects followed the decorators, and the lines of their buildings, like flower stalks bending with the wind, began to sway. The style of the nineteen-hundreds – then known in France as the 'modern style', and in England as 'Art Nouveau' – asserted itself in the Exhibition in Binet's monumental Gate; in the palaces of the Champ-de-Mars and the Invalides, in the furniture sections; but also outside the Exhibition, in the entrances of the underground railway, which had just been inaugurated; in various house and hotel façades, both in Paris (Castel Béranger, by Guimard, 14 rue La Fontaine; Ceramic-Hôtel, by Lavirotte, 34 avenue de Wagram) and at Nancy. Its inventors, Gallé and Majorelle, both came from that city. The Grand Palais and the Petit Palais, seemingly to stand for ever, were simply a return to the eclecticism of Charles Garnier. Nevertheless the Grand Palais, whose execution was divided into three lots, had in its interior, by

Louvet, a bold metal construction, a great glass house, which to this day serves for a large variety of crowded assemblies – exhibitions, horse shows, etc.

The 1914 war postponed the holding of another international exhibition until 1925. Then came the so-called Exhibition of the Decorative Arts. As the name suggests it gave first place to decoration and in part constituted a prolongation of the 1900 and modern style. But it also contained several bold assertions of the value of reinforced concrete. It brought into the limelight such names as Perret, Tony Garnier, Mallet-Stevens. In the *Esprit-nouveau* pavilion, Le Corbusier was preaching 'purism' and the total elimination of ornament.

The Exhibition of 1937 was perhaps of less significance; at least we have not yet grasped it. It certainly was of value for the clarity of its plan, the work of that master of town planning, J. Gréber. The errors of arrangement which had marred so many previous exhibitions were naturally avoided. The two remaining buildings, the New Trocadéro, called the Palais de Chaillot and the new Museum of Modern Art, both in reinforced concrete, have been variously judged.

CHAPTER THREE

THE TOWN AND TOWN PLANNING

THE architecture of a town is often called *town planning*, in spite of the fact that urban arrangement is immensely complicated, involving administration, traffic control, sanitation, and calling for the expertise not only of architects but of lawyers, engineers, surveyors, and doctors. The current equation of town planning and architecture shows that in the public opinion town planning is first and foremost architecture. This is perhaps an ideal; it is certainly not a reality. History shows us that in certain periods town planning was the affair of administrators, engineers, and surveyors, and that architects took no part in it. It is true that it also shows us that the result has generally been unfortunate.

The realm of urban architecture is the external appearance of the town, that is to say its plan and the placing of public open spaces, particularly squares. Man can dominate these features, on condition, of course, that he so desires, for it has very often happened that, showing no interest in it and letting the town take shape and grow by chance, he has become aware too late of the perils of a disorder no longer capable of remedy. Such an effort of organization, when it existed, was inspired by very varied factors – defence, traffic, hygiene, and beauty. It can almost be said that one or the other took the lead according to the period.

¶ THE MIDDLE AGES

Town planning was not invented in the nineteenth century or by Haussmann. Hellenistic and Roman towns were already masterpieces in this respect. And in many cases the birth and development of medieval cities were by no means left to chance.

Plan. The majority of French towns are of Gallo-Roman origin, that is to say, they were already in existence at the beginning of the Middle Ages – Paris, Lyons, Toulouse, Bordeaux, Reims, Arras, Orleans, Rouen, Tours, Dijon, Nîmes, etc., are among these. They have passed through the Middle Ages preserving more or less their original plan, formed by the right-angled crossing of a *cardo* and a *decumanus*, but, above all, expanding and being enriched by additions so substantial and so varied that generally we have difficulty in recognizing the early nucleus and its outline.

We need record only what happened in Paris. At the beginning of the Middle Ages the Gallo-Roman town, established principally on the left bank of the Seine, had been destroyed by the fires kindled by the great invasion of the third century. Paris got smaller, retreating to the Île de la Cité within the shelter of a surrounding wall. Outside this, small groups of buildings or suburbs gradually made their appearance. Some were of religious origin, villages set round the great abbeys of the outskirts of Paris: Saint-Germain-des-Prés, Sainte-Geneviève, Saint-Victor, Saint-Marcel, to the south; Saint-Germain-l'Auxerrois, Saint-Martin-des-Champs, and later the Temple, to the north. To the north, too, at the head of the bridge, there was a collection of merchants around the Place de Grève. To the south, a little later, grew the University. Thus, between the fifth and thirteenth centuries, the city spread in all directions. A conscious attempt was made to extend the city wall to take in progressively all these growths. In 1190 and 1210 Philip Augustus, and later Charles V at the end of the Middle Ages, marked out a new and ever vaster Paris; and their walls became so many concentric layers round the old Lutetian trunk. Their example was taken up by Louis XIII, Louis XVI, and Louis-Philippe. These three stages, the reduced, the enlarged, and the unified town may be recognized in the history of all the Gallo-Roman cities. Reims was formed by the joining together of the city and the suburb of Saint-Remi; Arras by that of the city, the suburb of Saint-Vaast, and a merchant community; Toulouse, by that of the city and the suburb of Saint-Sernin; Troyes by that of the city and a merchant community originating from the Champagne fairs; and so on.

Other towns are noticeably younger. Some have grown up within living memory (bathing resorts or garden cities). The seventeenth century saw the birth of Versailles, the sixteenth that of Le Havre. Nevertheless, a particularly great effort was made in creating new towns at the end of the Middle Ages, between the twelfth and fifteenth centuries. It was stimulated both by general economic factors such as the clearing and exploitation of land, often under the impetus of religious communities, and by two political factors: the Albigensian Crusade and the Hundred Years War.

The history of the French village is still far from being written. A study of its plan would be of considerable help. In a number of cases we find two main principles asserting themselves: envelopment and attraction. Envelopment takes place when a series of houses are erected round a building particularly precious either for its moral value or for its material solidity in relation to defence – generally, the church. The attraction of traffic by this building gives rise to a series of roads directed towards it. In this way is formed the type of pattern known to town planners as *radio-concentric*, that is, made up of radii and circles, like a spider's web. The design is naturally not very clear because it has been traced spontaneously without the use of rule or compass. For the most part this analysis applies only to humble villages, but the magnificent plan of Bram (Aude) is that of an already important rural township.

The new towns of south-west France have a more geometrical plan in a completely different spirit; chess-board fashion, their straight streets are parallel or at right angles to one another. A greater individual creative force can be seen in their history and the documents sometimes speak of the *Lotisséesurs*, that is the surveyors who marked out the plots. Originally they were a kind of colonial outposts founded, at the limits of their domains, either by the kings of France and the counts of Toulouse, opponents in the Albigensian war, or by the kings of France and the kings of England, neighbours and rivals on the confines of the Garonne and the Massif Central. Locally they were given the name of *bastides*. Many have remained district centres; others such as Montauban, Villefranche-de-Rouergue, Libourne, Carcassonne, have risen higher in the administrative hierarchy.

The two ruling ideas of the planners were to reserve a large open space for the market and to have plots with easily calculable surface areas; hence the rectangular blocks of houses with the public square and market in the centre. However, it would be incorrect to suppose that these plans – there are more than two hundred of them – are all the same and present the rigorous geometrical pattern of the American towns of the nineteenth century. The form of the block is very occasionally square (Mirande, Grenade-sur-Garonne), but more often rectangular, so that innumerable combinations of proportions as well as different rhythms are possible (Montpazier, Sainte-Foy-la-Grande). Sometimes also the straight line bends. Although it has occasionally happened that, regardless of the site, a rigid squaring has been imposed on a slope (Montflanquin, Lot-et-Garonne), other plans, such as those of Cordes or Montréjeau, with their lines following the curves of the slope, harmoniously combine the effort of art and the demands of nature.

Open spaces and squares. Except in these new towns, public open spaces and particularly squares were singularly restricted in medieval French towns. In the old Gallo-Roman cities the market was held in the open street. Even the church had no square in front of it; it was a house among houses. Surrounded on three sides either by a cemetery or by other buildings, it had only one façade to the street with, generally speaking, no open space of importance leading up to it. In Paris the churches of Saint-Merry and Saint-Séverin are still situated more or less like this – at the most they fill the corner at the meeting of two streets. The idea of creating a square whose ornament was to be provided by the church only appeared with the Renaissance in Italy and later still in France, since one of the first examples in Paris was the Place de la Sorbonne, in the mid seventeenth century.

Even the streets were generally anything but spacious, lined by arcades or narrowed by shop-stalls and the ever-increasing projections of the upper storeys of the houses. But this does not mean that these towns must be thought of as human ant-hills, quite deprived of air and light. If public open spaces were rare, private ones were many, particularly convent gardens. The town was still half rural. Poultry yards, rabbit hutches, stables and fields were close to the houses, and the agricultural calendars carved on the façades of the cathedrals did not represent an escape for the citizen, but an everyday reality.

In the new towns, on the other hand, not only were the streets wider (26 feet at Montpazier, while in Paris, in the same period, only one street reached 23 feet), but the squares were spacious. At Créon (Gironde) of a total of nine blocks, a whole one was given up to the square, roughly 11 per cent of the complete area. It was reached from the corners, not from the middle of the sides. The square was surrounded by arcades linked together so as to give the impression of an enclosed space. Some towns still have very fine examples of this pattern – Montauban (arcades rebuilt in the seventeenth century after the original design), Montpazier, Sainte-Foy-la-Grande, etc. – with narrow, oblique passages for carts at each corner.

Fortifications. Military architecture also had a part to play, though from the sixth to the eleventh century no fortifications were built. But before and after this period the surrounding wall was one of the essential elements of the town. It is again in the south that the finest examples have survived – at Carcassonne, Aigues-Mortes, Villeneuve-lès-Avignon. The fortifications of the city of Carcassonne include an inner rampart, erected by the Visigoths, dating back to the fifth century, and an outer rampart of the end of the thirteenth century. The first is 1,305 yards long; the second 1,638 yards. They are defended by sturdy towers of varying shape – round, square, and semi-circular. Between the two are the *lices*, open passages of variable width, on an average of 23 to 26 feet. Two gates only give access to the interior, the Porte d'Aude and the Porte Narbonnaise. Both, and especially the latter, are equipped with every means of defence – drawbridge, portcullis, and bartizan.

At Aigues-Mortes, St Louis had already built the tower of Constance when, in 1279, Philip the Bold concluded a treaty with the Genoese contractor Boccanegra, who undertook to erect the ramparts of the town. They form a slightly irregular rectangle, with a perimeter of about 1,640 yards. The walls, made of big stones carefully set and heavily rusticated, average 23 feet in height. They are flanked by fifteen towers, apart from the tower of Constance, placed externally in a rounded indentation.

The fortifications of Villeneuve-lès-Avignon, rather more recent, were started during the time of Philip the Fair, but were built mainly during the second half of the fourteenth century, to guard the frontier of the Languedoc region towards the Rhône. It is French work of which the finest and the most formidable element is the gate, framed between two enormous cylindrical twin towers (Towers of King John).

Among other French towns whose walls are still fairly well preserved we may mention the thirteenth-century ramparts of Provins; those of Avignon, of the fourteenth century (though these were in part destroyed in 1906); for the fifteenth century the important defences of the Breton towns, Guérande, Saint-Malo, Hennebont, Dinan, Vannes, Fougères, and Mont-Saint-Michel. Of the walls of Paris, built by Philip Augustus and Charles V, only scattered remains survive and not all are made the most of, such as the so-called Tower of John the Fearless in the rue Étienne-Marcel or a tower in the court of the Crédit Municipal, rue des Blancs-Manteaux. But certain miniatures, notably a page of the Breslau *Froissart*, give us a better idea of Charles V's ramparts.

¶ TOWN PLANNING IN THE CLASSICAL AGE

The period of classical town planning may be said to extend through the sixteenth, seventeenth, and eighteenth centuries, coming up even to 1815, for in this field the First Empire was no more than the executor of the Ancien Régime. The dominating factors in this period were aesthetic and theoretical considerations, the desire to make towns conform to a certain ideal of beauty. It may be noted, however, that in the eighteenth century, under the influence of England and Holland, practicality and the taste for comfort were not necessarily sacrificed to magnificence.

The principles. The principles of this classical town planning were laid down by sixteenth-century Italy; but France contributed largely to their perfection. The essential elements were:

(a) The straight line. It cannot be said that there were no straight streets in the Middle Ages since – as we have just seen – the rectilinear outline dominated the plan of the majority of the new towns. But this was merely the result of a division into rectangular plots considered as the simplest method, not the outcome of any theoretical adhesion to an ideal. On the contrary, classical town planning gave the straight line a theoretical superiority. It saw in it the very expression of human reason and will. Descartes has summed it up admirably: 'Thus these ancient cities which, having begun as small villages, have become with the passage of time large towns, are usually so badly planned that ... to see their curved and unequal streets one would say that it was chance, rather than the will of a number of men exercising their reason, which disposed them in this way' (*Discours de la Méthode*, second part); a mystical rather than a logical point of view, for there can be as much reason and geometry in a regular curve as in a straight line. This mysticism of the straight line did not, in any case, end with the eighteenth century. It was this, much more than preoccupation with the movement of traffic, which dictated Haussmann's vistas and which still inspires many town planners nowadays. They believe themselves freed from all dogmatic approach, while they are simply obeying the most academic routines.

(b) Monumental perspective. A rule which seems to have been admitted by all those who loved the beauty of towns is that in any street the eye must be arrested somewhere, must come to rest on something. Vistas must be limited. But there are several ways of satisfying this demand. It was met, quite naturally, in the old medieval towns, by the curved streets.

No more than a part of each street could be seen, and that never the same. The part displayed changed at every step. Those who have walked down the splendid curve of Oxford High Street know well the magnificent result that can be obtained by so simple and so elastic a design. For this natural limitation the classical town planner substituted a deliberate limitation, obtained by a monument built for the purpose – the Panthéon at the end of the rue Soufflot; the Madeleine at the end of the rue Royale; the Odéon theatre at the top of the rue de l'Odéon. Straight road and terminal building were the two elements necessarily linked in this aesthetic, for the combination underlined man's mastery and the character of work or art which he meant to give the town. One of the consequences of this principle was the transformation of the design of squares: openings in the middle of the sides were substituted for openings in the corners, and streets crossed in the centre, for a fine monument situated at this crossing provided terminal perspective for a greater number of streets. Another consequence was the layout of the town plan, or fractions of it, in which several streets converged towards the same building or radiated from it. In the Versailles of Louis XIV, three great avenues led up to the palace. Le Nôtre, who probably conceived this idea, wanted to reproduce it in the same period in Paris, in front of the Tuileries gardens – the Cours-la-Reine is one of the three avenues, the Champs-Élysées the second, and a third, symmetrical with the Cours-la-Reine, on the other side of the Champs-Élysées, remained a mere plan. On the other hand, the system is complete at the rear façades of the Invalides and the École Militaire. The finest example is the Place de l'Étoile, where twelve avenues radiate round the Arc de Triomphe.

(c) The programme. This is the term given to the obligation imposed on all the houses of a certain part of the town – street, square, district – to obey a given programme, that is, to conform to a general design. Although again an Italian invention, the finest applications of it are in France. One of the first examples there was carried out in Paris, when, between 1500 and 1510, the Pont Notre-Dame was rebuilt. It was still flanked by houses on both sides and all these had to be alike – brick with stone dressing and gables over the street, and a ground floor with arcades and shops. A hundred years later, at the beginning of the seventeenth century, when the rue Dauphine was created as a continuation of the Pont-Neuf, the inhabitants were ordered to 'make the fronts of their houses all in the same manner, for it would be a fine ornament to have at the end of the bridge this street forming one long façade'. The houses of the Pont Notre-Dame have disappeared; those of the rue Dauphine have ceased to observe the programme, if indeed they ever did conform to it; but the rue de Rivoli, on the west side, the work of Napoleon I, offers the finest example of the application of this principle.

¶ THE ROYAL SQUARES

It was on squares rather than on streets that the monarchy imposed a plan. The squares built in France in the seventeenth and eighteenth centuries represent the highest expression of classical town planning, above all those known as the royal squares, because they were meant to act as a setting for the statue of a sovereign. Unfortunately they have suffered greatly since they have lost the statues which were their justification, and not all have found an adequate substitute. They had been carefully set away from the main traffic currents, since it had been intended to ensure their calm and serenity, but the nineteenth century cut into them and exposed them to the noise of town and traffic. It did not recognize that supreme law which rules not only towns but all human activities – fitness for use. A street or a square cannot serve any purpose. There are great traffic arteries (*autostrade*, for example); there are streets for trade or residence; there are squares which are road-crossings and others which are stopping places. Neither the Middle Ages nor the classical period had made this mistake.

Paris has kept, though in a somewhat mutilated form, five royal squares: four are of the seventeenth century – the Place Dauphine, the Place des Vosges, the Place des Victoires, and the Place Vendôme, to which the eighteenth century added the Place de la Concorde. Most of the large French provincial towns also have one. They were so fine and became so well known that the rest of Europe borrowed the idea and the model.

The Place Dauphine occupies the western point of the Île de la Cité, which provides a resting-place for the Pont-Neuf on its way across the river. At the beginning of the seventeenth century there was only a stretch of waste land, the 'clean sheet' of which Descartes spoke, on which the mind could work at will. About 1605 the Place Dauphine was laid out on it, a triangle well adapted to the tapering form of the island. It had only two openings, one at the apex, the other at the base. All the houses were alike, built in brick and stone with slate roofs; the three storeys included a ground floor with filled-in arcading. The statue was that of Henri IV. It occupied the apex of the triangle, a position unique in the history of royal squares, but we are at the beginning of this history, and the final form was not to be found at the first experiment. Besides, the king was facing the square and not the river, which was enough to indicate the real link. What remains to-day of this delightful ensemble? The square has been broken open, the base of the triangle having disappeared in 1874 when the Palais de Justice was completed; the statue was overthrown during the Revolution, and that which is now in its place was re-established in the nineteenth century. As for the houses, rising to two, three, or four storeys, with their arcades broken, roofed in the most diverse ways, they no longer bear any relation to one another. Only the two skilfully restored houses at the apex, opposite the statue, show us the original pattern; but of the square as a whole we can have no idea except through engravings, particularly the fine plan of Paris attributed to Turgot (1737).

The Place des Vosges was for a long time called the Place Royale, as if it represented the royal square at its most perfect. Its design goes back to 1606, and the whole was completed in 1612. It is a square of about 500 feet a side, in which the houses have kept their uniform appearance; they are in brick and stone with open arcades on the ground floor forming a continuous covered walk; there are two storeys and dormer windows, and great slate roofs. Three corners of the square were closed in. A street ran out of the fourth corner, and two other streets ran from the centre of the main sides under two higher pavilions called the King's and the Queen's Pavilions. The statue was that of Louis XIII. Though the architectural ensemble remains intact a second corner has been opened up opposite the already existing one and traffic and a bus route now cross the square, which was so carefully isolated originally that one can go right through the rue Saint-Antoine just next to it, one of the great arteries of Paris, without suspecting its existence.

The Place des Victoires and the Place Vendôme are both dedicated to Louis XIV and are the work of the great classical architect, Jules Hardouin-Mansart. We have already met his work in the Dôme church at the Invalides, and in the greatest of the Grand Monarque's three Versailles. The architectural arrangement here becomes much more magnificent. We can hardly call these houses, for they are palaces, decorated this time with antique orders. The Place des Victoires, whose original plan, dated 1685, is in the Archives nationales, is circular. It was almost contemporary with the Place Royale at Dijon and the Bosquet de la Colonnade at Versailles, two other works by J. Hardouin-Mansart, all three being closely related in shape. The circle was broken into by three streets only. It was the most withdrawn of the royal squares, a kind of sanctuary of royalty. Night and day great torches burned before the statue. The formation of the rue Étienne-Marcel has made it to-day one of the busiest of Parisian crossroads. Mansart's façades have been transformed into shops and made gaudy with business signs. Nothing of the nobility of the square survives, any more than in the Place Dauphine. Seeing it now, we cannot even imagine what it was three centuries ago.

The Place Vendôme, on the other hand, has preserved its dignity, but it is greatly spoilt, even though its architecture has remained intact, by the Vendôme column, substituted for the statue, which does not harmonize in either style or proportions with the architectural background. Above all, Mansart's square was almost an enclosed space, a rectangle with the corners cut off, crossed by only one street which led almost immediately in each direction to two magnificent vistas – the portal of Orbay's Capuchin convent and the convent of the Feuillants, the church of which had a doorway by François Mansart. These were pulled down to allow of the formation of a great traffic artery from the boulevards to the Seine.

Several great provincial towns had also wished to dedicate a square to Louis XIV, for example Tours, Pau, Caen, Dijon, Lyons, Rennes, Montpellier. The square in Montpellier, transformed into a garden at the end of the eighteenth century, has become the Promenade du Peyrou. That of Lyons, now the Place Bellecour, has remained unfinished. The finest is the one at Rennes, designed by Jacques Gabriel at the time of the reconstruction of the town, after the great fire of 1721. It is a simple rectangle, at the end of which an older building, the Palais de Justice by Salomon de Brosse, was left standing; but the other three sides, planned by Gabriel with a great Ionic order over a high base, though almost unknown, can be counted among the most perfect works of French architecture. In them can be seen the part played by town planning in the work of Mansart and Gabriel, the greatest names in French architecture.

The work of Gabriel is to be seen once more in the squares of Louis XV. These are more numerous and their history is better known, for they were the subject of the magnificent compilation by Patte, *Monuments à la gloire de Louis XV* (1765). The principal are at Rennes, Bordeaux, Nancy, and Reims, and among them, in Paris, the Place de la Concorde takes its place. They represent a perfect series, each original in its own way.

The squares of Bordeaux, and the Place de la Concorde in Paris, are the work of the two Gabriels, the one by the father, the architect of Rennes, the other by the son, the architect of the École Militaire, and both are close to great rivers the view of which neither architect sought to hide. Yet the problem in the two cases was anything but similar. At Bordeaux buildings were erected on three sides; in Paris on one only, the other two being sufficiently defined by the masses of greenery of the Tuileries and the Champs-Élysées. Furthermore, while the Bordeaux square is self-contained, that of Paris forms part of a larger whole including also the rue Royale and the church of the Madeleine, which is the terminal perspective of the former.

At Rennes and at Nancy we find a completely different situation and a new idea – that of a group of squares. At Rennes the Place Louis XIV and the Place Louis XV communicate diagonally. Since both of them had a statue, pains were taken to vary the position of the monument. Louis XIV stood, as always, in the centre of the square. Louis XV was set right against the façade of the Hôtel de Ville. At Nancy there is a succession of three squares, Place Stanislas, Place de la Carrière, and the Hémicycle. The first alone was a royal square, and in fact was originally given the name and effigy not of Stanislas but of Louis XV. Héré designed the architectural elements, linked up at the corners by gilded gates designed by the virtuoso locksmith, Jean Lamour, but he did not make them identical. On one side, towards the west, he lowered them systematically so as to leave the horizon of hills and the Malzéville plateau in full view.

The Place Royale at Reims (Legendre, 1756–60) was the last of the French royal squares and the most classical, perhaps the most perfect. As in Paris and Nancy, it was part of a larger whole – the lay-out of the complete town centre and the creation of a great street (the present rue Colbert), joining the square to the town hall.

The Place Royale at Reims served as prototype for the Place Royale at Brussels; that at Bordeaux for the Praça do Comercio in Lisbon (after 1755). The Amalienborg square in Copenhagen, like the Place de la Concorde in Paris, is linked up by a short street to a great domed church; it is still more directly derived, in its square plan with cut-off corners, from a square created by Mansart at Versailles to serve as approach to his church of Notre-Dame, called to-day the Place Hoche.

¶ THE PARIS OF NAPOLEON I

Napoleon I had great ambitions for Paris. He wanted to make his capital 'not only the loveliest town which ever has existed, but the loveliest that can exist'. The principles of Napoleonic town planning were not new – the great imperial creation, the rue de Rivoli, was the typical application of the ideas of rectilinearity and uniformity which we have analysed above; the Arc de l'Étoile is the finest expression of monumental perspective. What we do find here for the first time is the 'break-through', that is, the laying down of wide straight streets to give perspective and vistas, involving the systematic demolition of parts of the city formerly built up and the disappearance of works of art often of considerable value and importance. The rue de Rivoli, the rue de Castiglione, and the rue de la Paix are examples of this. The emperor was all the more heavy-handed as regards what he found before him because he was personally insensitive to the delicate subtleties of the aesthetics of proportion and indifferent to a past which was not that of his dynasty. So with him begins what may be called demolition planning.

Attention must also be drawn to the desire to imprint the mark of antiquity on Paris, to revive imperial Rome. We have already met with this in the case of church architecture. We have said too that the architects of the Empire invented nothing, that they simply reduced to the status of pastiche what had previously been free imitation and, all things considered, original. It was the same here. Louis XIV and his successors had already dreamed of the hall-mark of antiquity. The gates of Paris in the reign of Louis XIV (Porte Saint-Denis, 1672, by Blondel; Porte Saint-Martin, 1674, by Bullet) were Roman triumphal arches without the name. But the triumphal arch by Daviler at the entrance to the Peyrou at Montpellier and that by Héré at the entrance to the Place Stanislas at Nancy had both the name and the reality. Under Napoleon I imitation was more literal. Not only were there triumphal arches (the Étoile and the Carrousel) but also columns (the Vendôme column copies that of Trajan), and above all temples – the Madeleine was the Temple of Glory, facing the Palais Bourbon, the Temple of Law.

¶ MODERN TIMES. HAUSSMANN

The history of town planning in the nineteenth century is dominated by the name of Haussmann. In him we have not an architect like Mansart or Gabriel, but an administrator. Napoleon I had reduced architects to the secondary rôle of executive agents. Haussmann's work is much less original than is generally believed. His principles and methods were in large part those of Napoleon I – vistas opened up by demolition, submission to the ideas of the straight line, uniformity and perspective. The scale of application alone was changed. All the same, he brought with it a certain concern for the practical, which we shall define later.

Haussmann's work aroused the most violent controversy. To judge the question impartially, we must remember first of all that Paris, about 1850, was without doubt a sick city. This was the result of the economic revolution which dominates the whole history of this period, the birth of large-scale industry following on certain technical discoveries, the best-known of which are related to the use of steam-power. From this resulted a series of facts deriving from one another like so many theorems – the concentration of workers round the factory, a revolution in the means of transport, a migration of the population of the countryside into the town. The movement was so rapid that the towns could not deal sufficiently quickly with the problems which faced them. From the beginning of the nineteenth century in all the countries of Europe, one after another, they became sick. Since then the town planner has never been able to give priority to aesthetic considerations. Having become a doctor, he has had to relieve the miseries from which men suffer and die. The great need is to cure the unhealthy town. Did Haussmann understand this? That is the whole question.

We cannot study here the stages of the sickness of Paris.

Only a few symptoms can be pointed out. The city reached, about 1850, a population of a million. The suburbs grew uncontrolled and without any general plan; in the centre, the old over-populated districts with their sordid, narrow streets often became the haunts of misery and crime. The descriptions of Balzac and Eugène Sue have a sinister eloquence. It may be objected that these are novels and that the search for effect naturally made the writer exaggerate. But the deplorable state of urban organization was proved by the numerous disturbances which occurred after 1830. It is sufficient to note the districts where the principal episodes took place and where the feelings that moved them were roused. The most bloody scenes of the 1830–4 period were set in the Île de la Cité (the affair of the Archbishopric, 1831), the Croisée de Paris (the riot at the convent of Saint-Merry, 1832), and, close to the latter, the rue Transnonain, of still more lugubrious memory; it was there that, until a few years ago, the unsavoury Block Number One could still be seen. The tactics of the rioters were always the same: street brawls were made easy by the narrowness of the public thoroughfares in those quarters. A couple of upturned carts, a few chairs, and a mattress or two were sufficient to barricade them. Behind this barricade the rebels resisted without difficulty, since the regular army could neither advance in a body nor use their long-range arms.

The transformation of the plan. Haussmann worked on three main problems. First and foremost, the two districts which riots had shown to be particularly dangerous – the Cité and the Croisée de Paris. In the Cité, he destroyed so many houses and streets that he reduced it to being nothing more than a collection of public buildings round Notre-Dame. Right through the middle of the island he cut the boulevard de la Cité, flanked by the Tribunal de Commerce and the city barracks, now the Préfecture de Police. To the west, one half of the island was almost entirely occupied by the Palais de Justice; to the east the open space before Notre-Dame became an immense parade ground, from which no one even thought of removing the Hôtel-Dieu, though Patte had suggested it a good hundred years earlier.

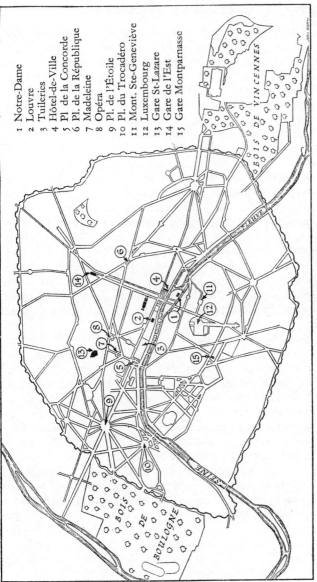

1 Notre-Dame
2 Louvre
3 Tuileries
4 Hôtel-de-Ville
5 Pl. de la Concorde
6 Pl. de la République
7 Madeleine
8 Opéra
9 Pl. de l'Etoile
10 Pl. du Trocadéro
11 Mont. Ste-Geneviève
12 Luxembourg
13 Gare St-Lazare
14 Gare de l'Est
15 Gare Montparnasse

Map of Haussmann's Paris

The 'Croisée de Paris' is the crossing of two great axes: one, north to south, has always been indicated by the rue Saint-Martin and the rue Saint-Jacques; the other, east to west, was represented in the mid nineteenth century by the rue Saint-Honoré, the rue de la Verrerie, the rue Sainte-Croix de la Bretonnerie, and the rue Saint-Antoine. These basic elements were considerably enlarged by Haussmann. From north to south the great artery was cut which bears in succession the names boulevard de Strasbourg, boulevard Sébastopol, boulevard de la Cité, and boulevard Saint-Michel. From west to east the rue de Rivoli was prolonged to meet the rue Saint-Antoine; the whole space between the Louvre and the Tuileries, still encumbered with houses, was cleared; the Place Saint-Germain-l'Auxerrois was created; the Place de Grève, widened and made more regular, became the Place de l'Hôtel-de-Ville. The actual crossing, the intersection of the rue de Rivoli and the boulevard Sébastopol, was situated at the Châtelet. The Place du Châtelet was laid out and joined directly to that of the Hôtel-de-Ville by the avenue Victoria. Nearby, the Halles, enlarged and rebuilt, kept their traditional site.

Secondly, Haussmann turned to the boulevards. Paris already had two lines of boulevards, one of them incomplete; there were the old series of the inner boulevards on the site of the city walls of Louis XIII and Charles V, to the north of the city only; and the outer boulevards, following the walls of Louis XVI's *Fermiers généraux*, to the north and south. The boulevard Saint-Germain was cut along the left bank of the Seine to form a continuation of the former. In this way a complete circle was inscribed around the Cité; the Concorde and the Bastille were linked up both by the north and the south. As for the outer circle of boulevards, at some points it was even doubled – on the left bank the boulevard Arago, boulevard Saint-Marcel, and boulevard de Port-Royal ran closer in round the Montagne-Sainte-Geneviève, through which, moreover, was cut the rue Monge. On the right bank, the wide boulevards Magenta and Voltaire radiated from the Place de la République; the canal Saint-Martin was even covered in to create a supplementary strategical line, the boulevard Richard-Lenoir.

Finally, large works were carried out in the west of Paris, all for the purpose of creating crossroads from which started great main streets all laid out symmetrically in relation to one another:

(1) The Carrefour de la Madeleine. The boulevard Malesherbes was added to balance the boulevard de la Madeleine. It led nowhere, and what is more it broke up the Parc Monceau into two parts; the west part disappeared.

(2) The Carrefour de l'Opéra. The Opéra was begun by Garnier in 1851. Before it opened the avenue de l'Opéra, begun only in 1879. The rue du Quatre Septembre, towards the Bourse (Stock Exchange), was set symmetrically to the rue de la Paix, created under the First Empire. Behind is the boulevard Haussmann, completed only in 1925, and the rue La Fayette; they make a straight line about three miles long.

(3) The Place de l'Étoile. This was already in existence as the meeting point of several avenues, and their number was increased to twelve. The irregularity of the various segments was skilfully masked. Hittorff established a pattern for the façades of the houses bordering on it. The neighbourhood, until then almost deserted, quickly filled up. The avenue des Champs-Élysées began to acquire all its present life and popularity.

(4) The Place du Trocadéro (then called Place du Roi-de-Rome). The Butte de Chaillot was flattened out. The avenue de l'Empereur (the present avenue Wilson) was opened up towards the Place de l'Alma; the avenue Kléber linked it with the Place de l'Étoile.

The principles behind the work. In the controversy, often very heated, which arose over Haussmann, the great administrator generally figured as the supporter of practical town-planning and defender of easy movement of traffic; his adversaries represented theoretical and purely aesthetic planning. This is quite a false viewpoint. Haussmann concerned himself very little with movement, at least that of carriages and pedestrians. His work, as we shall see, was in this respect rather unfortunate and his aims lay in quite another direction. He admits, in his *Mémoires* (Vol. II, p. 523) that he was not interested in the problem of circulation. 'The Emperor,' he writes, 're-proached me for sacrificing too much for the sake of straighten-ing out the streets and searching overmuch for vistas to justify the direction of the public thoroughfares. In London, he used to say, they are concerned only with satisfying the needs of traffic movement as adequately as possible. My invariable reply was, "Sire, the people of Paris are not Englishmen." ' So, while Napoleon put the question of circulation to the fore, Haussmann admits that he disagreed with him.

The ideas behind Haussmann's policy have already been stated: the classical aesthetic of straight line and vista, plus a certain practical idea unrelated to circulation but concerned with police strategy, rendering barricades, popular insurrec-tion, and street warfare impossible.

There are many proofs of this. First of all come the declara-tions of Haussmann himself. This is how he defined the lengthening of the rue de Rivoli – 'In this way was assured the complete opening-up of the great artery which not only links up the Louvre with the Hôtel-de-Ville, but the Place de la Concorde with that of the Bastille, the barrier of the Étoile with that of the Trône, by means of a direct, spacious, monumental, and more strategic communication'. (*Mémoires*, Vol. III, p. 21). The last term of this ascending catalogue is the most important one. A closer look at Haussmann's plans will serve to illustrate this. Why this profusion of streets around the Montagne-Sainte-Geneviève, if not to surround the student quarter, considered hostile to the imperial régime? Why were the boulevards Magenta and Richard-Lenoir built if not to allow the troops installed in the great barracks which Haussmann had built in the Place du Château-d'Eau (present Place de la République) to bar the way against rioters who might sweep down from Belleville or out of the Faubourg Saint-Antoine?

The observance of classical aesthetics is no less easily demonstrated. The discussions with Napoleon have been reported. One of Haussmann's proudest achievements was the straight three-mile stretch of the rue La Fayette. Here again, Cartesian aesthetics join hands with strategy. In straight wide streets cavalry charges are possible; regular troops can use their long-range arms and face the insurgents in file. The search for symmetry is evident in the crossroads of western Paris. This design appears in the Place de l'Étoile, the Place and Avenue de l'Opéra. Finally, Haussmann would have liked to have given monumental vistas to all his great streets. Unfortunately his taste was mediocre and intention is not enough to create a work of art, though it is undeniable that he desired to do so. For this reason the Tribunal de Commerce was given a dome to provide the boulevard Sébastopol with a vista.

Should we add to these considerations, as is sometimes done, those of hygiene and fresh air? Haussmann's treatment of the Parc Monceau and the Luxembourg gardens (preserved with difficulty by a violent reaction of public opinion and the resistance of the Emperor) prove that he did not look upon either as indispensable.

Judgement on the work of Haussmann. Haussmann's work aroused violent criticism even in his lifetime, leading to his dismissal in 1870, and still does so to-day. It has also had passionate defenders. Which side shall we take?

The financial arguments, although they were the principal matter of attack by the opposition under the Second Empire, may here be left aside. The costs were heavy but not unendurable and many of the works were remunerative. Two criticisms remain, artistic and social.

Artistic criticism has been expressed in the phrase, 'Haussmann's vandalism'. The roads cut during the Second Empire caused the disappearance of many historical monuments, churches, private houses, etc. Notre-Dame was irremediably spoilt by the treatment of the space before it. The balance-sheet of these destructions has been drawn up on several occasions – at the time they occurred, by de Lasteyrie (*Les Travaux de Paris*, Paris, 1861), and latterly by G. Pillement (*Destruction de Paris*, 1941). The accusations are overwhelming. However, we must allow that if all these demolitions were inevitable to improve a situation which had become impossible, we should have no right to blame Haussmann for them. The living have more rights than the dead. But most of them could have been avoided by a slight bending of the straight line and above all, as in London, by the frank adoption of the curve; in any case, they in no way remedied the ill they pretended to cure.

A perhaps even more serious criticism was that the changes heightened the distinction between social classes and increased the distance between rich and poor. The creation of a luxury city on the west of Paris has had disastrous results. Until that time the great industrialists lived in the Marais, the Faubourg Saint-Antoine, not far from their workers, sometimes under the same roof. 'Everybody knew everybody else, from the first floor to the sixth,' wrote Nestor Roqueplan. 'When a workman's wife fell sick, the lady from the first floor went up to care for her. The master reaped the benefit of this in times of revolution. The husband of the woman who had been looked after stood as guarantee for the bourgeois before the rabble who had risen to pillage and mishandle the odious property-owner.' Louis Lazare, in his studies on *Les Quartiers pauvres de Paris*, had pointed out the danger of large-scale demolitions; according to him, they would surely bring about disorder. In fact, if Haussmann had hoped to put an end to revolts, the insurrection of the Commune in 1871 must have shown him that he had had very little success. His work did not prevent it; and a strict analysis of the causes of the Commune would show that it was in some measure responsible.

At least, say Haussmann's defenders, Paris owes to him the best of its main traffic arteries. Thanks to him the tide of traffic can flow well enough, and would do so even better if Haussmann had planned on a still large scale. The answer to this must be that it was not due to him that improvement came about, but quite apart from his influence. His strategical preoccupations had an effect that he did not seek to obtain and the roads made for soldiers have been used for traffic, but the relief was only temporary, and the greater traffic difficulties with which Paris is still faced may be attributed to Haussmann.

His roads are something like academic exercises, fine designs on paper, nice straight lines, drawn in this way because their authors found them pleasant to look at. And such is what many amateurs understand by town planning. But never – except for the strategic routes – was the question asked: are they necessary? Actually, many of them are not. The boulevard Malesherbes does not lead anywhere: its only justification is to act as counterpart to the boulevard de la Madeleine. Others link up buildings which have little or no need to communicate with each other – the rue du Quatre-Septembre, in the beginning, ran simply from the Opéra to the Bourse. Why, people asked at the time, should a building which is used only by day be linked to another which is used only at night? On the contrary, others to which a wide and easy approach was indispensable were completely overlooked. This was the case with the railway stations. One station only, the Gare de l'Est, was adequately treated by the Second Empire, and that before the arrival of Haussmann; but nothing was done for the Gare Saint-Lazare, whose position is to-day one of the dangers of Paris. Nothing was done, when everything was easy to do. The approach to the Gare Montparnasse through the rue de Rennes was so badly planned that the latter, although it could easily have been made otherwise, comes up against a historical monument of the first order, the church of Saint-Germain-des-Prés, and its continuation beyond this point now raises the most thorny problems.

The real difficulty in Paris was – and still is – the bad lay-out of the generating centres of traffic; for example, the industries in the very heart of the city. Haussmann had no suspicion of this and greatly aggravated the difficulty. The vacating of the rich apartments of the Marais by their occupants gave them over to a series of undertakings whose place is anywhere but the centre of a large city. The decadence of this fine neighbourhood, as Alphonse Daudet sketched it in *Fromont jeune et Risler aîné*, is greatly to be lamented. The worst mistake was the strengthening of the position of the Halles Centrales, which Boffrand in 1755 had suggested should be removed, and which have so disastrously increased the difficulties of traffic movement in the heart of Paris. The two terms of the problem were these: Where should the vital centres be placed?

How should communication between them be assured? Haussmann was a bad doctor because he did not recognize and did not even look for the causes of the illness. And moreover, except for the 'west end', which, in any case, was part of the city, he did not even attempt to establish a plan for the extension of Paris.

CHAPTER FOUR

GARDEN PLANNING

THE garden has long been the necessary complement of the house. When private gardens became rarer, public gardens took on a greater importance in the town. Therefore the study of garden planning is often linked up with that of architecture. However, the two arts differ in many ways; no harsh sentence like the collapse of a building lies in wait for the badly planned garden. But they do offer certain similarities.

The first uses materials provided by the mineral, the second those of the vegetable world. The understanding of flowers and trees is as indispensable to the gardener as is that of the nature of rocks or the composition of concrete to the architect.

Both gardeners and architects are at once designers, painters, and sculptors. Garden planning can be reduced to design, to a mere elaboration of horizontal lines; a garden can please on paper merely by the outline of its flower-beds and the disposition of its alleys, even though the former be no more than green turf edged with plain boxwood borders. It can become a combination of colours if, no longer content with harmonious or regular pattern, it draws on the rich palette of flowering plants, seeking to rival an Oriental carpet. Finally, the gardener becomes architect and sculptor when he uses trees. On the one hand he has to study the relation of their volumes; on the other, he can cut them like simple stone, sculpt them like a block of marble or terracotta, and give the most varied and strange forms to the yew. A garden in which trees dominate changes its name and becomes a park.

Each of these three aspects of garden planning has been supreme in its turn. But the spirit in which these elements have been treated, sometimes subordinating them to human reason, at others making man submit to nature, has also changed, bringing with it another source of variety and another principle of chronological division. These are the two essential factors in garden planning: the material structure and, if it may be so called, the moral structure. Historians specializing in this subject have generally given much less attention to them than to complementary ornament, the statues, vases, fountains, which in reality are to garden planning only what furniture is to architecture.

¶ THE MIDDLE AGES

Garden planning in the Middle Ages is known to us from ancient texts and a few miniatures in illuminated manuscripts. The four essential parts listed in treatises on gardening are 'the orchard, the kitchen garden, the flower or "bouquet" garden, and the medicinal herb garden'. This list gives more importance to utility than to pleasure. This does not prove, however, that there was a fundamental difference between these and later centuries, since in modern times we do not disdain fruit and vegetables either, and there was a kitchen garden even at Versailles. But the meaning of the terms has changed somewhat, or rather a hierarchy has been introduced. Just as architecture is an art only on condition that it goes beyond mere construction, so the art of gardening is concerned only with the pleasure garden, leaving the others to horticulture or pharmacy.

Going back to the principles of classification mentioned above, we can say that the pleasure garden in medieval France was a design, and a severely pruned design, in which man imposed his will mercilessly on nature. There were no trees, only green turf and flowers; but the latter, which hardly varied, do not seem to have been the essential element. It was a garden, not a park, and treated on the strictest geometrical lines. In this respect, it already had the spirit of the garden 'à la française' and of the 'Grand Siècle'. But this geometry was much more monotonous, in that it was not an ordered composition. The garden was a collection of small squares, separated by identical alleys. There was no subordination to a centre or axis. It had a rectangular design analogous to that of some of the new towns of the late Middle Ages. All round the outside was a wider alley, covered by a tunnel-shaped arbour. This is the kind we find, for example, in the *Livre des chants royaux* (Bibliothèque Nationale). In the miniature of the *Très riches heures du duc de Berry* reproducing the Palais de la Cité in Paris (June in the Calendar) we also find arbours of vines or roses rising over the walls like a frame.

Literature acquaints us with another element, the terraces or high meadows, small stretches of turf overlooking a broader horizon, which implies that medieval gardeners knew how to create and use differences of level in garden sites. But it was rare for the ornamentation of these gardens to consist only of plants. The Middle Ages, like the Romans, introduced birds and animals and also architectural and sculptural ornament. The simplest form of this was a fountain at the intersection of two alleys. The descriptions of royal gardens at the end of the Middle Ages, notably those of Charles V at the Hôtel Saint-Paul, tell us of menageries and aviaries; there was a 'lion-house', which is still recalled by the name of the rue des Lions-Saint-Paul, made into a road when the site was developed for building in the sixteenth century.

§ THE SIXTEENTH CENTURY

It is probable, however, that with the exception of the kings and a few great nobles, people in France preferred the useful to the pleasant. Towns and castles hemmed in by walls left little space for fantasy. In the thirteenth century the Italian Brunetto Latini wrote, 'The French have large houses, with good paintings and good rooms ... they are skilled in making green terraces, vegetable gardens, and apple orchards.' While praising the French way of life, he considers it to be directed mainly towards the practical. This is why Italy and her gardens set out purely for pleasure appeared to the French nobles of Charles VIII and Louis XII as a new world, an unknown delight. A society such as they had never imagined, better dressed, exquisitely scented, lived happily under a glorious sky in beautiful gardens. Though he could not take the sky, Charles VIII at least brought back with him tailors, perfume-makers, and gardeners. One of the most important personalities mentioned in the wages list of 1496 and one whose services were employed in France until his death, was the designer of gardens 'dom Passolo', Pacello da Mercogliano.

The words 'Italian gardens' evoke the luxuriant paradises of the Roman campagna, the Villa d'Este with its leafy alleys and its thousand fountains, or Florence and the Boboli gardens. But we must be careful over dates. Here, as in architecture, there was a break between the two halves of the century. The Italian gardens of the end of the fifteenth century were still formal and geometrical, very near to the Middle Ages. Those we have just mentioned are Baroque creations and were to come later. Tasso spoke of the 'happy disorder which reigns there, so that, to see these places, one would believe that nature alone was responsible'. This is indeed one of the features of the Baroque. Another is the search after surprise, the desire to astonish, which asserts itself at every step; and a third is the complexity of elements in which all the senses can find delight.

At the beginning of the sixteenth century there was still a long way to go. The gardens of Mercogliano at Amboise, Blois, or Gaillon, as Du Cerceau shows them to us in his *Les plus excellents bâtiments de France*, closely resemble those of the *Livres des chants royaux*; they are simply squares subdivided into smaller squares, but planned without any directing axis – a juxtaposition of elements, not a composition; geometrical, but not geometry. Where then lay the innovations and the contributions of foreigners? In the first place, these gardens were much larger. They have as great a claim to our attention as the house itself; those at Blois cover an area five or six times that of the palace. We may also suppose – but suppose only, since Du Cerceau has left us engravings, not miniatures – that they owed more to colour, that the flowers were more abundant and more varied, that the designer became more and more of a painter. Later came the complements, the fantasies of the

Italian garden – grottoes, such as those of Bernard Palissy at Écouen or the Tuileries, and then fountains.

In the plan itself two notable changes appeared at the end of the century. The first was the application of embroidery patterns (*parterres de broderie*) to flower-beds. Larger areas were substituted for the small squares, and the bed acquired unity. At the same time the increased importance of colour was confirmed, for they are described as being 'in the fashion of a Turkish carpet'. This invention is often attributed to Claude Mollet; but according to Mollet himself the honour is due to the architect Dupérac, who was commissioned in 1582 to transform the gardens at Anet, where Mollet was then working. He traced out a fine garden 'forming one single compartment divided up by wide alleys'.

The second change was in the composition, now conceived as a whole and with a symmetrical axis. As early as the beginning of the sixteenth century Bramante had given axial symmetry to the Belvedere gardens in the Vatican. Before him, in Italy as in France, gardens could be looked at or crossed indifferently in any direction; there was neither top nor bottom, right nor left. Such a directing line, the key to the plan, exists in the Belvedere. The invention of embroidery-patterned flower-beds and the substitution of the single great square for a multiplicity of small ones provided the necessary lay-out for it. In the fine project of Charleval for Charles IX (*c.* 1575) the whole garden was planned in relation to an axis and – even more important – this axis was the same as that of the house. Garden and house were bound together. The same principle of composition was applied to Saint-Germain-en-Laye, where also the site forced Salomon de Caux to design a terraced arrangement, for which the Villa d'Este furnished the prototype.

¶ THE CLASSICAL GARDEN

From now on were present the essential elements of the classical garden, termed 'à la française'. Le Nôtre was to use them with genius. He created proportions and vistas with a superiority which gained him the foremost place. The formula had already been found before his time, but this does nothing to diminish his renown. 'In a game of tennis the same ball is used, but one player places it better'; this remark of the classically-minded La Bruyère may well be applied to the classically-minded Le Nôtre.

These gardens 'à la française' were happily described by L. Corpechot as 'gardens of intelligence'. There are laws of the mind, and according to these man must shape nature. The first of these laws is order: to give an intellectual significance, an organization to what are no more than scattered elements. A garden 'à la française' is a lesson in order. At the time of Louis XIV it was also a lesson in grandeur.

These fine garden designs call to mind the great contemporary town-planning schemes. Le Nôtre designed the plan of the town at Versailles, symmetrical with that which he had just produced for the park: three avenues converged in front of the château on the one hand, three at the top of the grand canal on the other. In Paris, the same pattern is found: the Champs-Élysées, prolonging the axis of the Tuileries, was to have been balanced by two symmetrical avenues.

Among the forerunners of Le Nôtre we must name Boyceau and André Mollet. Boyceau de la Barauderie, supervisor of the royal gardens, wrote a *Traité du jardinage selon les raisons de la nature et de l'art*, which was published only in 1638, after his death. 'All things,' he says, 'however beautifully they may be chosen, will be defective if they are not ordered and placed in proper symmetry.' About 1620 he designed the great embroidery-patterned flower-beds of the Luxembourg; but numerous and charming souvenirs from Italy here counteracted French logic in its search for expression. André, son of Claude Mollet, after having been 'first gardener to the king', became, about 1650, 'Master of the gardens of the most serene Queen of Sweden'. In 1651 he published at Stockholm his *Jardin de plaisir*, the theory of which comes even nearer to Le Nôtre. Before the house, situated 'in an advantageous site', runs a great alley of elms and lime trees; near the house, the embroidery-patterned flower-beds; further off, the stretches of

green turf, the trees and spinneys. Nor were the vistas of the
alleys neglected, all of which were to end at some statue or
fountain. Does not this already read like a description of
Versailles?

Le Nôtre is supreme by the size of his compositions, vast
schemes comparable to the most vast architectural schemes,
and by his recognition of the importance of trees, which he
treated in masses so as to obtain clear-cut volumes. With him
the French garden conquered the third dimension. And finally
he carried the day with his feeling for space – we are told that
he could not bear limited views. A few anecdotes told by
Saint-Simon give a clearer definition of his character. The
historian says that he had no use for flower-beds because they
lend themselves too much to virtuosity of pattern and play of
colour, appealing to the senses rather than to the intelligence.
We know also that in his opinion the garden ought to remain
the province of the gardener; the attraction of the shrubberies
ought to depend on the successful arrangement of trees,
flowers, and water, not on the beauty of garden sculpture or
applied architectural ornament. Louis XIV, taking him one
day to the Colonnade shrubbery which Mansart had just
installed, pressed him to give his opinion; he replied, 'What
would you have me say, Sire? You have made a gardener
of a mason. He has served you according to his trade.'
And yet it is difficult for us, lacking the same professional
preoccupations as Le Nôtre, not to admire Mansart's success.

The contrast between Le Nôtre's art and Italian Baroque
would be still more evident if so many foreign elements had
not slipped into his gardens, elements to which it has become
the habit to attach as much, if not more, importance as to
the general composition and structure. We have named Mansart, but Le Brun must not be forgotten. But compare, for example, the treatment of water in France and Italy: in Italy cascades and the play of fountains were used to provide perpetual
movement. Le Nôtre loved the tranquil splendour of great
calm pools, for which the delightful expression 'mirrors of
water' was invented.

Three names sum up the career of Le Nôtre: the Tuileries, Vaux-le-Vicomte, and Versailles.

The comparison of the Tuileries, as redesigned by him, with its lay-out in the sixteenth century is striking. In 1579 the garden, as Du Cerceau recorded it, was chequered by a series of alleys parallel or at right angles and all of the same width; although all the squares were not equal, the general appearance was that of a chess-board, and each square was self-sufficient. One of the alleys did indeed end at the centre of the palace façade, but it was given no more importance than the others, and it certainly could not be said that the plan of the garden was subordinated to that of the building. Then came Le Nôtre. The heart of the garden remained as a chess-board, but the central alley was very much widened, clearly stressing its supremacy and its rôle as an axis, the more so that it commands various groups of ornamental pools on which secondary alleys converge. From a collection of different elements an organic whole has been created. The importance given to pools should also be noticed. The trees, not yet treated in masses, formed only a border, for the old framework could not be destroyed.

At Vaux-le-Vicomte, for Fouquet, Le Nôtre had a clear site before him. Here was scope for creation, and Vaux was the result of a single burst of planning (1654–61). We know that he had numerous collaborators – gardeners, florists, fountain-makers. His rôle was that of overseer, the master designer controlling the plan and organizing the distribution of space. In front of the house is a great open space filled by embroidery-patterned flower-beds and pools of water, here framed by two masses of trees. The trees had not been able to grow very high in the seven years before the opening ceremony of 17 August, 1661. They were to some extent symbolized by shrubberies, but the division of light and shade was clearly marked. From either side of this light-filled axis, the two areas of shade answer each other like an echo. The vista terminates in a grotto.

At Versailles the creative spirit was again at work, but in gradual, or rather successive, phases. The garden, or as we must call it here, the park, passed like the palace itself through several stages. Only the last need be spoken of here. In front of the buildings, on the same terrace on which they stand, are ornamental ponds. On a lower level stretches the large vista of the *Tapisvert*, a green carpet between two masses of foliage, two symmetrical and geometrical volumes. On the horizon, closing the perspective, is another stretch of water, the Bassin d'Apollon. To this was added, as at Vaux, a rich decoration of vases and statues; but we have already said that for us this is not the essential. Le Nôtre was at least responsible for their arrangement, and when we look closely it is surprising to see with what care everything was foreseen and calculated. The decorative detail may vary from the Tuileries to Vaux and Versailles, but the three compositions are certainly similar and born of the same spirit.

¶ THE ROMANTIC GARDEN

The opposite of the French garden is the English garden. This contrast depends on the different reply which the two give to the fundamental question asked above – shall man or nature dominate?

But was the English garden, also known as the landscape garden, really invented in England? During Le Nôtre's own lifetime a very odd character, Charles-René Dufresny, dramatic author and garden designer, had set himself up as such in a completely opposite sense to that of the creator of Versailles. 'He needed,' says his biographer, 'obstacles to overcome, and when nature did not provide him with any, he created them for himself; that is to say, of a clear site and a flat piece of land he made a hilly one, so as to create limited vistas by setting up mounds of earth. ... Such were the gardens of Mignaux, near Poissy, and such also those which he laid out in the Faubourg Saint-Antoine.'

To leave, or rather to seem to leave nature free, means substituting sinuous paths for straight alleys and, of course, renouncing the symmetrical axis; it means giving up the treatment of trees in masses, still less in geometrical masses, ceasing to arrange shade in systematic contrast with light, letting the two interpenetrate and the trees stand isolated or form irregular groups on green turf; preferring lawns to flower-beds; giving up the horizontal terrace; accepting as a setting for the garden a site as irregular as possible; if necessary, creating such irregularities. But to leave nature free does not mean to exclude architectural ornament. We find it in the English garden as in the French, and sometimes it is the same in each, which proves well enough its secondary character. So Greek temples sprang up in the most rambling gardens, such as the Temple de l'Amour at the Petit Trianon or the Naumachie in the Parc Monceau. But rustic houses, Chinese pagodas, and Gothic ruins are also to be seen.

France has produced such magnificent examples of these English gardens that it would be better to give them a more general name, more characteristic of a spirit than a period – that of 'romantic gardens', for example, if we admit that Romanticism, like Classicism, is eternal.

We find them as early as the eighteenth century at Bagatelle, and above all at Versailles itself, where the park of the Petit Trianon contrasts with that of the main palace. The paths wind over green lawns through which runs a stream. The trees regain their individuality: we can photograph or draw a tree in the Petit Trianon, but in the Descente de Latone we see only the foliage as a whole. Ornament is provided by the Temple de l'Amour and the charming little houses of the Queen's Hamlet, designed by Mique, each surrounded by a small garden enclosed by an open wooden paling. At Betz, Hubert Robert provided a décor for the Princess of Monaco – Chinese bridge, Druid temple, feudal tower, that is to say as crumbled and ruined as could be desired, even an inscription in Old French, and a valley of tombs dedicated to the memory of the knights of the Holy Land.

In the nineteenth century the taste for the romantic garden became firmly established, particularly during the Second Empire, in the great parks created on the personal initiative of Napoleon III. We can hardly quote the name of Haussmann in connexion with them, since he was, as we have seen, a slave to geometry. On the contrary, they represent the personal taste of the Emperor, formed by a long exile in London. Among the most famous are the Bois de Boulogne and the Bois de Vincennes, the Parc de Montsouris, and above all the Buttes-Chaumont, where the cliffs, which the engravings of the period were at great pains to render impressive, seemed to be especially provided for the apprenticeship of some budding Tartarin.

Here again the influence of the garden décor on that of the town may be noticed, though the impact was considerably delayed. It is found in the garden cities which flourished at the beginning of the twentieth century; Foyer Rémois, near Reims, the garden cities of the Paris suburbs, and the residential quarters of the new European towns of Morocco.

The Principal Hôtels of the Classical Period in Paris

CLASSIFIED BY ARRONDISSEMENT AND STREET*

(A) *Right bank of the Seine (from west to east)*

❡ VIII ARRONDISSEMENT

Rue du Faubourg-Saint-Honoré:
    31. Hôtel de Blouin (H. Pillet-Will)
    39. Hôtel de Charost (British Embassy)
    51. Hôtel d'Évreux (Élysée Palace)
    85. Hôtel de La Vaupalière
    96. Hôtel Le Camus de Maizières (Ministry of the Interior)

❡ I–II ARRONDISSEMENTS

Place Vendôme
    The whole.
Rue des Petits-Champs:
    8. Hôtel du Président Tubeuf (Bibliothèque nationale)
    45. Hôtel de Lulli
Rue Colbert:
    12. Hôtel de Nevers
Rue La Vrillière:
    1 and 3. Hôtel de La Vrillière (Bank of France)
Place du Palais-Royal:
    Palais Cardinal (Palais-Royal)
Rue de Richelieu:
    21. Hôtel Dodun

❡ IX–X ARRONDISSEMENTS

Rue de la Rochefoucauld:
    66. Hôtel Rousseau
Rue des Petites Écuries:
    44. Hôtel Botterel-Quintin

*For a list of the successive owners of each building, see Rochegude et Dumolin, *Guide pratique à travers le vieux Paris* (New edition, 1923), and Jacques Hillairet, *Évocation du Vieux Paris* (3 vols., 1952-4).

Rue de la Tour-des-Dames:
 1. Hôtel de Mlle Mars
 3. Hôtel de Mlle Duchesnois
 9. Hôtel de Talma
Rue de Trévise:
 32. Hôtel de Bony
Rue du Faubourg Poissonnière:
 30. Hôtel Chéret
Rue d'Hauteville:
 44. Hôtel Bourrienne
Rue Pierre-Bullet:
 6. Hôtel Gouthière

¶ III–IV ARRONDISSEMENTS

Rue Michel-le-Comte:
 28. Hôtel d'Hallwyl
Rue du Temple:
 57. Hôtel Titon
 71. Hôtel d'Avaux
 79. Hôtel de Montmor
Rue des Archives:
 78. Hôtel Amelot de Chaillou
Rue des Francs-Bourgeois:
 60. Hôtel de Soubise (Archives de France)
Rue Vieille-du-Temple:
 47. Hôtel de Hollande
 87. Hôtel de Rohan (Archives de France)
Rue François-Miron:
 68. Hôtel de Beauvais
 89. Hôtel du Président Hénault
Rue Geoffroy-l'Asnier:
 26. Hôtel de Châlons-Luxembourg
Rue de Jouy:
 7. Hôtel d'Aumont
Rue Saint-Antoine:
 21. Hôtel de Mayenne
 62. Hôtel de Sully
Rue Pavée:
 24. Hôtel de Lamoignon
Rue de Sévigné:
 23. Hôtel Carnavalet (Musée Carnavalet)

29. Hôtel Lepelletier de Saint-Fargeau (Bibliothèque Historique de la Ville de Paris)

Rue de Thorigny:
  5. Hôtel Salé

Rue de Turenne:
  23. Hôtel Colbert de Villacerf

Place des Vosges:
  The whole.

Rue des Tournelles:
  28. Hôtel Mansart de Sagonne

Quai des Célestins:
  2. Hôtel de Fieubet

Rue de Sully:
  3. Arsenal (Bibliothèque de l'Arsenal)

(B) *Île Saint-Louis*

Quai de Bourbon:
  13 and 15. Hôtel Le Charron
  21. Hôtel de Jassaud
  29. Hôtel de Boisgelin

Quai d'Anjou:
  1. Hôtel de Lambert
  17. Hôtel de Lauzun

Quai de Béthune:
  16 and 18. Hôtel d'Astry
  20. Hôtel Lefebvre de la Malmaison

Rue Saint-Louis-en-l'Île:
  51. Hôtel Chenizot

(C) *Left bank of the Seine (from east to west)*

¶ V ARRONDISSEMENT

Rue du Cardinal-Lemoine:
  49. Hôtel of the painter Le Brun

¶ VI ARRONDISSEMENT

Boulevard Saint-Michel:
  60 *bis.* Hôtel de Vendôme (École des Mines)

Rue de Vaugirard:
　17. Palais du Luxembourg
Rue de Tournon:
　6. Hôtel de Brancas
　10. Hôtel de Concini (Barracks)
Rue Garancière:
　8. Hôtel de Rieux
Rue de l'Abbaye:
　3. Abbatial palace of Saint-Germain-des-Prés
Rue des Saints-Pères:
　28. Hôtel de Fleury (École des ponts et chaussées)
　56. Hôtel de La Meilleraie
Quai Malaquais:
　5. Hôtel de Garsaulan
　9. Hôtel de Hillerin
　17. Hôtel de La Bazinière (École des Beaux-arts)
Rue Visconti:
　21. Hôtel de Rannes
Boulevard Montparnasse:
　25. Hôtel de Vendôme

¶ VII ARRONDISSEMENT

Rue de Varenne:
　45. Hôtel Janvry
　47. Hôtel de Boisgelin (Italian Embassy)
　57. Hôtel de Matignon (Presidency of the Council of Ministers)
　73. Hôtel de Mme Juillet
　77. Hôtel Biron (or de Moras) (Musée Rodin)
　78. Hôtel de Mlle Desmars (Ministry of Agriculture)
Rue de Grenelle
　15. Hôtel de Bérulle
　75. Hôtel de Furstenberg
　79. Hôtel d'Estrée (Russian Embassy)
　87. Hôtel Pâris de Marmontel
　101. Hôtel Rothelin (Ministry of Commerce)
　110. Hôtel de Rochechouart (Ministry of Education)
　116. Hôtel Le Coigneux (Mairie of the VIIth arrondissement)
　127. Hôtel du Châtelet (Ministry of Labour)
　138. Hôtel de Noirmoutiers
　142. Petit Hôtel de Chanac (Swiss Legation)

Rue Saint-Dominique:
  1. Hôtel Amelot de Gournay
  14–16. Hôtel de Mailly et de Brienne (Ministry of War)
  28. Hôtel d'Auvergne (Maison de la Chimie)
  57. Hôtel de Monaco (Polish Embassy)
Boulevard Saint-Germain:
  246. Hôtel de Roquelaure (Ministry of Public Works)
Rue de l'Université:
  24. Hôtel de la Monnoye
  51. Hôtel du Président Duret
  126. Hôtel de Bourbon (Chambre des Députés)
  128. Hôtel de Lassay (Présidence de la Chambre des Députés)
Rue de Lille:
  64. Hôtel de Salm (Légion d'honneur)
  78. Hôtel de Boffrand (German Embassy)
Rue Saint-Guillaume:
  14. Hôtel de Mortemart
  27. Hôtel de Mesme (École des sciences politiques)
Rue du Bac:
  46. Hôtel de Roye
  118. Hôtel de Clermont-Tonnerre
Rue Bertrand:
  11. Hôtel Masserano
Rue Monsieur:
  12. Hôtel de Mlle de Bourbon-Condé

Biographical Notes on the
Principal Architects Mentioned in the Text

ALPHAND, JEAN-CHARLES. Engineer. Worked with Haussmann. Designed gardens, parks, and public walks in Paris during the Second Empire. Cf. Alphand, *Promenades de Paris*, 1867.

ANTOINE, JACQUES-DENIS. Paris, 1733–1801. Member of the Academy, 1773. Some important work in Paris. Apart from some private houses (Hôtel de Maillebois, Hôtel de Jaucourt, Hôtel de Fleury), he built the Hôtel des Monnaies (1771–5), rebuilt the Palais de Justice after the fire of 1776, and built the portico of the Hôpital de la Charité. His fame was such that he was called to Switzerland (Hôtel des Monnaies, Berne) and to Spain.

AUBERT, JEAN. ?–1741. Member of the Academy, 1720. Architect to the Prince de Condé; worked in this capacity at Chantilly (Stables, 1720–35) and at the Palais-Bourbon. Other important works are the Hôtel Peyrenc de Moras or Hôtel Biron in Paris, the rebuilding of the abbey of Châalis.

BACHELIER, NICOLAS. Architect and sculptor from Toulouse, born towards the beginning of the sixteenth century, died in 1556. Although documented as a 'master mason', he seems to have worked mainly as a figure sculptor. In the buildings where he worked he seems to have been entrusted with the decoration (doors, windows, chimneys, rood-screens, altar-pieces, etc.). He certainly worked on some of the main houses of Toulouse: Hôtel de Bagis (Hôtel de Pierre, 1538), Hôtel Buet (1540), Château de Saint-Jory (1545), Hôtel d'Assézat (1555), probably the Hôtel du Vieux-Raisin (Hôtel Béringuier-Maynier). He was also responsible for the gateway of the Capitole (1546, now in the Botanical Gardens), and the entrance to the Collège de l'Esquile (1555). See also H. Graillot, *Nicolas Bachelier, imagier et maçon de Toulouse*, Toulouse, 1914.

BALLU, THÉODORE. 1817–85. Built the church of Sainte-Clotilde together with Gau, and the church of the Trinité in Paris.

BALTARD, VICTOR. 1805–74. Worked with Haussmann who entrusted him with the rebuilding of the Central Markets (Halles) and the church of Saint-Augustin.

BARRÉ, NICOLAS. ?–?. In Paris, *circa* 1770, he built the Hôtel Grimod de La Reynière, decorated by Clérisseau and one of the first manifestations of French neo-classicism. From 1774 to 1779 he advised on the plans for the Place Royale in Brussels.

BAUDOT, ANATOLE DE. 1834–1915. A follower of Viollet-le-Duc. One of the first architects to favour the use of reinforced concrete. Built the church of Saint-Jean in Montmartre. Set forth his ideas in *L'Architecture, le passé, le présent*, 1916.

BÉLANGER, FRANÇOIS-JOSEPH. Paris, 1745–1818. Architect and designer. One of the most open and inventive minds of his age. First architect to the Comte d'Artois for whom he built Bagatelle (1779) and redecorated the Château de Maisons. Under Louis XVI, he was responsible for many private houses in the region of the Chaussée d'Antin, in Paris. With his brother-in-law Dugourc, he was, from then onwards, one of the creators of the Empire style, full of reminiscences of the antique. This did not stop him from being one of the first upholders of the use of iron (Halle aux Blés, 1802). During the Empire he was entrusted with the erection of slaughter-houses, a job he carried out very well. See also Stern, *F.-J. Bélanger*, Paris, 1932.

BIART, COLIN. Born at Amboise, 1460, died probably after 1520. Took part in the greatest buildings of his time: the châteaux of Amboise, Gaillon, Verger, the bridge of Notre-Dame in Paris. He acted as consultant at Bourges and Rouen, and seems to have been one of the most important personalities in French architecture of the early Renaissance. See also P. Lesueur, 'Colin Biart, architecte et maçon de la Renaissance', *Gazette des Beaux-arts*, 1929, tome II, pp. 210–31.

BLONDEL, JACQUES-FRANÇOIS. Architect and decorator. The main representative of an eighteenth-century family of architects, born probably in Rouen, 1705, and died 1774. He opened a school of architecture in Paris, 1739. Professor at the Academy, 1756. Known principally as a theorist, through two important works: *L'Architecture française* (1752–6) and the *Cours d'Architecture* (1771–7), completed by Patte. He did some practical work at Strasbourg (town planning, town hall, theatre) at Cambrai (Archbishop's Palace), and at Metz (Place d'Armes).

BLONDEL, NICOLAS-FRANÇOIS. Engineer and architect, born at Ribemont (Aisne) in 1618, died 1686. Made his career in the army and navy, drew up many town plans (La Martinique,

Rochefort) and plans of fortifications. Professor of Mathematics at the Collège de France. Academician and professor, 1671. Author of numerous theoretical works, the most important of which is the *Cours d'Architecture enseigné à l'Académie royale* (1675, 1683, 1698). Supervisor of building in the city of Paris; built the Porte Saint-Denis (1672). Cf. Mauclaire and Vigouroux, *Nicolas-François Blondel*, Laon, 1938.

BOFFRAND, GABRIEL-GERMAIN. Born in Nantes 1667, died in Paris 1754. Architect and engineer. Member of the Academy, 1709. Inspector General of Highways and Bridges, 1732. Considerable work in Paris and in Lorraine, partly known through his compilation: *Le Livre d'Architecture*, 1745. In Paris he was responsible for the Hôtel Amelot de Gournay (1712, 1 rue Saint-Dominique), his own house (1713, 80 rue de Lille), the decoration of the Arsenal for the Duchesse du Maine (1718–28), the enlargement and decoration of the Hôtel de Soubise (1735–40), the decoration of the Petit-Luxembourg, etc. In Lorraine, he took over from Jules Hardouin-Mansart as architect to Leopold of Bavaria. He built the cathedral of Nancy, the church of Saint Jacques at Lunéville, the Hôtel de Craon, the colonnade of the Palais du Gouvernement at Nancy, the châteaux at Junéville and Haroué, the Château de la Malgrange (unfinished). Considerable reputation abroad: worked for the Elector of Bavaria (pavilion of Bouchefort near Brussels, plan for the archiepiscopal palace at Würzburg) and for the Elector of Mainz (plan for La Favorite near Mainz).

BOULLÉE, ÉTIENNE-LOUIS. Paris, 1728–99. Member of the Academy, 1762. In Paris, he built or remodelled several houses on the eve of the Revolution, especially the Hôtel de Brunoy. Later, he gave himself up to meditating gigantic projects, which naturally remained on paper. He held the title of architect in chief to the King of Prussia. See also H. Lemonnier, *La Mégalomanie dans l'Architecture à la fin du 18ième siècle* (*Architecture*, 1908); H. Rosenau, *Boullée's Treatise on Architecture*, London, 1953.

BRONGNIART, ALEXANDRE-THÉODORE. Paris, 1739–1813. Member of the Academy, 1781. He directed, under Gabriel, the work at the École Militaire. He later became one of the strongest supporters of a return to antiquity, which was the source of his inspiration in the Capuchin friary in the Chaussée d'Antin in 1783. His style is less severe in a few charming houses (Hôtel Masserano; Hôtel de Condé, rue Monsieur). Under the Empire, he was entrusted with the building of the Bourse (1808). See also J. Silvestre de Sacy, *Alexandre-Théodore Brongniart*, Paris, 1940.

BRUANT or BRUAND, LIBÉRAL. Paris, *circa* 1635–97. Architect to the king, 1663. Member of the Academy, 1671. Provided the overall plan for the Salpêtrière. His fame rests on the plans for the Invalides, where he was in charge at the start of the building.

BULLANT, JEAN. *c*. 1510–78. Came from a family of master-masons; had travelled in Italy. Early in his career was in the service of the Montmorencys, for whom he worked at Écouen and who recommended him to Henri II. Surveyor of the King's Works, 1557. Fell into disgrace on the death of Henri II, and gave himself up to theoretical writings. In 1564, he published *La Règle générale d'Architecture, étude des cinq ordres de colonnes,* a work which met with great success and was reissued in 1568 and 1619. Catherine de' Medici restored him to favour in 1570 and he regained his title of Surveyor. Worked for the queen at the Tuileries, Saint-Maur, the Hôtel de Soissons in Paris, of which there remains the column in the Halle aux Blés.

BULLET, PIERRE. Paris, 1639–1716. Member of the Academy, 1685. Responsible in Paris for the Noviciate of the Jesuits (St Thomas d'Aquin) and for numerous houses. Architect to the City of Paris, he built the Porte Saint-Martin (1674). As theorist, he published *L'Architecture pratique,* 1691.

BOYCEAU, JACQUES. Gardener. Designed the flower-beds of the Luxembourg. Wrote a *Traité de jardinage selon la raison de la nature et de l'art,* which was published only after his death, in 1638.

CAUX, SALOMON DE. Born *c*. 1576 in the neighbourhood of Dieppe, died *c*. 1636. Engineer and architect. Worked a long time in Germany, especially at Heidelberg.

CEINERAY, JEAN-BAPTISTE. 1722–1811. Architect and town planner. Responsible for the plans of several squares and the principal *quais* at Nantes.

CELLÉRIER, JACQUES. Dijon, 1742–1814. Built several theatres in Paris, especially the Ambigu (1770), the Variétés (1807), and the theatre at Dijon, finished after his death.

CHALGRIN, JEAN-FRANÇOIS. 1739–1811. Member of the Academy, 1770. Built one of the first and most frequently imitated of French neo-classical works: Saint-Philippe-du-Roule (1774–84). He also built at that time several fine houses in Paris and

Versailles (Hôtel de la Vrillière). During the Empire, he provided the designs for the Arc de Triomphe de l'Étoile, finished long after his death.

CHAMBIGES, PIERRE. The most important member of a remarkable architect family. His father, Martin Chambiges, worked at the end of the fifteenth century and at the beginning of the sixteenth on the completion of several great cathedrals (Sens, Troyes, Beauvais). Pierre himself worked at Chantilly for the Montmorencys (1525–30), and on the rebuilding of Saint-Germain-en-Laye for François I (after 1540), perhaps on the Hôtel de Ville of Paris. This matter has caused considerable controversy (see Marius Vachon, *Mémoire au Conseil municipal*, 1903) there are full references in P. Lesueur, *Dominique de Cortone, dit le Boccador*, Paris, 1928, a summary of conclusions. Pierre II Chambiges, son or nephew of the former, worked in 1567 on the Petite Galerie of the Louvre.

CHASTILLON, CLAUDE. 1547–1616. Architect, engineer, engraver. Drew up the plans for the Hôpital Saint-Louis in Paris (1607–12), and for a Place de France, the carrying out of which was prevented by the death of Henri IV. Author of *La Topographie française*, published after his death, in 1648.

CHENAVARD. 1798–1838. Architect and decorator of the romantic period. Compiled the important *Recueil de décorations intérieures*, 1837.

CHERPITEL, MATHURIN. 1736–1809. Member of the Academy, 1776. Built the Hôtel du Chatelet (1770–1, now the Ministry of Works, 127 rue de Grenelle) and the Hôtel de Rochechouart (1777, now the Ministry of National Education, 110 rue de Grenelle), in Paris.

CHEVOTET, JEAN-MICHEL. 1698–1772. Member of the Academy, 1733. He built the Pavillon de Hanovre (1760), now removed to the park of Sceaux, for the Maréchal de Richelieu, in Paris.

CLÉRISSEAU, CHARLES-LOUIS. 1772–1820. Studied at the French Academy in Rome, 1746. During his Italian stay, he accompanied Robert Adam on his visit to the ruins of Spalato. Member of the Academy, 1777. In Paris, decorated the Hôtel Grimod de La Reynière, c. 1770. Built little (Château Borély, Marseilles; Hôtel du Gouvernement, Metz). Important mainly as a draughtsman; some of his drawings, acquired by Catherine II in 1779, had great influence in Russia; others are preserved in the Sir John Soane Museum in London.

CONTANT D'IVRY, PIERRE. 1698–1777. Member of the Academy, 1728. In Paris worked on the convent of Panthémont, rue de Grenelle (1747–56), for the Duke of Orléans on the Palais-Royal and at Saint-Cloud. Built Arras cathedral. His most important work was to have been the church of the Madeleine, at the end of the rue Royale; he provided the plans for it, but only the foundations were laid.

COTTART, PIERRE. Mid seventeenth century. Architect to the king. Built the so-called Hôtel des Ambassadeurs de Hollande (47 rue Vieille-du-Temple) and the city hall at Troyes. See also *Recueil des œuvres de Pierre Cottart, architecte*, 1686.

COTTE, ROBERT DE. Paris, 1656–1735. Pupil and assistant of Hardouin-Mansart, he became his brother-in-law in *c.* 1683, and succeeded him in many of his appointments. Member of the Academy, 1687. Architect to the King, 1689. Director of the Gobelins Factory, 1699. First architect to the king after the death of Hardouin-Mansart, 1708. Worked with the latter on the Place Vendôme and the chapel at Versailles. His personal works are: numerous houses in Paris many of which are destroyed, such as the Hôtel des Mousquetaires (rue du Bac), the Hôtel du Maine, etc. On the other hand, the Hôtel d'Estrées has survived as the Russian Embassy (1713, 79 rue de Grenelle). Other Parisian works are the façade of Saint-Roch, the decoration of the choir of Notre-Dame; in the provinces, he built the episcopal palaces of Strasbourg and Verdun, and at Lyons the Place Bellecour. Outside France he worked for the Elector of Cologne at Bonn, for the Elector of Bavaria, for Victor-Amadeus II of Savoy, for Philip V of Spain, etc. Cf. Pierre Marcel, *Inventaire des papiers de Robert de Cotte*, Bibliothèque nationale, 1906.

COURTONNE, JEAN. Paris, 1671–1739. Member of the Academy, 1728. In Paris built several private houses, of which the Hôtel de Noirmoutiers (138 rue de Grenelle) and the Hôtel Matignon (57 rue de Varenne, 1721) survive. He published an *Architecture Moderne*, 1728.

COUTURE, GUILLAUME-MARTIN. Rouen, 1732–99. In Paris, directed the rebuilding of the Palais de Justice after the fire of 1776. He carried on the work at the Madeleine after Contant d'Ivry.

CRUCY, MATHURIN. 1749–1826. Architect and town planner from Nantes. Built most of the Graslin district, towards the end of the eighteenth century: the Place Royale and the Place Graslin, the Théâtre and Cours Cambronne.

CUVILLIÈS, FRANÇOIS. Soissons, 1698–1768. Pupil of de Cotte. First architect to the Elector of Bavaria. Worked much in Germany (Amalienburg, Munich), and published pattern books of decoration.

DAVILER, CHARLES-AUGUSTIN. 1653–1701. Studied at the French Academy in Rome, 1676–81. Back in Paris, worked for eight years in the office of Hardouin-Mansart. Disliking his subordinate position, he settled in the provinces, at Montpellier. Architect to the États de Languedoc, 1693. Worked all over the south: Montpellier (Porte du Peyrou, several houses), Béziers (Bishop's Palace), Alès (cathedral). His *Cours d'Architecture*, 1691, had a great success and was reprinted several times.

DAVIOUD, GABRIEL-JEAN-ANTOINE. 1823–81. Worked with Haussmann, who entrusted him with the building of two theatres in the Place du Châtelet.

DEBROSSE or DE BROSSE, SALOMON. Born *c.* 1562 at Verneuil-sur-Oise, died 1626. Grandson of Jacques I Androuet Du Cerceau. A Protestant. Architect to the king. Built the Luxembourg and probably (though it is also attributed to Clément Metezeau) the façade of Saint-Gervais. The Palais de Justice at Rennes was built from his plans after his death. He also built the Château de Coulommiers and the Protestant church at Charenton (both destroyed). See also Jean Pannier, *Salomon de Brosse*, 1911.

DELAMAIR, PIERRE-ALEXIS. 1675–1745. Architect to the Soubise family. In 1705 began restoration and transformation of the old Hôtel de Guise in the Marais (courtyard and façade of the Hôtel de Soubise, now the Archives de France) and building of the Hôtel de Rohan. Disgraced in 1710, he was replaced by Boffrand.

DELORME, PHILIBERT. Born in Lyons *c.* 1515, into a family of master masons; died Paris, 1570. When twenty, he stayed three years in Italy (1533–6), mostly ·at Rome, where he met Cardinal du Bellay, who a little later entrusted him with the building of the Château de Saint-Maur (1540–4). In high favour from the beginning of Henri II's reign, he was appointed Surveyor of the King's Works and was entrusted with the oversight of the works at Saint-Germain, Fontainebleau, Villers-Cotterets. For Diane de Poitiers he built the Château d'Anet.

Fell into disgrace at the king's death in 1559, and was replaced by Primaticcio. He devoted himself to theoretical writings: *Nouvelles Inventions pour bien bâtir et à petits frais*, 1561; *Architecture* (only one volume published), 1567. In 1563 he returned to favour and Catherine de' Medici entrusted him with the Tuileries and the great gallery at Chenonceaux. Cf. H. Clouzot, *Philibert Delorme*, 1910; Jean Prévost, *Philibert Delorme*, 1948.

DERAND. 1588–1644. Architect to the Society of Jesus. Built, together with Martellange, the church of the Jesuit Fathers, Saint-Paul-Saint-Louis, in Paris. Published in 1643, *L'Architecture des voûtes*. Cf. P. Moisy, 'L'Architecte François Derand', *Rev. de l'histoire de l'Église de France*, 1950.

DESGODETS, ANTOINE. Paris, 1653–1728. Studied at the French Academy in Rome, 1674. Member of the Academy, 1698. Architect to the king, 1699. Above all a theorist, he became professor at the Academy of Architecture. Published numerous works: *Les Monuments antiques de Rome, dessinés et mesurés très exactement*, 1682; *Des ordres de l'architecture*, 1719.

DORBAY, FRANÇOIS. Paris, 1634–97. Son-in-law and assistant of Le Vau. Member of the Academy in 1671. Worked with his father-in-law on the Collège des Quatre-Nations, the Louvre, the Tuileries, and Versailles. In 1667 he was a member, with Le Brun and Perrault, of the artists' commission asked to provide a plan for the Louvre façade. In Paris he built the façade of the convent of the Capuchins (1689), which completed the architectural ensemble of the Place Vendôme.

DUBAN, FÉLIX-LOUIS-JACQUES. 1797–1870. One of the main representatives of nineteenth-century eclecticism. A great admirer of and expert in the Italian High Renaissance, he preferred it to antiquity as a model. Built the library of the École des Beaux-arts and the Hôtel Pourtalès (1826).

DUC, JOSEPH-LOUIS. 1802–79. Restored the Palais de Justice. Built the column of the Bastille.

DU CERCEAU, JACQUES I ANDROUET. c. 1510–85. To him are attributed the châteaux of Verneuil and Charleval and the choir of Montargis. He is especially famous for his engravings, the most important series of which, *Les Plus Excellents Bâtiments de France* (two volumes published, in 1576 and 1579), contain engravings of the main châteaux of the period in France.

DU CERCEAU, BAPTISTE. c. 1545–90. Eldest son of the preceding; the last of the great French architects of the sixteenth century.

A document of 1586 calls him 'counsellor to the king, and his architect in ordinary'. He worked on the Pont-Neuf.

DU CERCEAU, JACQUES II. *c.* 1550–1614. Appears in 1602 as architect and surveyor of the royal works.

DU CERCEAU, JEAN I. Born *c.* 1585. He was architect to the king in 1617, and was responsible for some of the most important houses in Paris at the beginning of the seventeenth century, among which are the Hôtel de Sully (rue Saint-Antoine) and the Hôtel de Bretonvilliers (destroyed; the finest house on the Île-Saint-Louis). See also Geymuller, *Les Du Cerceau, leur vie et leur œuvre*, Paris, 1910.

DUGOURC, JEAN-DÉMOSTHÈNES. Versailles, 1749–1825. Draughtsman. Brother-in-law of Bélanger. Under Louis XVI, he played a considerable part in the formation of the Empire style.

DUPERAC, ÉTIENNE. Born at Paris before 1544, died in 1604. Architect, painter, engraver, gardener. Stayed a long time in Italy. Architect to the Duc d'Aumale. As garden planner, the invention of embroidery-patterned flower-beds and the planning of the gardens of Saint-Germain-en-Laye, executed by Claude Mollet, his pupil, are attributed to him.

DURAND, JEAN-NICOLAS-LOUIS. 1760–1834. Professor at the École Polytechnique. A supporter of architectural rationalism. His theoretical works are still found to-day in all architects' libraries.

EIFFEL, GEORGES. Dijon, 1832–1923. Engineer, contractor, and architect. Apart from the Eiffel Tower (1889) and the Garabit viaduct, he built the dome of the Nice Observatory (together with Garnier), the railway-station at Pest in Hungary, and several exhibition halls. See also Jean Prévost, *Eiffel* (*Maîtres de l'art moderne*), 1929.

FONTAINE, PIERRE-FRANÇOIS-LÉONARD. 1762–1853. Percier's inseparable collaborator; but Fontaine, a better courtier, received the official honours, notably the appointment of Chief Architect to the Emperor. Later employed by Louis XVIII and Louis-Philippe. Both architects were responsible for the first stages of the completion of the Louvre, the lay-out of Compiègne, l'Arc de Triomphe du Carrousel, and the Chapelle Expiatoire. Their work as decorators is even more important. They issued in 1833, *Le Parallèle des principales résidences des souverains d'Europe* on their restorations. For almost half a century, Fontaine was supervisory architect of the Louvre and the Tuileries, resigning after 1848. See also M. Fouché, *Percier et Fontaine* (*Grands artistes,* undated).

FRANCINE. Architects and garden planners of Italian origin but naturalized French. The father, François de Francine, died in 1688; he had been superintendent of water supplies and fountains, and in this capacity took part, from 1662, in the work at Versailles. His son, Pierre-François de Francine (1654–1720) succeeded him in his office.

GABRIEL, JACQUES. 1667–1742. The Gabriel family, one of the great architectural dynasties of the eighteenth century, was related to Hardouin-Mansart and Robert de Cotte. Jacques Gabriel's father had worked on the Palais-Royal and on the Château de Choisy for Mlle de Montpensier. Jacques himself became a member of the Academy in 1699, chief engineer of Ponts et Chaussées, 1716; succeeded Robert de Cotte as first architect to the king, 1734. Architect and town planner. In Paris he built or drew up the plans for many houses, in particular the Hôtel Peyrenc de Moras (Hôtel Biron). At Versailles, he supervised the decoration of the royal apartments (Queen's Bedroom, 1735). In the provinces, he built the Bishop's Palace at Blois, the façade of the cathedral of La Rochelle, and worked on the cathedral of Orléans. As engineer he built many bridges at Blois, Lyons (bridge of la Guillotière), Poissy, Charenton, Saint-Maur, Pontoise, L'Isle-Adam, Pont-Saint-Maxence. As town planner, he drew up the plans for the reconstruction of Rennes after the fire of 1720, those of the Place Royale at Bordeaux, etc. In many of his works, especially at the end of his life, he was assisted by his son, A.-J. Gabriel.

GABRIEL, ANGE-JACQUES. 1698–1782. Son of Jacques Gabriel. Member of the Academy, 1729. Took part in his father's works; succeeded him as first architect to the king, 1742. Until then his career was closely associated with that of his father. His main works were carried out at Versailles and in Paris for the king. He built the École Militaire (1751), the Place de la Concorde (1754), and began the Petit Trianon at Versailles (1762). He also built the Versailles Opéra and drew up plans for a total rearrangement of the palace, which was begun (Gabriel wing facing the court of honour). He also carried out important works at the Louvre, Fontainebleau, and Compiègne. Cf. De Fels, *Ange-Jacques Gabriel,* 1912; abridged edition, 1924; Gromort, *A.-J. Gabriel,* 1933.

GARNIER, CHARLES. 1825–1898. His plans for the new Opéra

were chosen in the 1861 competition; he then took charge of its building. He also built the Casino of Monte Carlo (1878–9) and created the prototype of the large luxury flat of modern Paris.

GIRAL. A family of architects who worked in the eighteenth century at Montpellier. Étienne Giral was born at Montpellier, 1665. At the beginning of Louis XIV's reign he collaborated in the planning of Le Peyrou. His son, Jean-Étienne Giral, built the Château d'Eau of Le Peyrou and numerous houses in Montpellier, among them the Hôtel Saint-Côme. Cf. A. Fliche, *Montpellier* (*Villes d'art célèbres*), 1935.

GITTARD, DANIEL. 1625–86. Architect and engineer, collaborator of Hardouin-Mansart. Member of the Academy, 1672. Worked on the fortifications of Belle-Isle. In Paris, he planned and began the church of Saint-Sulpice and the façade of Saint-Jacques-du-Haut-Pas; in Dijon he worked on the Palais des États (1685).

GONDOIN, JACQUES. 1737–1818. Member of the Academy, 1774. His main work is the École de Chirurgie, of which he made an important collection of engravings, *Description des Écoles de Chirurgie*, 1780.

GRAPPIN. A family of French architects from the Gisors district. To the sixteenth century belong Robert Grappin and his three sons: Michel, Jacques, and Jean I, as well as his grandson, Jacques II. Cf. L. Regnier, *La Renaissance dans le Vexin*, 1886.

GUILLAUME DE SENS (William of Sens). Second half of the twelfth century. Supposed author of the cathedral of Sens, but his name is only recorded with certainty a little later, when his plans were chosen for Canterbury cathedral, 1175.

GUIMARD, BARNABÉ. ?–1792. French architect settled in Brussels, where from 1775 he supervised the laying out of the Place Royale.

HÉRÉ, EMMANUEL. Nancy, 1705–63. Architect in chief to Stanislas Leszczinski, 1740. His two main works are the Place Stanislas and the royal chapel of Bonsecours at Nancy. He himself described the first of these in his *Plans et élévations de la Place Royale de Nancy et des autres édifices qui l'environnent, bâtie par les ordres du roi de Pologne, duc de Lorraine*, 1753. He also drew up the *Recueil des plans, élévations et coupes, tant géometrales que perspectives des châteaux, jardins et dépendances que le roi de Pologne occupe en Lorraine* (two volumes, no date). See also A. Hallays, *Nancy* (*Villes d'art célèbres*, no date).

HITTORFF, JACQUES. Cologne, 1792–1867. Architect and archaeologist. One of the first to realize that antique temples and statues were painted in colours. In 1827, he published his *Architecture ancienne de la Sicile*. Built the church of Saint-Vincent-de-Paul, the Gare du Nord, the circus of the Champs-Élysées, and directed the replanning of the Place de la Concorde.

HOREAU, HECTOR. 1801–72. One of the main exponents of iron architecture in the mid nineteenth century. Produced a remarkable plan for the London Great Exhibition of 1851. In opposition to Baltard, he brought about the adoption of iron for the Central Markets of Paris. See also Jeanne Doin, *Hector Horeau*, Gazette des Beaux-arts, 1914.

JARDIN, NICOLAS-HENRI. 1720–99. Grand Prix de Rome, 1741. Member of the Academy, 1771. Worked mostly in Denmark where he built the Frederick church at Copenhagen.

JEAN DE CHELLES. Mid thirteenth century. Began the reconstruction of the transepts of the cathedral of Paris.

JEAN DESCHAMPS. End of the thirteenth century. Introduced the Gothic style of the northern French cathedrals to the south. Worked on the cathedrals of Clermont-Ferrand, Limoges, Narbonne, Rodez, Toulouse.

LABROUSTE, HENRI. 1801–75. One of the leaders of the rationalist school of the mid nineteenth century. A great supporter of iron building, he used it for the Bibliothèque Sainte-Geneviève (1844–50), and the reading-room of the Bibliothèque nationale (1868). He was less successful as a whole with the alterations he imposed on the former Bibliothèque du Roi and he pulled down, without reason, the building by Robert de Cotte in which the collection of medals was housed.

LASSURANCE (CAILLETEAU, *called*). Two architects bore this name. The father, Pierre (?-1724), became a member of the Academy in 1699. Architect to the king, he did much work for Hardouin-Mansart and Robert de Cotte, who, to believe Saint-Simon, drew from him their plans, their drawings, their inspiration. The son, Jean (*c.* 1690–1755), built in Paris the Hôtel Bourbon together with Giardini, and the Hôtel de Lassay. Architect to Mme de Pompadour, he altered the Hôtel d'Evreux (now the Élysée Palace), built Bellevue, the Hermitage at Versailles and the Hôtel des Réservoirs.

LASSUS, JEAN-BAPTISTE-ANTOINE. 1807–57. Architect and archaeologist. Restored Saint-Séverin and the Sainte-Chapelle. Built several neo-gothic churches, among them the church of Belleville and the church of Saint-Nicolas at Moulins. He had

begun with Viollet-le-Duc the restoration of Notre-Dame de
Paris, but his collaborator finished it alone. He published together with Darcel the *Album* of Villard de Honnecourt, 1858.

LE BAS, HIPPOLYTE. 1782–1867. Went with Murat to Italy as a
hussar of his guard. In Paris, built the basilica of Notre-
Dame-de-Lorette (1823–6).

LE BLOND, JEAN-BAPTISTE. Architect, town and garden planner.
In Paris, built the Hôtel Vendôme (École des Mines). Entered
the service of Peter the Great of Russia (1716), who commissioned him to prepare a plan for Saint Petersburg (never
executed). He wrote the treatise *De la théorie et de la pratique du
jardinage*, 1709, for which Dézallier d'Argenville assumed the
credit. See also B. Lossky, *J.-B.-A. Le Blond, architecte de
Pierre le Grand. Son œuvre en France*, Prague, 1936.

LE BRETON, GILLES. A very little known architect of the sixteenth century. Built the new buildings at Fontainebleau, under
François I.

LE CARPENTIER, ANTOINE-MATHURIN. Rouen, 1709–73. Member of the Academy, 1756. Built many houses in Paris.
Drew up the plans for the new town hall at Rouen, which
were never carried out.

LEDOUX, CLAUDE-NICOLAS. Born Dormans (Marne), 1736;
d. 1806. Under Louis XVI, built in Paris and the neighbourhood a series of houses: the Hôtels d'Hallwyl, de Mlle Guimard, de Mme de Thélusson (in Paris); houses for Mme du
Barry (Versailles and Louveciennes); the house of Monsieur
de Saint-Lambert (Eaubonne); the Château of Bénouville
(near Caen, Normandy). Member of the Academy, 1773. In
his capacity of architect to the Farmers-General, he planned the
magnificent town at the salt pits of Arc-et-Sénans in Franche-
Comté (1773–5). This led to his building the theatre of Besançon.
In Paris, he designed the pavilions of the so-called Enclosure
of the Farmers-General. Imprisoned in 1793, he occupied his
captivity by compiling a large work, *L'Architecture considerée
sous le rapport de l'art, des mœurs et de la législation*, 1804. His main
works were also described in the *Architecture de C. N. Ledoux*,
two volumes, 1847. Cf. G. Levallet-Haug, *Claude-Nicolas
Ledoux*, 1934; Raval and Moreux, *Ledoux*, 1944.

LE DUC, GABRIEL. ?–1704. Architect to the king. In 1665 was entrusted together with Le Muet with the continuation of work
on the Val-de-Grâce. Built several houses in Paris.

LEFUEL, HECTOR-MARTIN. Versailles, 1810–81. Grand Prix de

Rome, 1839. Chosen by Napoleon III as architect in chief of the Louvre and the Tuileries. He carried out the joining-up of the two palaces begun by Visconti.

LEGENDRE, JEAN-GABRIEL. Architect and engineer. Some important works in Champagne. Planned the Place Royale at Reims and built the Hôtel de l'Intendance (now the Préfecture of Châlons-sur-Marne). See also Berland, *L'hôtel de l'Intendance de Champagne*, Châlons-sur-Marne, 1928.

LEMERCIER. An important family of architects from the French Vexin. At the end of the sixteenth century, Pierre Lemercier worked on Saint-Maclou at Pontoise. He is also generally credited with the major part of Saint-Eustache in Paris. The greatest name in the family is that of Jacques Lemercier (1585–1654), architect to Louis XIII and Richelieu. In Rome, 1607–13. Built the Pavillon de l'Horloge at the Louvre (1624) and until his death directed the work on the square court. For Richelieu he built in Paris the Sorbonne (beginning 1629) and the Palais-Royal (Palais-Cardinal, 1629–36); the Château of Rueil (*c.* 1630); the château and the town of Richelieu (château, 1625–35; town, from 1633). He also holds an important place in religious architecture: the church at Richelieu, the Oratoire and Saint-Roch in Paris. Saint-Roch was his last work (1653). From 1646, he succeeded François Mansart at the Val-de-Grâce.

LEMUET, PIERRE. Dijon, 1591–1669. Built several houses in Paris, among them the Hôtel Tubeuf (Bibliothèque nationale). Published in 1623, *L'Art de bien bâtir pour toutes sortes de personnes*, second edition, 1647, where he described his main works. He succeeded Lemercier on the latter's death in the work on the Val-de-Grâce, and erected the dome.

LE NOTRE, ANDRÉ. Paris, 1613–1700. Head gardener at the Tuileries, 1637. Surveyor general of the royal works, 1657. His first great work was the park of the Château of Vaux for Fouquet (1655–61). Almost simultaneously (autumn, 1661) began his work on Versailles. He replanned the park several times and probably drew up the plan of the town as a complement to that of the garden. From 1664, he altered the Tuileries gardens. Other noteworthy works are: the parks of Saint-Germain, Saint-Cloud, Meudon, for the royal family; the gardens at Chantilly, for the Condé family; Pontchartrain and Dampierre, for noble families of the Parisian area; in the provinces the Bishops' gardens at Meaux, Bourges and

Castres. He also travelled in Germany, Italy, and England. See also J. Guiffrey, *André Le Notre* (*Grands artistes*), 1902.

LE PAUTRE, ANTOINE. *c.* 1621–91, architect and engraver. Architect to the king, 1655. Surveyor-general of works to the Duke of Orléans, 1660. Member of the Academy, 1671. His masterpiece was the Hôtel de Beauvais at Paris (1650).

LESCOT, PIERRE. *c.* 1510–78. Seigneur de Clagny, architect, scholar and man of letters, a friend of Ronsard and the humanists of the period. Personal friend of François I. Collaborated with Jean Goujon in the building of the rood screen of Saint-Germain-l'Auxerrois, now destroyed (1541–4). From 1546, worked solely on the building of the Louvre, collaborating once more with Goujon. Seems to have worked also, about 1556, on the Château of Vallery (Seine-et-Marne).

LE VAU. A family of architects. The father had probably worked at Fontainebleau. In the seventeenth century there were three brothers Le Vau, all architects. Much the best known is Louis Le Vau, born and died at Paris, 1612–70, architect to Louis XIV and of Versailles. Settled in the Île-Saint-Louis then being developed as building land. There he built, besides his own house, the Hôtels Lambert and Lauzun, and drew up the plans for the new church of Saint-Louis-en-l'Île. In 1655, he was appointed architect to the Louvre and the Tuileries to replace Lemercier. He gained fame by building the Château of Vaux-le-Vicomte for Fouquet, erected and decorated with the assistance of Le Brun and Le Notre, whom he was to meet again at Versailles. After the death of Mazarin, he designed the Collège des Quatre-Nations, 1661–2. Helped to quash Bernini's plan for the Louvre, 1666. The last years of his life were entirely taken up by Versailles. He held the titles of first architect to the king and surveyor and organizer of the royal works.

LIBERGIER, HUGUES. ?–1263. Built the church of Saint-Nicaise at Reims, where he was buried. His tombstone, which shows him holding the *virga geometralis* and a small model of Saint-Nicaise, is still extant.

LOUIS, VICTOR. 1735–1807. First prize for architecture, 1755. He erected the Intendance at Besançon (now the Préfecture), 1771–80. Called to Bordeaux to erect the Grand Theatre, his masterpiece (1775–80); he also built many houses in the town and the neighbourhood. He prepared a lay-out for the Place des Quinconces. As architect to the Duke of Orléans, he planned the garden of the Palais-Royal with the surrounding galleries, and built the theatre, now the Comédie Française. Cf. Marionneau, *Victor Louis*, 1881.

MANSART, FRANÇOIS. 1598–1666. Founder of the Mansart dynasty, was himself the son of an architect or a carpenter to the king. Did not go to Italy. Worked first with de Brosse at Coulommiers. His first Paris work was the façade of the Feuillants (1624 or 1629), followed by the church of the Visitation and the Hôtel de la Vrillière. He worked at the Château de Blois for Gaston d'Orléans *c.* 1636–8, but stopped after three years. He built the church of the Minims in Paris (1636), the Château of Maisons (1642–51), the Mazarin gallery (1644), the Val-de-Grâce (1645), from where he was soon dismissed. After 1645, he undertook much building in Paris for private patrons. In 1664, Colbert asked him for designs for the Louvre, in 1665 for a funerary chapel for the Bourbons at Saint-Denis, in 1666 for a triumphal arch in the Faubourg Saint-Antoine. Cf. A. F. Blunt, *François Mansart and the Origins of French Classical Architecture*, London, 1941.

MANSART, JULES HARDOUIN, *called* HARDOUIN-. Born in Paris 1646, died at Marly-le-Roi 1708. Grand-nephew by marriage of François Mansart, whose name he took in 1668. His career was rapid and brilliant. In 1674, when twenty-eight, he was commissioned by the king to build Clagny for Mme de Montespan. He then became and remained until his death the favourite of Louis XIV. Architect to the king, 1675. First architect to the king, 1685. Surveyor of the royal works, 1699. In the meantime, he was ennobled, created baron of Jouy and count of Sagonne. His works are numerous. For the king, he created the final Versailles of Louis XIV, including the new Orangerie and the Trianon, as well as several layouts in the park. He was wholly responsible for Marly, and in Paris for the domed church at the Invalides. As a town planner, he created the Place des Victoires and the Place Vendôme in Paris, and the Place des États (Place de la Liberté) in Dijon. He was at the head of a sizeable studio and had many collaborators: Lassurance, Daviler, Gittard and Robert de Cotte.

MANSART DE JOUY, JEAN HARDOUIN-. 1706–54. Grandson of Jules Hardouin, he designed the façade of Saint-Eustache in Paris.

MANSART DE SAGONNE, JACQUES HARDOUIN-. 1709–76. Brother of the preceding. He built the cathedral of Versailles.

MARESCHAL, JEAN-PHILIPPE. ?–*c.* 1765. Built the theatre at Montpellier, and designed the fine Jardin de la Fontaine at Nîmes.

MAROT. Family of architects and engravers. The best-known are Jean Marot, *c.* 1619–*c.* 1679, and his two sons, Jean II and Daniel.

MARTELLANGE, ÉTIENNE. Born at Lyons, 1568–1641. Architect to the Society of Jesus which he joined in 1590 as temporal coadjutor. In Rome from 1590 to 1604. Came back to France where he erected or supervised all the buildings of the Society. Worked especially in Paris (Saint-Paul-Saint-Louis, together with Father Derand), at La Flèche, Avignon, Roanne, etc. See also H. Bouchot, *Notice sur la vie et les travaux d'Étienne Martellange*, 1886; Bourde de la Rogerie, *Notice sur un recueil de plans d'édifices construits par les architectes de la Compagnie de Jésus*, 1904.

MEISSONIER, JUSTE-AURÈLE. Born Turin 1693; d. Paris 1750. Goldsmith and draughtsman. In 1726, put forward a plan for the façade of Saint-Sulpice. In his ornamental designs Meissonier is one of the most characteristic representatives of the Rococo style.

METEZEAU. A family of architects from Dreux. Louis Metezeau, *c.* 1562–1615, was architect to the king in 1594. Probably built the Grande Galerie of the Louvre and the Place Royale in Paris. May also have built the Place Dauphine. Clément Metezeau, 1581–1652, was his younger brother. Architect to the Duc de Nevers in 1610, built in this capacity the Place Ducale at Charleville. Architect to the king, 1615, replacing his brother. In 1623, built the church of the Oratoire when he was replaced by Lemercier. In 1627, during Richelieu's siege, he built the sea wall of La Rochelle. After 1630, he worked in Paris for private patrons, especially at the Quai Malaquais. He is mentioned in 1616 in the document relating to the façade of Saint-Gervais, which is often attributed to him. See also P. du Colombier, *Autour des Metezeau*, Humanisme et Renaissance, 1943.

MIGNARD, PIERRE. Born Avignon 1640, d. Paris 1725. Architect and engineer. Member of the Academy, 1671. Spent the first part of his life at Avignon, where he worked at the cathedral, the Hôtel-Dieu and the Hôtel de Forbin-Janson. In Paris, after 1671, he built the Porte Saint-Michel and the façade of the Collège Saint-Nicolas.

MIQUE, RICHARD. Born Nancy 1728, d. Paris 1794 (executed). The best-known representative of a family of architects from Lorraine in the eighteenth century. Chief engineer of the Ponts et Chaussées of Lorraine and Barrois, 1762. Surveyor and Controller-General of the works of Stanislas Leszczinski, 1763 (in succession to Héré). In Nancy, he built the Palais du Gouvernement, the Porte Stanislas and the Porte Sainte-Catherine; also the town hall at Pont-à-Mousson. He came to Paris in 1766 as Surveyor and Comptroller-General of works to Marie Leszczinska. He then built the Queen's Convent at Versailles (now the Lycée Hoche), the Carmelite church at Saint-Denis (now Justice de Paix). Member of the Academy and first architect to the king in succession to Gabriel, 1775. From 1780, he devised for Marie-Antoinette the charming hamlet of the Petit Trianon and supervised the decoration of the queen's apartments at Versailles and Fontainebleau. The last years of his life were troubled by the persecutions of a so-called brother who demanded a share of his inheritance from his father. The children of this brother ended by having him guillotined during the Terror. See also A. Hachette, *L'Affaire Mique*, 1928.

MOLLET, CLAUDE. Gardener to Henri IV and Louis XIII. Wrote a *Théatre des plans et jardinages*, published after his death in 1652. One of his sons, André Mollet, was gardener to the Queen of Sweden.

NICOLE, NICOLAS. 1702–84. Worked mostly at Besançon, where he designed the Hôtel de l'Intendance (finished by Louis) and the church of the Madeleine (1749, finished 1830).

OPPENORD, GILLES-MARIE. 1672–1742. Architect and decorator. Studied at the French Academy in Rome, 1692–8. Architect and surveyor of works to the Duke of Orléans. Took over the work on Saint-Sulpice after 1719 and built the porch of the south transept. Most important as a decorator, he played a very great part in the formation of the Regency style; (Hôtel de Pomponne, Place des Victoires, decoration of the Châteaux de Bercy, Rambouillet, etc.). See also Fiske Kimball, *Oppenord reconnu*, Gazette des Beaux-arts, 1935.

PARIS, PIERRE-ADRIEN. Besançon, 1746–1819. Member of the Academy, 1780. His main architectural works are in the Jura region: the Neuchâtel town hall, the hospital at Bourg-en-Bresse. He bequeathed to his native town a magnificent collection of drawings and manuscripts.

PATTE, PIERRE. 1723–1814. Architect and engraver; his fame

mainly rests on the magnificent compilation, *Monuments à la gloire de Louis XV*, 1765. He also wrote the *Mémoires sur les objets les plus importants de l'architecture*, 1769, and the completion and publication of the *Cours d'architecture de J.-F. Blondel* is due to him. In Paris he decorated the house of the Duc de Charost (rue Saint-Honoré, now the British Embassy) and built the church of Bolbec in Normandy. Architect to the Duke of Zweibrücken, he undertook works in Germany which are not known. See also Mae Mathieu, *Pierre Patte. Sa vie et son œuvre*, 1940.

PERCIER. 1764–1838. Inseparable collaborator of Fontaine. See FONTAINE.

PERRAULT, CLAUDE. 1613–88. Doctor and architect, he became known as a translator of Vitruvius. As a member of the commission asked in 1667 to draw up a plan for the Louvre façade, he played an important part and later supervised the building of the Colonnade. He wrote several books, among them his *Mémoires* and the *Ordonnance des cinq espèces de colonnes selon la méthode des anciens*, 1683. Cf. A. Hallays, *Les Perrault*, 1926.

PERRET, JACQUES. Second half of the sixteenth century. Came from Chambéry, was a Protestant and probably provided Sully with the plan for Henrichemont, meant to serve as a city of refuge for Protestants. In Paris, he published in 1561 a *Traité des fortifications et artifices* (subtitle: *Architecture et perspective*) (second edition, 1620).

PERRONET, JEAN-RODOLPHE. 1708–94. Architect and engineer. Member of the Academy, 1758. Director of the École des Ponts et Chaussées. Built many bridges, among them the Pont de la Concorde and the Pont de Neuilly.

PIERRE DE MONTEREAU or DE MONTREUIL, (PETRUS MUN-STEROLIS). Died 1267. The greatest architect of the second half of the thirteenth century. Built the Sainte-Chapelle of the Palais in Paris, the chapel of the Château of Saint-Germain-en-Laye, the Lady Chapel of Saint-Germain-des-Prés, the new nave at Saint-Denis. Completed the restoration of the transept arms of Notre-Dame de Paris begun by Jean de Chelles.

PEYRE, MARIE-JOSEPH (the Elder). 1730–88. Grand prix d'architecture, 1751. Member of the Academy, 1762. In Paris, built several private houses. His most important work is the Théâtre Français (now the Odéon), built in collaboration with de Wailly, 1779–82.

PEYRE, ÉTIENNE-FRANÇOIS. 1739–1823. Younger brother of the preceding. Grand prix for architecture, 1762. Member of the Academy, 1771. Worked mostly outside France and built the magnificent palace of the Elector of Trier at Coblenz.

RONDELET, JEAN-BAPTISTE. Lyons, 1743–1829. Finished the dome of the Panthéon. One of the organizers of the École Polytechnique and one of the leaders of French rationalism during the Empire. Wrote a famous *Traité théorique et pratique de l'art de bâtir*, 1802–17.

ROUSSEAU, PIERRE. Nantes, *c.* 1750–1810. In Paris, built the Hôtel de Salm (now the Chancellerie de la Légion d'Honneur).

ROUSSEAU DE LA ROTHIÈRE, JEAN-SIMÉON. 1747–? Decorator, worked with Gabriel and Mique on the decoration of the royal apartments at Versailles and Fontainebleau.

SAMBIN, HUGUES. Died between 1600 and 1602. Spent almost all his life at Dijon, where he carried out many works of carpentry and woodcarving. As architect, he drew up in 1581 the plans for the Palais Communal of Besançon (now Palais de Justice). He issued a collection of engravings, the *Œuvre de la diversité des termes, dont on se sert en architecture*, Lyons, 1572.

SERVANDONI, JEAN-NICOLAS. Florence 1695–Paris 1766. Came to settle in Paris in 1724 as stage designer. He worked mostly for the Opéra. In 1733, he proposed a plan for the façade of Saint-Sulpice which was accepted. He also organized numerous public fêtes with fireworks on the Seine. See also J. Bouché, *Gazette des Beaux-arts*, vol. II, 1910.

SOUFFLOT, JACQUES-GERMAIN. Born at Irancy (Yonne), 1713–80. Made several journeys to Italy and Rome, especially in 1749, when he accompanied Cochin and the Marquis de Marigny to Naples and Paestum. He had already done some work in Lyons (quays and bridges, the Hôtel-Dieu) when Marigny summoned him to Paris in 1755, as Surveyor of the king's works. In this capacity he made many plans for alterations in Paris and in particular advised on the Place Royale at Reims, but he was occupied mainly by the building of the church of Sainte-Geneviève (Panthéon) which he left unfinished at his death. See also Mondain-Monval, *Soufflot. Sa vie, son œuvre, son esthétique*, 1918.

TEMPLE, RAYMOND DU. Architect to Charles V during the second half of the fourteenth century. Built the spiral staircase of the Château of the Louvre.

TURMEL, CHARLES. 1597–1695. Jesuit architect. He seems to

have succeeded Martellange *c.* 1634 as inspector of the Society's buildings in France. Worked especially on the college and church of the Jesuits at Blois.

VALLIN DE LA MOTHE, JEAN-BAPTISTE-MICHEL. 1729–1800. Worked mainly in Russia, where he was called by Catherine II and lived for sixteen years (1759–75). He built several palaces in Saint Petersburg, among them the Academy of Fine Arts, and his teaching had great influence.

VAUBAN, SÉBASTIEN LE PRESTRE DE. 1633–1707. Not only the great military engineer familiar to everyone, but a town planner and architect as well. He drew up the plans of the towns he brought into being (Neuf-Brisach, Longwy, Mont-louis, Mont-Dauphin, etc.), and both in these and in other towns which he simply fortified he erected certain buildings, particularly the churches at Givet, Briançon, etc. He restored the châteaux of Aunay, Ussé, and others. His memoir, entitled *Plusieurs maximes bonnes à observer pour tous ceux qui font bâtir*, is a complete treatise on building. See also J. Lazard, *Vauban*, 1934.

VAUDOYER, LÉON. 1803–72. Grand Prix de Rome, 1825. Restored the church and refectory of Saint-Martin-des-Champs and built the Conservatoire des Arts et Métiers. His chief work was the cathedral of Marseilles.

VIGNON, PIERRE-ALEXANDRE. 1763–1828. Chosen in 1807 by Napoleon as architect for the Temple of Glory, which later became the church of the Madeleine.

VILLARD DE HONNECOURT. First half of the thirteenth century. His MS. notes and sketches were published by Lassus and Darcel, *Album de Villard de Honnecourt*, 1858, and constitute our best source of information on the training of an architect in the Middle Ages. As a builder, the cathedral of Cambrai and the collegiate church at Saint-Quentin are attributed to him, though uncertainly. He worked in Hungary.

VIOLLET-LE-DUC, EUGÈNE-EMMANUEL. 1814–79. Architect and archaeologist. Begetter of the new Historical Monuments Department, a task for which he prepared himself by a close study of all the great medieval buildings. He was in charge of the principal restorations undertaken during the Second Empire. He was also important as a historian and a theorist His *Dictionnaire raisonné de l'architecture française*, 1854–68, and *Dictionnaire raisonné du mobilier français*, 1858–75, are still essential works, in spite of the criticism which his views on

Gothic architecture have lately incurred. His *Entretiens sur l'architecture*, 1863–72, is one of the bases of modern architecture.

VISCONTI, LUDOVICO. Rome 1791–Paris 1853. Son of the famous archaeologist Ennius Visconti. Naturalized in France 1799. Directed the decorations on the occasion of the return of the ashes of Napoleon I in 1840. He was then commissioned to construct the Emperor's tomb at the Invalides. In 1851, drew up a plan for the joining the Tuileries and the Louvre, which was carried out by Lefuel.

WAILLY, CHARLES DE. 1729–98. Grand Prix d'architecture, 1752. Member of the Academy, 1767. Important mainly as a decorator (Hôtel de la Chancellerie d'Orléans in Paris). Built, together with Peyre the Elder, the Théâtre Français (now the Odéon).

WILLIAM OF SENS. See GUILLAUME.

Index

Plate references are in italics